Augustus Henry Mounsey

A Journey through the Caucasus and the Interior of Persia

Augustus Henry Mounsey

A Journey through the Caucasus and the Interior of Persia

ISBN/EAN: 9783743318205

Manufactured in Europe, USA, Canada, Australia, Japa

Cover: Foto ©ninafisch / pixelio.de

Manufactured and distributed by brebook publishing software (www.brebook.com)

Augustus Henry Mounsey

A Journey through the Caucasus and the Interior of Persia

A JOURNEY THROUGH THE CAUCASUS

AND THE

INTERIOR OF PERSIA.

BY

AUGUSTUS H. MOUNSEY, F.R.G.S.,

SECOND SECRETARY TO HER MAJESTY'S EMBASSY AT VIENNA.

WITH A MAP.

LONDON:
SMITH, ELDER & CO., 15, WATERLOO PLACE.
1872.

[ALL RIGHTS RESERVED.]

PREFACE.

THE following narrative has been compiled, at the suggestion of a friend, from the notes which I jotted down almost daily during my travels in the East; and it is published by the advice of other friends, and in the hope that, in the dearth of books on Persia, it may not be without interest for the public, or useless to travellers who may follow my route.

When, after knocking about in Europe for several years, circumstances unexpectedly rendered it necessary that I should take up my residence in Persia for a considerable period, I found that my knowledge of that country was of the most meagre description. Beyond reading *Haji Baba* and a *Diplomate's Residence in Persia*, my thoughts and studies had never carried me eastwards of Constantinople, and I had merely that hazily golden, but, alas! deceptive idea of the East which one gathers from imaginative works, such as *Vathek* and the *Veiled Prophet*. The *Haji* had always appeared to me rather as a highly-drawn and amusing caricature than, as it really is, one of the most correct pictures of real life, whilst the "Diplomate's" pages had left on my mind but a very faint impression of Persia and Persians.

The day will come, I presume, when we shall have "Murray's" Guide Books for Central Asia and the vast regions which the compilers of English Atlases term Independent Tartary. As yet, however, we are without these aids to the traveller; and though many excellent works, both historical and descriptive, have been written about Persia, we have none in the style of those well-known red volumes which are the *vade-mecum* of the British continental tourist.

Time failed me to consult the admirable but ponderous volumes of Ker Porter, Malcolm, and Kinneir, or even Lady Shiel's excellent narrative of her journey to the Persian capital;[*] and I was, therefore, obliged to make inquiries amongst friends and acquaintances as to my route, and the preparations necessary for the journey. But Persia was evidently a *terra incognita* to most of my friends; some of them talked of Ispahan as its capital, others had a dreamy sort of idea that Tehran was the metropolis, whilst

---

[*] All these works are out of print, and copies of them are difficult to obtain.

several were totally ignorant of the existence of the latter town.

As to outfit, one gentleman who had passed some years of his youth in Iran, recommended me to take a supply of watch-glasses and crystal wine-coolers; another, lately returned from it, said an English saddle and a portable bed were all the extra kit I should require; and a third, who had sojourned in the land for four or five years, hesitated at counselling me to provide myself with a supply of brandy and sherry, and pronounced a fur coat for the journey to be completely superfluous.

Under these circumstances, it is not surprising that I should discover later that I was not as fully equipped as I ought to have been, and it may therefore be well to indicate, at once, a few of the necessaries, which my experience leads me to recommend to those who may follow in my steps, namely:

Fowling-piece, revolver, and ammunition; light bedstead (the lightest I know are made in Russia, and occupy little more space than an ordinary gun-case); sheets, blankets, &c., and waterproof covering; portable India-rubber bath, japanned iron washhand-basin, plates and cups; knives (a large one for the pocket, with corkscrew, is most useful), forks and spoons; English saddle, fitted with holsters and saddle-bags, and bridle; portable medicine-chest; a small supply of brandy; preserved meats and soups. The traveller should be prepared for the extremes of heat and cold, and accordingly provide himself with a pith helmet, strong riding-boots, and breeches; veils and spectacles for protection of the eyes; several linen suits for summer; fur coat, felt boots (reaching to the knee), and a plentiful outfit of woollen and flannel clothing for winter.

The easiest method of reaching Tehran is by the Russian route, and probably the best season for setting out is September. Leaving Nishni Novgorod about the 15th of that month, there would be time enough to visit the Persian capital, Ispahan, Persepolis, Shiraz, Shapoor—in fact, the most interesting places in the country—before the cold weather sets in; and from Bushire the traveller might proceed home *viâ* India, Baghdad, Egypt, or wherever inclination might lead him, for the winter.

In conclusion, I wish briefly to advert to two points which stand out rather prominently in the foreground of my sketches, viz. the moral obliquity of the Persian's character, and the fatigues and difficulties of travelling in his country and in the Caucasus.

As regards the first point, it must be borne in mind that the Persian's character has been formed, to a very great extent, by the system of government under which he has so long lived. His natural disposition is amiable, intelligent, imaginative, and docile; and it would, therefore, be a source of great regret to me if, by dwelling too much on the defects of the former and too little on the good qualities of the latter, I should have diverted from him the sympathy and assistance of which he at this moment stands so much in need.

The winters of 1870 and 1871 were unusually dry throughout the country. Very little snow fell, and still less rain; the rivers and springs were dried up, the crops failed, and for the last eighteen months there has been a famine in the land. Hundreds of people have died of starvation, and though the harvest this year promises to be a good one, there must necessarily be much misery and suffering for some time to come. A committee of gentlemen has long been engaged in London in collecting subscriptions and forwarding relief to the sufferers, but the appeal thus made has met with but limited success. If these pages should enlist the sympathies of any of my readers in favour of the Persian Relief Fund, they will not have been written in vain.

With reference to the second point, I, perhaps, met with a larger share of fatigue than usually falls to the lot of the traveller, partly in consequence of my complete ignorance of the country, and partly on account of the season of year at which I entered it.

Fatigue and a certain amount of difficulty there must always be; but those who do not mind roughing it will be more than compensated for both: in the Caucasus, by the natural beauties of the scenery, in Persia, by the novelty of the manners and customs of the people, the interesting remains of ancient times, and the charm of perfect freedom of movement and action.

Vienna, May, 1872.

CONTENTS.

CHAPTER I.
Across Europe to Constantinople—The Black Sea—Sinope—Samsoon—Trebizonde—Batoum 1

CHAPTER II.
Poti: Its Importance and Future—Russian Project for connecting Petersburg and Odessa with Turkistan by Steam—The Rion, or Phasis—The Skoptsi—Mingrelia—Kutäis 14

CHAPTER III.
Posting in the Caucasus—The Telega and Post-House—Camels—Suram—Georgia—Gori—Accidents on the Road—Chapars............................ 28

CHAPTER IV.
The Bragrations—Tiflis—Its Bazaar—The River Kura—Environs—Hospitality at Tiflis -Theatre—Georgian Ladies—Cossacks—Character of the Georgians—Schamyl—Present State of the Caucasus—Departure for Persia... 37

CHAPTER V.
The Plain of the Kura and Valley of the Akstaf—Snow—Pass of Dilijan—Lake of Goutche—Legend about its Trout—Erivan...................... 51

CHAPTER VI.
Armenia and Armenians—St. Gregory the Illuminator—Etchmiadzin—Traditions relative to the Ark's Resting-place—Mount Ararat—Nakhitshevan—Julfa—The Araxes 64

CHAPTER VII.

Arrival in Persia—Persian Cookery, Towns, Post-houses, and Caravansaries—Oriental Hospitality—Feringhee—Tabreez—General Features of the Country — Population — Heir-Apparent to the Throne— Government—Visit from an Official Personage—Character of Persians—The Bāb.. 83

CHAPTER VIII.

Departure from Tabreez—Some of the Discomforts of Posting—Turkmanchai—Mianeh—Lost in the Snow—Zenjan—Sultania—Kasvin— The Assassins—First Impressions of Tehran 108

CHAPTER IX.

Situation and General Appearance of Tehran—A Persian House— European Colony—The Telegraph—Food—Wine—Skating—The Shah's Practical Jokes—The Persian Army—Hunting and Hawking —Horses.. 127

CHAPTER X.

Rhé—The Guebres—Religion of Zoroaster—The Ramazan and Bairam —Bazaars—Persian Women—New Year's Day—The Shah—His Palace—Reception of the Diplomatic Body, and Grand Salaam—A Debt of Honour... 148

CHAPTER XI.

Preparations for a Caravan Journey—Start for Ispahan—Valley of the Angel of Death—Devils—Koom—Kashan—The good Emir— Ispahan—Palaces of Forty Pillars and Eight Paradises—Armenian Quarter—Shaking Minarets—Rifle-Practice—Manna........................... 170

CHAPTER XII.

Fellek and Chub—Persian Doctors—Yezdicaust—Abadeh—Antelopes and Mouflons—Pasargadæ—Tomb of Cyrus—Plain of Merdasht— Naksh-i-Rustem—Tomb of Darius—Sassanian Bas-Reliefs—Bahram Gour and his favourite Wife—Persepolis—Tragic Story of a Lutee Bashee—Bendemir 192

CHAPTER XIII.

Shiraz—Tombs of Hafiz and Saadi—March Southwards—Partridge-shooting—Vale of Wild Almonds—Asylum—Passes of the Old and Young Woman—Ruins of Shapoor—Sculptures—Statue of Sapor—A Garden at Kazeroon—Environs of Shiraz—The Sword of the State—A Nomad Chieftain—Mirza Mahommed Reza 223

CHAPTER XIV.

Return Northwards—Second Visit to Persepolis—Naksh-i-Rejeeb—Istakr—Oujān—Disagreeable Reception in an Eeliaut Encampment—A Flight of Locusts—Pistols *versus* Daggers—Summer Quarters—Persian Ideas of Europe—Massacre of Jews—Trout-fishing and Snipe-shooting 252

CHAPTER XV.

A Persian Marriage — Khorassan — Kermanshah — Tag-i-Bostan — The Loves of Ferhad and Shireen—Bisitoon—Dancing-Girls—Hamadan—Tombs of Esther and Mordecai—Climate—Sunnies and Shiahs—Passion-Plays 284

CHAPTER XVI.

Tehran to Resht—Enzelli—Ashorada—Turcomans—Baku, Astrakhan, and the Volga 316

APPENDIX.

Routes 335

Map showing Mr Mounsey's Routes through the Caucasus and Persia

A JOURNEY THROUGH THE CAUCASUS

AND

THE INTERIOR OF PERSIA.

CHAPTER I.

ACROSS EUROPE TO CONSTANTINOPLE—THE BLACK SEA—SINOPE—SAMSOON—TREBIZONDE—BATOUM.

ON a cold drizzling November morning in 1865, I left the great metropolis shrouded in its congenial fog, and rolled down with the mail to Dover.

The usual inconveniences of the Channel passage are but too well known. There was just time on landing at the Calais quay to gulp down the pale ale which, from the excited manner in which they recommend it to all, the white-aproned garçons evidently consider a sovereign remedy for the internal derangements induced by the passage, when away rattled the express to the Belgian frontier and Brussels.

French first-class railway-carriages are the least convenient in Europe, and French conducteurs, with the administrative talent which characterizes their nation, take particular care that each compartment shall have its full complement, before an extra car is added to the train. So, to avoid the inconveniences of their huddling system, I made straight for Vienna, by way of Cologne and Passau, and there being nothing to see and no very agreeable companions to talk to, occupied my mind by watching the varied grades of deference shown to the traveller as we journeyed along.

In France and Belgium the " Oui, Monsieur " and " Non, Monsieur " of the officials, pronounced in a dry business-like fashion, smacked somewhat of the democratic universal-suffrage idiosyncracy of the inhabitants of those countries; further on, as we get past Cologne and on to the Rhine, a casual " Herr Baron " varies now and then the grating monotony of " Ja, mein Herr," and would indicate that the doctrine of "fraternité, égalité," &c. has not yet effaced from the sluggish German mind every landmark of the feudal ages; whilst the salutations of " Herr Graf," " Euer Gnaden," and, as we approach Vienna, " Euer gräfliche Gnaden," which universally meet the ear in Bavaria and Austria, are melancholy proofs that the levelling civilization of the West has not yet shed its light on the benighted people of these truly conservative states, where the members of all classes of society still show respect unmingled with servility to their superiors in the social scale, and each man is still content to appear to the world as he really is.

> Es gibt nur 'ne Kaiserstadt,
> Es gibt nur 'ne Wien.

So sing the inhabitants of Vienna; and they might with equal justice add that they, "the Viennese, are unique in the world." Such a pleasure-seeking population, and one so easily amused, does not exist elsewhere. Good-humoured, good-natured, not overburdened with education, nor schooled into pedantry, like the denizens of the capital which Bismarck has made Imperial, but gifted with a natural 'cuteness and kindliness of manner quite exceptional in Germany, the Viennese merrily pass the time away in their dear old Kaiserstadt, intent on enjoying the present and perhaps somewhat too careless of the future.

With a pang of regret I quitted this abode of light hearts, and with Strauss's last valse still ringing in my ears, was borne along up the beautiful Sämmering and down past Grätz and Laybach, until a sight of the blue waters of the Adriatic notified our approach to Trieste. Here I bade adieu to railways, and comfortably installed on board one of the Austrian Lloyd's boats, steamed away down south towards Istamboul.

Antivari, the port of Scutari, was our first halting-place, and here we shipped a foretaste of the East, in the shape of a pasha's wife, accompanied by two old male attendants and several female slaves. The lady herself was of European parentage, and, as one of my female fellow-passengers informed me, possessed much more mind than is commonly found in a harem. She was pretty too, allowed her face to be seen now and then, and spoke French and German. The slaves seemed dirty and ill-drest, but not unhappy; and the old male attendants were, I presume, so flabbergasted the first day by their mistress's disregard of Koranic precept on the subject of veils, that they never showed their own visages during the rest of the voyage.

Though cholera had disappeared from Trieste full three weeks before we left it, the enlightened Government of Greece had such a tender regard for the health of its subjects, that it still kept up quarantine, and we were thus prevented landing at Corfu and Syra. The usual gale caught us off Cape Matapan, with the exception of Gibraltar, the most southernly point of continental Europe, and we consequently missed seeing the hermit, who, they say, keeps a solitary look-out from its bluff headland o'er the blue waters of the Mediterranean. Stormy weather retarded us too in the Archipelago, and it was not until the morning of the seventh day that we cast anchor in the Golden Horn.

Twenty-four hours is not much for Constantinople. Time enough, however, to visit St. Sophia, to ramble through the great bazaar, and walk through Pera to Old Stamboul, to have a chat with old friends, and eat an excellent dinner at the ambassadorial table.

The sun shone brightly as we steamed, on the 17th December, up the Bosphorus. Even then, almost midwinter, the scene was lovely, such as once seen can never be forgotten : a perfect paradise, if such there be on this earth's crust ; and when at sunset I took a farewell look at the fast receding shores of Europe, all was calm and still—everything portended a fair voyage across the dreaded Black Sea.

Widely different was the scene which presented itself next morning to my waking eyes. We were driving along the Asiatic coast ; stern and inhospitable it looked—bleak rocks rising perpendicularly from the water, and succeeded by mountains clothed with forests of pine. The land was covered with a mantle of snow, while all around the sea was black, save where lashed into angry foam by the hurricane. The heavens looked like lead, and now and then a snow-storm shrouded our vessel in what might be termed white darkness. With a perversity which I have only witnessed on the Black Sea, the waves came dashing in upon us, and almost over us, from all sides, and as the vessel pitched and rolled and thumped about in the storm, it was difficult to prevent oneself being shot out of the cabin windows. Our captain, a fine tall Dalmatian, with excessively Pan-Slavist tendencies (he showed me the arms of the future Slave empire, and his diploma as member of some society, which is to effect its constitution), looked anxious as, towards dusk, a huge sea took the ship at right angles, and deluged our decks from prow to stern. As darkness closed in upon us things got worse, and he determined to make for Sinope. The difficulty was to find it. Its lighthouse is a wretched concern, and snow, hail, and sleet were not calculated to render its light more apparent than usual. At length, during a fair interval, we got a five minutes' glimpse of it some two or three miles off, and, steaming straight for it, luckily entered the harbour without accident, at about 10 P.M.

Sinope is stated to have been founded by one of the Argonauts, and to have been colonized by Milesians. Xenophon and his Greeks, having, on their long homeward march, first come in sight of the Black Sea on the heights above Trapezus (Trebizonde), paid a visit to Harmene, one of its ports; and Diogenes and the great Mithridates first saw light within its walls. It likewise furnished Apelles with a red earth from which he compounded one of his four principal colours, and has lately become known as the scene of the destruction of the Turkish fleet by the Russians during the Crimean War. Strabo speaks of its advantageous position as a port. "It stood," he says, "upon an isthmus that joined the peninsula to the mainland, having on each side a port where great quantities of tunny were taken as they swam along the coast from their breeding-ground in the Palus Mæotis (Sea of Azoff) to the Bosphorus. The peninsula was surrounded by sharp rocks, which made all access difficult: the land above the town was very fertile, and laid out in beautiful gardens: the city was well built and adorned with a place of exercise, a market, and magnificent porticoes."

As we lay here storm-bound for forty-eight hours, I had plenty of time to make comparisons between the present and the past—very much in favour of the latter. The present town, if indeed worthy of that name, is a collection of mean-looking houses, containing perhaps 1,000 inhabitants; and a ruinous old castle, probably of Genoese construction, which formerly defended the approach to the harbour, is its only interesting building.

All was now covered with snow, and looked bleak and cheerless. However, mustering up our courage, we went on shore, and walked through a narrow street or two, out on to the rising ground above the town, to the cemetery—an unenclosed bit of ground, disproportionately large for the actual number of inhabitants. Here we thought we discovered traces of the magnificent porticoes above mentioned, in the shape of slabs of white marble and bits of broken columns scattered about and peeping here and there out of the soil. Returning to our boats, we passed some hours in the apparently sole amusement of Sinopians—grebe-shooting. Strabo's shoals of tunny are now metamorphosed into swarms of grebes of various sorts, and the natives derive considerable profit from the sale of their skins, which are bought up by a French agent for a franc or a franc and a half apiece, and exported to Paris to adorn the black-velvet mantles *de ces dames*. We succeeded in bagging several of different sizes, and continued the sport next day, until, luckily, towards evening the storm subsided, and our

Dalmatian captain, to our great joy, hoisted the Blue Peter.

Some ten hours' steaming and we reach Samsoon (Amisso of the Greeks), situated close down on the waters of a bay backed on the land side by hills of considerable altitude; the lower slopes covered with olive plantations, while higher up fir-forests stretch away into the interior of the country. As at Sinope, a Genoese castle is the most picturesque building in the town, which we perambulated through half-melted snow and much mud. The bazaar is a miserable-looking place, containing nothing worth purchasing but pheasants at six and woodcocks at two francs the brace. Samsoon is, however, a town of considerable trade, being a sort of depôt of European goods for the interior of Asia Minor. Much Turkish tobacco is likewise exported hence to Stamboul and elsewhere, whilst a post-road connects it with Mosul and Baghdad.

A post-road! Once in Asia, let all preconceived ideas and knowledge of highways and byways be dismissed from the mind; let Macadam be forgotten, and the results of the labours of parish overseers and district boards be consigned to oblivion. Let it be distinctly understood that a Turkish or Persian post-road has not been made by the hand of man, and that his feet alone have contributed to render it what it is—a series of parallel tracks, beaten perhaps for centuries by the feet of men and quadrupeds, but totally ignorant of the impress of wheels, running straightway up hill and down dale, regardless of wind-breaking ascents and neck-breaking descents, over plains and through bridgeless rivers and torrents, from one town to another. At intervals varying from ten to thirty miles, as the case may be, are villages and post-houses, where fresh horses may be procured, the simplest necessaries of life obtained, or a halt made.

Such are the high-roads of those parts of Asia to which European civilization has not yet penetrated, and they seem to answer pretty well the wants of the inhabitants, for few attempts have yet been made to ameliorate them; perhaps on the principle, not long ago prevalent in Spain, that bad roads keep away unpleasant visitors, the fallacy of which has been so eminently proved by our late expedition to Magdala.

After this digression upon roads, we resume once more our watery way. Calm and bright weather has succeeded the storms of two days ago, and we get along smoothly and comfortably to Trebizonde, 180 miles from Samsoon, having touched during the night at Keresoon.

"Θάλαττα! Θάλαττα!" shouted the Greeks, as, after their long tedious march through the wastes of Asia, they viewed once more, from the hills above Trapezus, the waters of the Euxine, and they no doubt sang many pæans and poured out frequent libations at the welcome sight. But "circumstances alters cases," as remarked the maid, who had sworn eternal service to her mistress, when announcing her approaching marriage and giving notice to quit; and we hailed the prospect of leaving salt water behind us for twelve hours with as much joy as Xenophon did his approach to it. It was a lovely winter's day, and Trebizonde, nestling down on the shore, under the shelter of its elevated old castle and crumbling walls, in their turn commanded by picturesquely wooded hills, rising amphitheatre-like around the town, quite came up to what I had heard of its beautiful position.

Having travelled from Vienna with Count L——, first Aide-de-Camp of the Grand Duke Michael, I went with him and his family to a capital déjeuner at the house of the Russian Consul-General. And after breakfast we all rode through the town and away westwards for about three miles, until we reached an old Byzantine church, St. Sophia, I believe, by name, beautifully situated in a sort of verdant esplanade surrounded on the land side by hills, and looking down on the now sparkling waters of the sea, some sixty or eighty feet below. The church was in process of being converted into a mosque, and the pasha of the province, a fine tall and portly old Turk with a long white beard, was inspecting the works as we rode up. All the frescoes, with which the internal walls were covered, were being scraped off, all vestiges of the cross destroyed, and the exterior of red stone, adorned with a frieze from biblical or saintly history, was receiving a substantial coating of whitewash. The pasha appeared to take much interest in the progress of conversion, but found time to address us a few polite phrases.

Returning homewards we passed the cemetery, thickly planted with tall cedar-trees, and rode up to the castle, the oldest building in the town, and as usual in these parts, attributed to the Genoese. It is in a ruinous state; in its loftiest tower three or four guns seemed ready at any moment to descend from their carriages; and neglect and decay were visible everywhere. After paying a visit to the English consul, whose first-born was found standing sentinel-like on a terrace in front of the house, waiting for a few shots at the usual evening flight of woodcocks, I rejoined my friends on board at 8 P.M., and early next morning we entered the Bay of Batoum.

Errors in orthography are inelegant, but generally productive of no greater harm than a comical mistake or remediable misunderstanding. They may, however, have very serious consequences, and my Russian friends here related to me an instance of this, which, although I must leave to them the responsibility for its historical accuracy, ought to be a warning to careless spellers. Two streams fall into the Black Sea, they said, at a short distance to the east and west of Batoum, and the names of these streams are, with the exception of one letter, identical. When the frontier line in this quarter of the world was being negotiated between Russia and Turkey, the former power was naturally anxious to include Batoum, the only good harbour on the eastern shore of the Euxine, within its territory, and, in order to obtain this object, to extend its frontier to the most westernly of the two streams. In drawing up the treaty, however, that one little letter, which alone marked the difference in their names, was omitted, and the eastern stream became and has remained the division between the two countries.

Russia would certainly have gained great advantages by the acquisition of Batoum. It possesses naturally the principal requisites of a good harbour. There is deep water close into the shore, and the high overhanging cliffs of a spur of the Gouriel mountains protect it from wind and weather. These facilities for the establishment of a naval station and arsenal close to the Turkish frontier would, if turned to account, have greatly added to her strength in the Black Sea. She would have found there, too, a ready-made commercial port, much better adapted to accommodate a trade which may soon take vast proportions, and to which I shall presently refer, than any which the work of years and the expenditure of millions can ever create at Poti.

At present Batoum contains nothing but some squalid-looking huts; but the smooth blue waters of its bay and the surrounding quasi-perpendicular rocks, glittering in their snowy mantles, looked beautiful on this sunny winter's morning.

Travellers for Poti here leave the steamer which has brought them from Constantinople, and embark on a smaller one for the rest of the voyage; but no smaller vessel being forthcoming on this occasion, time too being precious, our Dalmatian captain agreed to take us on to our destination. So after an hour's halt for communication with the authorities, we steamed out of the harbour, along a low forest-covered coast, and soon caught a first glimpse, far away to the northeast, of the great Caucasian Alps, and their tall snow-covered peaks sharply defined against the clear blue sky. What with examining these with our telescopes, watching the evolutions of the myriads of grebe, teal, and waterfowl of every description which swarmed around us, and drinking, at breakfast, numerous bumpers of champagne to the health of our captain of Pan-Slavistic tendencies, our three hours' run from Batoum passed quickly and pleasantly, until, somewhere about noon on the 23rd December, we cast anchor about half a mile from the bar of the classical and auriferous Phasis.

Looking eastwards from the deck of our steamer, our view embraced a long reach of flat coast extending from the Gouriel, which we had passed on the right, to the outlying spurs of the great Caucasian chain on the left, being the eastern limit of a plain some sixty miles by seventy. This plain is covered by the Mingrelian Forest, is surrounded, except towards the western or sea side, by high mountains, and is traversed from east to west by the Phasis, or Rion, as it is now called, which debouches in the Black Sea at Poti. Thither we will now proceed.

CHAPTER II.

POTI: ITS IMPORTANCE AND FUTURE—RUSSIAN PROJECT FOR CONNECTING PETERSBURG AND ODESSA WITH TURKISTAN BY STEAM—THE RION, OR PHASIS—THE SKOPTSI—MINGRELIA—KUTÄIS.

My Russian friends were now about to enter their own country, so the count donned his A.D.C.'s uniform, and we entered, bag and baggage, a barge manned by soldiers which had come over the bar to meet us. Crossing the bar of the Rion is frequently a dangerous proceeding, but we had perfectly calm weather, and entering the river without difficulty, rowed a few hundred yards up-stream through the forest to what is called the town of Poti. The first sight of it recalled vividly to my mind Mr. Dickens's picture of Eden. The remains of an old Turkish fort, the walls of which were fast being demolished, as I afterwards learnt for the sake of converting their materials into cement, three or four oblong wooden houses, painted white and green and raised on log platforms a few feet above the marshy, oozy soil, and a few miserable-looking huts, all scattered at random, as it were, along the left bank of the stream, hardly came up to my idea of a town, and, for a moment, I was under the delusion that we had only a faubourg before us. Only for a moment, however, for running alongside one of the white and green houses, we were ushered by its owner into the "Hôtel Colchide," and out of another appeared the town commandant in full fig to pay his respects to the A.D.C.

The internal accommodation of our new abode corresponded entirely with its external appearance; walls and floors were completely bare, and as to furniture there was as little as possible. We had luckily had a good breakfast on board, and that and our champagne libations induced us to shut our eyes to the dark side of that or any other picture. Our French host and hostess, too (where does one not find French hotel-keepers?), though apparently somewhat fever-stricken, were obliging; and so, having ordered everything that could be got for dinner, off we set in our barge to inspect the works which the Russian Government have commenced with a view to constructing a port. Before we get there, however, it were well to complete the picture of the town by adding that, at right angles to the portion already described, there is a street—that is, a certain number of wooden structures, houses, huts and cabins, dotted down in the forest in two straight lines, with a muddy interval between them—and that here and there, hidden amongst the trees, there are others of a similar style.

The soil, on which stand these diverse habitations, is here, as indeed throughout the whole of this plain, fertile to a degree and completely stoneless, but marshy and oozy in consequence of its very slight elevation above the water-level. It is covered with a most luxurious vegetation; magnificent forest-trees of many varieties, festooned to the topmost branches by the wild vine, and a tangled and impenetrable mass of brushwood and jungle below, are as evident proofs of Nature's largess in this region as they are truthful indicators of the prevalence of deadly fever and ague. The forest comes right up to, or rather into, the town, and if I add a small river steamer and a few idle barges and small craft, moored along the banks of the stream, I have mentioned all worthy of notice at Poti.

A short distance above the town, the river runs its waters into two channels, separated from each other by a small delta some hundred yards across, and it is on the northern of these—the town being on the southern channel—that the Government are attempting to form a port. The great difficulty to be surmounted is the want of water on the bar, outside which there is, at no great distance, a depth of thirty feet, rapidly increasing to sixty and one hundred and twenty feet. It is proposed therefore, as the colonel of engineers who directs the works informed us, to drive the bar into the sea, and, with a view to this object, wooden piers, several hundred yards in length, have been constructed on each side of the river's mouth, confining the stream and rendering the current more powerful. Though very rough and incomplete, these piers *—which are to be replaced by quays of stone as soon as the

---

* Destroyed by a storm in 1867, and being now replaced, as I am informed, by cast-iron ones.

railway now in course of construction towards Tiflis is capable of bringing down the necessary material—have already had the effect of deepening the channel to a certain extent, as appeared from the soundings shown me, and the colonel was confident that he would finally have seventeen feet of water in his port. If this hope be realized, Poti will to some extent compensate the Russians for the non-acquisition of Batoum, and may become a place of a good deal of importance in a commercial point of view. Indeed my sanguine Russian acquaintances already talked of it as the future Liverpool of the Euxine.

As a means of developing the resources of the Caucasus this port is of the utmost necessity, and a railway connecting it with Tiflis is hardly less so. The works for the latter have been carried on for some years by the Government, who employ a considerable portion of their army on them, under the direction of half-a-dozen English engineers. But little progress had, however, yet been made; and though the embankment was far advanced in the direction of Kutäis,* about seventy-five miles from the sea, no bridges or stonework had been commenced, and it was calculated that it would require five years to finish the line to Tiflis. Thence it is to be prolonged to Baku on the Caspian, a distance of about 300 miles; and when this is terminated, Russia will have a line of steam communication from Odessa and her southern Eu-

---

* The railway is now opened from Poti to Quiril. May, 1872.

ropean provinces to the port of Astrabad at the southeastern corner of the Caspian Sea.

With the prospect of soon possessing the whole of Turkestan and Tartary, by the acquisition of the Khanats of Khiva and Bokhara, and the vast steppes which separate them from the northern Persian frontier, the Russian Government must be most anxious to complete this line of railway, which will form the most important link in a long chain of projected steam communication with those distant regions. Steamboats, touching at all the ports on the southern coast of the Caspian, at present run from Astrakan to Ashorada, a small island belonging to Russia at its south-eastern extremity. Were the Caucasian Railway and Port of Poti completed, all the trading operations of Europe with the northern and north-eastern provinces of Persia would inevitably follow this route, instead of being, as at present, carried on by means of caravans of camels and mules, which tramp wearily up and down the 1,100 miles between Tehran and Trebizonde.

Another line of steamers is to be established between Astrakan, Baku, &c. and the north-eastern corner of the Caspian; whence, according to a pamphlet lately published by General Romanoffski, who commanded in Turkestan for some years, three roads are to start eastwards. One will be carried from the Bay of Krasnovod along the old bed of the Amou Darya to the Sea of Aral. Another will cross from the Mertvi Kultuk Bay to Tchernycheff on the same sea. Neither of these routes presents any great physical difficulties to the construction of railroads. From the Sea of Aral steamers will eventually run up the Gihon or Syr-i-Darya;* and thus during summer, or as long as the Volga and Amou Darya are navigable, St. Petersburg and Odessa will be placed in direct steam communication with Khojend. Troops may then be moved from the Volga to Turkestan in a fortnight, the army of the Caucasus will become the reserve for that province, and Russia will find, what she professes is her only object in these Central Asian conquests, a vast outlet for her manufactures. Between 1825 and 1850 her trade with this part of the world increased 300 per cent., and is no doubt capable of great development. All sorts of

---

* In connection with this subject the *Golos* published an article, sometime last year, of considerable interest. Goods, it stated, are now sent from Samara (on the Volga) to Orenberg, and thence to Fort No. 1, on the Syr-i-Darya by land, a distance of 1,500 versts, through barren and uninhabited steppes. Were the Caspian route open, they would be shipped to the Bay of Krasnovod, and thence be forwarded by water, viâ the old and present beds of the Amou Darya and Syr-i-Darya to Bokhara and Tashkend. In 1868, Russian trade with Bokhara reached the sum of 20,000,000 roubles, but was not expected to increase, the population of the Khanat being little more than 1,000,000. Around Kashgar there was a region, cut off from China by the late revolution, which contained 20,000,000 inhabitants. There was the market for Russia, as plenty of cotton could be grown there, and there were no manufactories of any sort. The trade with Tashkend, in the same year, amounted to 30,000,000 roubles, and could be much developed.

Steamers already (May, 1872) ply on the Syr-i-Darya, and coal has been discovered in the vicinity.

cotton—as good, it is affirmed, as that of the United States—can be grown in Turkestan; much silk is produced there; coal exists; and there is a probability of the discovery of gold and silver.

These are some of the more remote possibilities which are dependent on the completion of the Poti, Tiflis, and Baku Railway; its immediate effect in developing the resources of the Caucasus itself would be equally great. The forests of Mingrelia and Imeritia contain abundance of fine timber; their plains are capable of producing cotton, hemp, and tobacco; the vine is indigenous; the finest walnut-wood grows on their hills, and underneath them lie hidden vast treasures of mineral wealth. Apropos of walnut-wood, a traveller for one of the largest furniture manufactories in Paris, whom I met at Tiflis, told me that as it was no longer to be found in Europe, his firm had sent him there to procure a supply, which he had obtained, but did not know how to forward to France. Eventually it was sent to the Caspian in bullock-carts, then up the Volga, then down the Don, and so viâ the Sea of Azoff and Black Sea to Marseilles.

It would appear that, in very ancient days, the products of the East found their way to Europe through the Caucasus. Pliny thus describes their route. "Arrived at Bactra (Balk) the merchandise descends the Icarus as far as the Oxus, and thence is carried down to the Caspian. It then crosses that sea to the mouth of the Cyrus (Kura), where it ascends the river, and on going ashore is transported by land for five days to the banks of the Phasis (Rion), where it embarks once more and is conveyed down to the Euxine." From this statement it is apparent that both the Rion and the Kura were then much deeper than at the present day, for instead of there being merely five days' land journey between the points where they cease to be navigable, sixteen full marches must be reckoned. A further proof of the change that has taken place in their beds and the volume of their waters, may be inferred from the facts that the galleys of Pompey ascended the Rion, and that Seleucus Nicator had, some 2,000 years ago, a project for uniting the Euxine and Caspian by means of a canal.* Such a project would hardly have been conceived had not these rivers then afforded greater facilities for navigation than they do at present.

Meanwhile innocent, no doubt, of all speculations like the above as to the future importance of Poti, 750 soldiers were working away at the harbour, sawing up timber in a steam-mill, probably the first steam-engine of any sort in the Caucasus, driving in piles, &c. There we will leave them to return in our barge to dinner at the "Colchide."

The commissariat resources of Poti are fortunately superior to those of Dickens's "Eden;" they had all been put in requisition by our hostess, and a tolerable meal was the result. Our host, who waited on us,

---

* The idea of a canal between the two seas has again been broached in the Russian papers, but, I should say, without any prospect of being realized. May, 1872.

being of a speculative turn of mind, had led a somewhat adventurous life, dabbling a little in all sorts of enterprises. Gold-seeking had been the last, and he showed us some diminutive nuggets, varying in size from a pin's head to a split pea, the produce of his searches in the sands of the Phasis; a few droppings in fact of the precious metal which a modern Munchausen would say had fallen from Jason's fleece.

About 11 A.M. next day we were all ready for a start in a small steamer, which we hired for the moderate sum of 400 francs for the sixty or seventy miles' trip up the river; when at the last moment it was discovered that our passports, taken from us on our arrival by the police authorities (for Poti in its misery has a police-force, and, maybe, quite a hierarchy of other authorities), had never been restored. A soldier was at once despatched for them, but returned saying the office was closed: so we started without them, and received them next morning by an express on horseback. Had I been alone, I presume I should never have seen mine again.

The Rion winds sluggishly through the flat forest-covered plain. Its waters are shallow and slimy, swarming at this winter season with myriads of wildfowl of every description—grebes, gray-duck, teal, &c.—which rose singly, in twos and threes, or in vast flocks, as we slowly steamed up the river. Its banks are fringed with lofty trees, festooned with tangled masses of luxuriant creepers, and with an impassable jungle of thorny undergrowth. Our steamer, a very tiny affair, drawing some three feet of water, was manned by members of that incomprehensible sect, the Skoptsi, whose tenets enjoin self-mutilation. It is possible, though I never heard it so stated, that they entertain other notions, as repugnant to imperialism as this extraordinary practice is subversive of the laws of nature; however that may be, the Russian Government do not tolerate their residence in Russia Proper, and, when discovered there, they are packed off to end their days on the Rion and other places in the Caucasus, whilst many of them seek a home at Bucharest and other places in the principalities. The specimens of this sect which I saw were fine-looking men, much cleaner, better dressed, and with a more well-to-do look than their less self-denying compeers; and I was told that they were equally superior to the latter in thrift, industry, and sobriety. The most highly-respected converts are those who join the sect with wives and a family.

About 4 P.M. we came to an anchor, and I accompanied the A.D.C. through mud and snow to inspect a regiment encamped in the forest, about two miles from the river, and employed on the railway. The men were lodged in wooden huts, thatched with branches—some 200 men to each hut. Their aspect was decidedly repulsive, for the muddiness of the place had communicated itself to their fatigue-dress and general appearance; the overcrowded huts seemed to have no ventilation, so that what with the bad air generated in them and the smoke of their large wood fires, the atmosphere was anything but agreeable. Outside, the camp was not cheery; half-melted snow, and a sea of black oozy mud, with now and then a dangerously deep pool of the same, being the general features: something like the camp of the Allies before Sevastopol, I fancy, without the excitement. A considerable portion of the railway embankment had been completed, after visiting which we retraced our steps in the dark to our steamer. A pretty fair dinner somewhat reconciled us to a hard berth in our clothes on the cabin table.

There is one advantage connected with this species of couch. One rises from it even in mid-winter without reluctance; there is no inducement to turn round and have another snooze; the sluggard would have been cured of his sloth had he been forced to sleep on a deal plank, and there was consequently no merit in being on deck at sunrise. It was Christmas morning, a most orthodox one, too. There had been a sharp frost during the night, and, as the sun rose in the clear blue sky, the snow-covered trees and ground sparkled and glittered merrily. Coming down from their inland feeding-ground, myriads of wild-fowl were hastening towards the sea, and, as we steamed slowly up stream towards our destination, the river seemed alive with the feathery tribe.

The scenery was similar to that of the previous day. We were still threading our way through the Mingrelian forest, amidst lofty trees crested with snow-covered garlands of wild vine, and, at rare intervals, cleared patches of ground which the presence of a log-hut on piles allowed one to infer were under cultivation. Few inhabitants or signs of life were, however, visible on shore, until, after passing a spur of the Gouriel chain which frowns boldly over the river, we came in sight of Maran, a considerable village and head-quarters of the Skoptsi in this part of the Caucasus.

Here we left our steamer: and, though the poorest of its species I ever embarked on, being somewhat inferior to a Thames tug, it was not without regret that we bade adieu for many a long month to the most ordinary indication of European civilization, the steam-engine. The Count's travelling-carriages were in waiting, and after seeing our baggage piled on a couple of waggons, and the loss of a good deal of time and much unmusical vociferation in Russian, off we went about sunset. Each carriage had a team of six puny little horses, four wheelers and two in front; one of the latter bearing a native, and the whole team being driven by another native perched on the footboard, just below the count and myself, who were seated on the box. "Poshol!" "poshol!" "Hup!" "hup!" shrieked the driver, and well wrapped in our furs, away we went over a flat macadamized road, at a pace which carried us over the twenty-seven miles in three hours and landed us in Kutäis about supper-time.

A tall handsome colonel of Cossacks, in the elegant uniform of his regiment, dark maroon caftan, and quite an arsenal of silver-mounted cartridge-cases on each breast, welcomed us with truly Russian hospitality (of which more anon) to an excellent meal, after which I was shown to a room engaged for me at the hotel. My day was not yet at an end, however, for in the saloon or coffee-room I found a couple of English engineers, employed on the railway, celebrating Christmas with punch and songs; in singing the one and drinking the other, they were ably seconded by a number of Russian officers, and the arrival of a new comer necessitated the emptying of a fresh bowl of a liquor so congenial to the tastes of both nations.

Kutäis, the chief town of Colchis, where Jason's long search was rewarded by the acquisition of the Golden Fleece, and where, to his discomfort, he met that veriest of tartars, Medea, is now the capital of Imeritia. Beautifully situated on the banks of the Phasis—here no longer the sluggish stream we quitted on issuing from the Mingrelian Forest at Maran, but a healthy mountain torrent—it is half-surrounded by picturesque hills and contains some 6,000 inhabitants. Its broad streets smack of Russian occupation, whilst its bazaar reminds us of its former possessors and their Asiatic origin.

From the heights overlooking the town, fine views are obtained of the rich country trending away towards Mingrelia. The surrounding district is most fertile; cotton of fair staple, wine which is drinkable and of course capable of much improvement, and smokeable tobacco, being some of its products; whilst flax (Herodotus I believe speaks of the excellence of

Colchian linen) might be grown to any extent. Imeritian women have long been celebrated for their beauty. Jason was no greenhorn, but a man who had travelled far and seen much, and therefore we may presume that Medea's charms were not inconsiderable; great too were the prices paid in the marts of Stamboul for the fair slaves of Colchis, and the present generation does not belie its repute, though the wintry season and several inches of snow in the streets greatly curtailed my opportunities of obtaining ocular demonstration of the fact. The climate is good: snow falls exceptionally, and, though the summer heats are great, they are free from the feverish elements which prevail in Mingrelia and along the eastern coast of the Euxine. Kutäis therefore may have an "Avenir."

CHAPTER III.

POSTING IN THE CAUCASUS — THE TELEGA AND POST-HOUSE — CAMELS — SURAM — GEORGIA — GORI — ACCIDENTS ON THE ROAD — CHAPARS.

THE traveller who, never having left the great highroads of Europe, is accustomed to well-padded railway carriages, first-rate steam-boats, or, at the worst, comfortable diligences and fine smooth roads, elegant hotels, restaurants, and buffets, would do well, on undertaking a posting trip during the winter in Russia, to forget such luxuries, and make up his mind to bear with equanimity the numerous trials and hardships which await him in a half-civilized country. A large stock of patience, good-humour, and robust health, are necessary to surmount them, and without these qualities he had better remain at home.

The "telega" is the vehicle generally used in posting. In the Caucasus it may be described as an oblong wooden box of the roughest sort, placed, without springs, upon four wheels, and capable of holding one traveller and his traps most uncomfortably. Even on the best of roads the jolting of such a machine would effectually dissipate all idea of comfort; on the very bad ones of the Caucasus it is simply beyond description. Bedded in straw, huddled in furs and wrappers, exposed to driving rains, pelting sleet and spattering mud, all control of one's actions ceases from the moment the yamtchik, or driver (whose retention of his seat on a narrow board in front has always appeared a miracle to me,) takes possession of the reins; all one's energies are thenceforward devoted to preventing oneself being jerked out of the waggon, or crushed by one's portmanteau breaking away from its fixings. *Ventre-à-terre* is the pace, maintained if possible throughout the stage, irrespective of ascent or descent, ruts, holes, road, or no road. A friend of mine once performed a journey after this fashion from Tiflis to St. Petersburg in nine consecutive days and nights; on his arrival at his destination, he was lifted more dead than alive from his telega: but habit is a second nature, and a journey of sixty or seventy hours in one of these vehicles comes quite natural to a Russian. One stage is, however, sufficient to make a stranger hail with delight his arrival at a post-house.

An average specimen of the latter contains a couple of travellers'-rooms, each furnished with a wooden tressel, a fireplace or stove, and, exceptionally, a chair and a table. The windows have frames, and sometimes glass in them. The post-master is obliged to supply wood for heating the stove once, at a fixed price; if more is required, at any price he likes to charge. He must further provide a "samovar," *i. e.*

an urn, heated from the centre with charcoal, and the best of all inventions for procuring a speedy supply of hot water. With these luxuries the traveller, whose ideas of travel are indissolubly connected with the well-padded railway-carriage, first-class saloon cabin, and luxurious hotel, will at once feel himself quite at home, and pass a most enviable night! Provided with the necessaries I have indicated, he unpacks his bed and bedding, food and drink, and *nécessaire de voyage;* he makes his tea and eats his supper. He is lord of all he surveys, and can sleep as long as he listeth, without fear of disturbance; for post-master and post-servant are not intrusive: they don't press their services on their guests, and generally *brillent par leur absence.*

If anxious to push on at once, he will always have time to make his tea and drink it without scalding his mouth, for the time gained by the *ventre-à-terre* pace is more than lost by the inexplicable delays of the post-house—delays which even the triple-sealed Padarojna (Government order for horses) can hardly curtail. As these three seals are only given to Government couriers and employés, the ordinary traveller must content himself with two, and submit himself to further delay. If unfurnished with any species of Padarojna, he had better perform his journey on foot.

Travelling with an A.D.C. of the governor of the country, I escaped some of the discomforts just mentioned, but even under these most favourable circumstances *on n'allait pas comme sur des roulettes.*

Leaving Kutäis in a snow-storm on the 27th, we were four hours in performing our first stage, and the snow still continuing, and having completely obliterated all traces of the road, it was then judged prudent to await the dawn; so I thus had an early opportunity of becoming acquainted with the wooden tressel and samovar.

Next morning the storm had cleared, and we drove through a beautiful country along winding affluents of the Rion, and through hills, covered, I was told, with rhododendron and azalia, and crested here and there with ruined castles and churches. One stage was over the worst of roads: nothing, it seemed to me, but a series of ruts, holes, streamlets, &c. The jolting, even in my friend's comfortable travelling carriage, was intolerable. After this we began to ascend towards the Col de Suram, a mountain pass, some 3,000 feet high. Henceforward the road was pretty good, though too narrow for much traffic, or, indeed, for the little that exists.

In one of its narrowest parts an incident occurred which revolutionized all my pre-conceived notions of the habits of that most mysterious of beasts, the camel. I say mysterious, because I have always heard that he is unknown in a wild state. What, then, is his history? Has he always been protected by the hand of man since the deluge? All other beasts of burden are found in some quarter of the globe in a state of nature. The wild ass scours the deserts of Khorassan; the horse careers at freedom on the vast plains of South America; we have the wild elephant and the wild ox. But the camel, who has heard of a wild camel? The author of the simile, "The Ship of the Desert," ought to be proud of the success of his definition. It has so indissolubly connected its subject with burning sands and fiery deserts that the ordinary European mind finds it almost impossible to conceive a desert without a camel, or a camel without a desert. Profound astonishment therefore seized me in that narrow bit of road on the Suram Pass,—a precipice and low stone parapet on one side, a perpendicular wall of rock on the other—at the sight of a long string of desert ships coming scrambling and shambling down the pass towards us in eight inches of snow. Astonishment yielded to disgust as, on closer acquaintance with the brute, a further pre-conceived notion of his moral qualities was likewise dissipated. There was just sufficient space to allow of our passage, and the yamtchik accordingly drove his team as close to the parapet as possible, on the supposition that the gentle and patient beasts would pass quietly on the other side. Not at all: the leader of the string planted himself right in front of us in the centre of the road, and there he stood, whilst his followers crowded after as far as their leading strings—each camel's head being tethered to his antecedent's tail—would allow, and all progress became impossible. In vain the drivers coaxed, swore, and belaboured: groans, grunts, and screams were the only response; until at last, having no desire to pass the night in the snow, as a last resource we succeeded by our united efforts in lifting the off-wheels of our vehicle on to the parapet, and thus rewarded the obstinacy of our opponents by letting them have their way.

Mr. Palgrave, in his interesting book on Arabia, has most truly portrayed the moral qualities of the camel, and my experience of the beast fully coincides with his description. More obstinate than the mule, the camel is likewise much less intelligent. Patience is not one of his virtues, for he protests to the best of his ability against the slightest imposition. Make him lie down, place a feather on his pack, and he will groan and scream as much as if he were receiving a load of three hundred-weight. He is stupid to a degree; give him his liberty, and he won't know what to do with it. He is, further, revengeful, and harbours rancour in his breast. He is a fool, an ass, and a brute.

Having thus vented our spleen, we drive on through the snow and the cold night wind, over the top of the pass to the post-house, where deep potations of hot tea in glasses and with a squeeze of lemon instead of cream, soon warm our half-frozen blood; and where, wrapped in our furs, we pass another middling sort of night on the wooden tressel. Glass in the windows to-night.

The summit of the Suram chain, just surmounted, forms the boundary between Imeritia and Georgia— two provinces different as night from day in their natural features. Here we bid adieu to forests and undergrowth and luxurious vegetation, to travel for hundreds of miles over bare brown plains amidst arid mountains and bald peaks—a land where nature sleeps. A mantle of snow, however, now concealed these features and necessitated an early start next morning; for we have eighteen hours' work, barring accidents, to Tiflis, and there may be camels on the road.

A gradual descent of five or six hours through a bleak and inhospitable region, and we reach our first Georgian town, Gori, prettily situated on a slight elevation overlooking the vast plain of the Kura, and in full view of the great Caucasian chain, and Elburz, its loftiest peak, where poor Prometheus paid the penalty for being in advance of the world, to the north. Mud walls and square turrets still surround the town, indicative of the insecurity which prevailed before the country came into the hands of its present rulers. Descending further into the plain, the prospect of reaching Tiflis becomes problematical. The warm sun has melted the snow, and as evening darkens into night, frost sets in again and the road becomes a mass of ice. As long as it is flat the horses keep their legs, God knows how, and we get along; but at the first insignificant hill the foremost of our three carriages comes to a standstill. In vain the merciless yamtchik applies his punishing thong; his team, shod with the round flat Asiatic shoe, slips, flounders, and finally succumbs in a heap.

Along the high-roads of the Caucasus there are, at intervals of fourteen or fifteen miles, stations of what may be called mounted rural guards. Chapar, Persian for courier, is the name still given them, and their duties consist in keeping the peace and escorting travellers who can exhibit to them orders to that effect. They are recruited from the natives, I believe, fairly mounted, armed with native-made rifles, which they carry slung in buffalo-hide cases on their shoulders, and the long knife, common to every Caucasian, and they wear the Cossack costume and paposh, a species of low busby, and a huge mantle of buffalo-skin called a bourka. I never had an opportunity of testing their courage, and have always heard that in case of attack, especially by superior numbers, they would make themselves scarce; but they are certainly useful in case of accidents to carriage or horses.

We had six of these gentry with us, and two of them at once cantered off to the nearest village in search of assistance, and soon returned with some twenty or thirty peasants. The horses were taken out and the carriages dragged to the top of the hill, or until we reached even ground and were again enabled to resume our ordinary pace. But if our horses were unable to drag us up hill, they were equally incapable of guiding us down; and as, for the best part of a stage, the road runs along the banks of the Kura, there was considerable danger in descending steep inclines of our being shot into its icy waters. Again and again were we obliged to unyoke our teams, attach ropes to the back-springs and axles, and by hanging on, chapars, travellers, and peasants, like so many living drags, steer our vehicles slowly to the bottom.

In ordinary winters difficulties of this nature seldom occur (there are others no doubt in their stead), for the valley of the Kura enjoys a very mild climate, but the winter of 1865-6 was particularly severe, and caused me here and during the rest of my journey to Tehran much more discomfort and delay than it is to be hoped usually fall to the traveller's lot. Our progress under the above circumstances was not great, but after passing a good portion of the night in the way just described, we at last, when within two stages of our destination, left the snow behind us, and, resuming our *ventre-à-terre* pace, at three in the morning clattered over the rough pavement of Tiflis. Half-an-hour later we were landed safely at my friend's hospitable table, and a hot supper with copious libations of the Russian's favourite wine, champagne, erased from our minds, for the moment at least, all recollection of the petty annoyances of the day.

CHAPTER IV.

The Bragrations—Tiflis—Its Bazaar—The River Kura—
Environs — Hospitality at Tiflis — Theatre — Georgian
Ladies—Cossacks—Character of the Georgians—Schamyl
—Present State of the Caucasus—Departure for Persia.

Tiflis is the capital of Georgia, which in 1801 became a Russian province, but was, previous to that date, an independent kingdom, under the sway of the most ancient dynasty in the world. The family traditions of the Bragrations trace their origin to King David; and it is evidently with reference to these traditions that Marco Polo states, in the history of his travels, which he dictated in his Genoese prison in the last years of the thirteenth century, that "in Giorgia hae un rè, il quale si chiama sempre David Melek, cioè a dire in Francesco David Re."* "Anticamente," adds this quaint old traveller, "a tutti gli rè che nascono

---

* The text quoted is that of the Crusca, transcribed by Michell Ormanni, who died in 1309. Marco dictated in French, but an Italian translation was published almost immediately after the appearance of the original.

"In Georgia the king is always called David Melek, *i.e.* King David. Formerly all the kings of that country were born with the effigy of an eagle under the right shoulder."

in quella provincia (Giorgia) nasceva un segno d'aquila sotto la spalla diritta." Though I frequently met a couple of scions of this ancient house, it was of course impossible to ascertain whether the sign of the eagle still graces their backs : its imperial neighbour perhaps no longer brooks the poor bird's existence even in effigy. One member of the family bears the title of Prince of Georgia, and remains faithful to the costume of his country—very broad inexpressibles, a plain caftan of dark material, secured by a handsome belt mounted with silver ornaments, the inevitable dirk, and a bonnet resembling the Polish cap. He is a handsome, agreeable man, but somewhat too fond of piping melodies on a silver flute, his inseparable companion.

The town, which contains some 60,000 Russian, Georgian, Armenian, Persian, Jewish, German, and French souls, occupies a long stretch of uneven ground on both sides of the river Kura, and is almost surrounded by an amphitheatre of brown barren hills, from the tops of which there is a fine view of the great Caucasian chain. It is a strange mixture of Asiatic and European architecture, and yet hardly European; for though its modern quarter, containing the Grand-Ducal palace, the theatre, public buildings, and the residences of the Russian authorities, civil and military, is laid out in broad streets and open squares, still the overhanging red roofs and projecting balconies of the houses, and more especially their bright green and blue walls, bear a decidedly Muscovite stamp.

The old part of the town is thoroughly Asiatic—

mud or sun-baked brick houses, with flat roofs and an almost complete absence of windows, narrow, unpaved lanes and alleys, and vaulted bazaars, being the prominent features. Here are the principal shops and mercantile depôts; here too is all the life of Tiflis. A thorough motley it is: the stately Persian with high lambswool hat and flowing jubbah,* the stolid Armenian, and lethargic Georgian, jostle against the Cossack and the Frank; the Russian lady, in the latest fashions from Paris, elbows the white-veiled figure of her Armenian sister and the dark blue inscrutable form of the denizen of the harem; long strings of camels silently thread their way through the throng, heavily-laden mules jingle their bells and chains, troops of unbridled donkeys demurely follow their leader. A babel of tongues salutes the ear—"Salam aleikum," "Zdrastwuyte," "Bonjour," "Guten Morgen." Here are vendors praising the quality of their goods, purchasers depreciating the same, bargaining and haggling on all sides—a scene, in fact, which can only be realized by one who has visited the confines of Europe and Asia.

The Kura, a rapid-flowing, impetuous river, cuts the town in two parts, as we have seen, and is traversed by several bridges, the most elegant and modern of which bears the name of Woronzoff, a former Governor-General. Chardin, who travelled through the Caucasus on his way to the Court of Abbas the Great

---

* A species of mantle, generally of broad-cloth, descending to the ankles.

in the beginning of the seventeenth century, and the history of whose travels is as interesting from his remarks on men and things as it is amusing from the quaintness of his style and the naïveté of his anecdotes, speaks thus of the river Kura: "C'est sur ce fleuve Kur que Cyrus, ayant été exposé en son enfance, sans y être submergé, il en prit son nom, au rapport des anciens historiens."

Without stopping to consider what amount of credit can be given to the legendary dicta of these "anciens historiens," amongst whom is Herodotus,—though he does not mention the exact spot where the infant Cyrus was abandoned—we may presume that here, amidst the arid brown hills which skirt the valley of the Kura, was passed, in the shepherd's tent, the first youth of the great founder of the Persian empire. A few months hence, and we shall see his last resting-place in the distant plain of Pasargadæ, and again find his name immortalized in the appellation, Kurāb (Persian-water of Cyrus), still borne by the stream which flows past the sparse remains of his once proud capital.

To judge from present appearances, the shepherd must have had some difficulty in providing for an extra mouth, for one is somewhat at a loss to imagine what flocks can find to eat on these hills. Around Tiflis their monotonous brown colouring assumes, I was told, for a week or two during spring, a sickly tint approaching to green, and at rare intervals in winter, as was the case this year, is relieved by patches of snow; but with these exceptions they are sterile and arid-looking to a degree, and shutting in the town, as they do, in a basin, are anything but agreeable to the eye. They shelter the town, however, from the cold winds, and render the climate as mild as that of the Isle of Wight.

Tiflis, I believe, takes its name from its warm springs, but I am ignorant of the language which gives the word that meaning. It is now the seat of government for the Caucasian Provinces of Russia; head-quarters of an army of 150,000 men, employed in frontier duty, in surveillance of the tribes, and to a very great extent in making roads; and the residence of the Governor-General, the Grand Duke Michael. His Imperial Highness, third brother of the reigning Emperor of Russia, here holds his Court, and thus in this distant little capital there is to be found most agreeable society, and an unexpected quantity of social resources.

All travellers in Russia have doubtless experienced and benefited from the well-known hospitality of its inhabitants. In the remote out-of-the-way corners of the empire this national characteristic is carried almost to excess. The Court being in mourning for the Hereditary Grand Duke, lately deceased, there were no balls or dancing; but society solaced itself with breakfast, dinner, and supper parties. Invitations to the latter showered upon me, so that during my visit of more than a fortnight I could only make use of my hotel, a rough-and-ready sort of place kept by Frenchman of course, as a dormitory. I was frequently honoured with invitations to the palace, and the exquisite urbanity and real cordiality of the reception given me by their Imperial Highnesses the Grand Duke and Grand Duchess, as well as the excessive kindness I experienced at the hands of all I came in contact with, have left a most charming and indelible souvenir in my mind. "Venez dîner aujourd'hui;" "Nous vous attendons demain à dejeuner;" "Mon cheval sera à votre porte cet après-midi;" "Je vous verrai dans ma loge ce soir." Such were the phrases continually resounding in my ears, and in this way hospitality was rendered doubly acceptable—as it always is *du reste* amongst Russians—by a complete absence of ceremony and formality.

"Je vous verrai dans ma loge ce soir." Those habitués of Covent Garden and of the Grand Opera who have ever heard of Tiflis, will be surprised to learn that it possesses a theatre, where all the fashionable operas are as well given as in any second-rate Western capital, and that the "Salle de Théâtre," though comparatively small, is one of the prettiest in the world—what the French would term a "bijou;" but a thoroughly Oriental one, for this essentially western institution is here completely eastern, even to the minutest details of its decoration. It is a hall such as one might expect to find described in the pages of the *Arabian Nights*, or portrayed, as an antechamber to the Palace of Eblis, by the author of *Vathek*. Arabesques, exquisite in their minute tracery and glowing colouring, adorn the dome, the base of which almost imperceptibly blends itself in the elegant intricacies of the honey-combed architrave, harmoniously supported in turn on a double tier of horseshoe arches, which form the boxes. At first sight one's thoughts are carried far away to the halls of the Alhambra, and souvenirs of Moorish legends crowd on the mind, until, amidst the impatient stamping of the parterre and the tuning of orchestral instruments, the curtain rises and Gounod's *Faust* recalls us from our reveries. Below, in the body of the theatre, there is a good deal of the motley we noticed in the bazaar, but in the boxes we see some of the far-famed Georgian beauties, in the costume of their country as at present worn. It consists of a circular, flat velvet cap, in form like that of a German student, *couleur à volonté*, embroidered with gold lace and spangled with pearls, which covers the top of the head and part of the forehead. From it descends a short veil of white lace, thrown off the face and falling gracefully on the shoulders, whilst the jet black hair is worn in long tresses, two of which descend in front. A dress of Parisian cut, and a mantle heavily embroidered or trimmed with rich fur, complete the costume. The features of the wearers are regular and handsome, rather than beautiful. Finely chiselled brows, large black liquid dreamy eyes, prominent semi-aquiline nose, and voluptuous mouth, are the general characteristics of this Georgian race, which would excel all others in beauty were it likewise gifted with expression. This very necessary item is seldom found, but where it does exist the face is perfect. I was fortunate enough to behold this perfection, but, alas! my complete ignorance of the Russian and Georgian languages was an insuperable bar to an intimate acquaintance with the owner.

Before quitting the opera, one word of eulogy to the orchestra. The musicians are Russian subjects of German origin, descendants of a colony of Würtembergers who, driven from their native country, in I don't know which year of the last century, by religious persecution, sought and found freedom of conscience amongst the Georgians. Preserving intact their taste for music, these children of the great Teutonic Fatherland form an orchestral body which, though inferior to those of the London, Paris, and Vienna operas, has not its equal in precision of execution, discipline and taste, in the whole extent of the land of song. Yes, of song: vocal, not instrumental music. Have any of the thousands who yearly pass a portion of the winter months in Italian cities ever had the good luck to hear a really good orchestra? And if not, has any one of them been able to account for the fact that an Italian audience, so astonishingly quick in detecting the slightest error in singing, the variation of a fractional part of a note up or down the scale, not only tolerates inferior instrumental music, but is apparently indifferent to any amount of want of harmony and to any number of false notes in orchestral performances? Discipline is one of the first requisites for an orchestra. Discipline cannot be maintained without perseverance ; perseverance, the passive form of which is so manifest in the lazzaroni, would seem to be wanting as an active principle in the minds of the Italian instrumental performers. It is to be hoped that this deficiency will not be forgotten in the regeneration of the now united kingdom, and that the success which has already crowned the efforts of the Bolognese to counteract it, will encourage other opera orchestras to follow in their steps.

To return to our Würtembergers. They have not only preserved their national taste for music, but many other habits and customs of the Fatherland. Riding through their quarter of the town, called the colony, the neat and solid houses, surrounded by their garden plots, looked to advantage as contrasted with the half-underground mud hovels of the Georgians and Orientals, and the somewhat flimsily-painted dwellings of the Russians of the same class and standing.

Near the colony is the parade-ground, where, through the kindness of the officer in command of the Grand-Ducal Cossack body-guard, I witnessed a truly novel equestrian exhibition. After being paraded, the men, about sixty in number, mounted on strong ugly little horses, were ordered to perform a sham skirmish. Forming themselves into two camps, each combatant attacked his opponent on his own hook and after his own fashion. Here was a fellow standing bolt upright in his saddle and discharging his musket at another, who, hanging pendent by his legs, returned fire from underneath his horse's belly : there a couple clinging like cats to the flanks and ribs of their chargers, and thus completely sheltering their own bodies, watched a favourable moment for pinking each other, though to me they almost appeared like a couple of riderless horses; whilst others flattened themselves at full length on their beasts' backs and manœuvred for the chance of some unguarded movement on the part of their foes. All this at full gallop, accompanied by a good deal of screaming and yelling. Other feats were then performed. Galloping with the head downwards in the saddle and the body and legs erect in the air seemed a favourite one; still more so, picking up a stone or even a coin at the same pace, the performer holding on the while to his saddle by his feet. A couple of hours of this sort of work seemed to be enough for horse and man, so closing up into a column four deep, the Cossacks marched home singing in remarkably good time a native chorus with an accompaniment of two kettledrums.

They are first-rate irregular cavalry, these Cossacks, strong well-built fellows, and active as cats. Their dress and accoutrements are similar in form, but each man is at liberty to choose the colour of his caftan, and of the sixty, mustered on this occasion, hardly two were alike: white and different shades of grey and maroon seemed the favourite colours. Instead of boots, they wear a species of buskin, of a very pliable leather, reaching to the knee, and in the place of soles, a pair of mocassins of the same material, fitting like a glove and leaving the foot in perfect freedom.

The cathedral of Tiflis is worthy of a visit from those who have never seen a Greek church. There are pretty rides to the Botanical Gardens and amongst the neighbouring hills; and to the district of Kahétie, famous in the Caucasus for its very palatable and wholesome wine. It is more powerful and warmer than Bordeaux, with somewhat less body than Burgundy, and is the best substitute for either of the French wines that I have tasted. Its good qualities are duly appreciated by the natives, whose greatest pleasure it is to set themselves down for a good steady long drink: indeed, it is only then that the Georgians give any sign of animation. In general they are lazy, indolent, apathetic, and ignorant, without ambition to rise in the world, and content to live on in their own sluggish way. The lower classes are principally cultivators of the soil, which they manipulate in the same old-fashioned jog-trot style as their ancestors for centuries before them. Amongst the higher, education is little heeded; a Georgian seldom rises to the senior class in his school or college, and considers further study unnecessary when he can jabber French. Such being the case, and there being few Russians in the country who are not either civil or military employés, all trade and commerce are in the hands of the Armenians, an active and enterprising race, whose views are so steadfastly and ceaselessly fixed on the main chance, that they have come to be designated as the "Jews of the East."

Though some of the mountain tribes continue now

and then to give trouble to the Russian Government, and though the latter is obliged to maintain a large force—200,000 men, I have heard—in the Caucasus, still its various races of inhabitants seem pretty well reconciled to their present rulers; to whom they certainly owe the little that has as yet been done for the advancement of civilization. That little may, as we have seen in speaking of the Poti-Tiflis and Baku Railway, at no distant day receive a vast extension, and not even the most ardent of Schamyl's romantic admirers will maintain that it could have been effected without the aid of Russia. Schamyl was a hero, no doubt, but then he was one of those heroes whose existence is incompatible with this progressive nineteenth century. Left to themselves and to heroes of this species, the Caucasians would to this day have been found in a state of barbarism, continually warring with each other, and warring merely for plunder.

Vastly preferable to such a state of things is Russian civilization, deficient though it may be in some respects. A police force is an acknowledged necessity of our times, and, just as amongst communities of men, there are criminals and malefactors whose attacks and outrages on their fellows are no longer compatible with social order as at present understood and practised, so likewise amongst communities of states there are unruly and worthless members whose existence can no longer be tolerated by the prevalent ideas of the century. Incapable of themselves of emerging from barbarism, they must either be swept from the face of the earth or submit to the guidance and domination of some other member of the community which has had the wisdom or the good luck to conform itself to those ideas. Russia having adopted them, was thus impelled not only by her geographical position, but also by the feeling of the age in which we live, to step in and keep the peace in the Caucasus, just as she is now by the same motives urged on to enforce the first rules of order and civilization on the recalcitrant khans of Central Asia. An Englishman, in the ardour of his patriotism, may regret and deprecate her approach to our Indian frontier; a cosmopolitan must rejoice that, whatever its intents, that approach will eventually replace barbarism by civilization.

But we must back to Tiflis, where the Russian new year, the 12th of January, is celebrated with an excess of hospitality which makes one almost forget the extraordinary severity of the winter. A good deal of snow has been falling, and the frost is so severe that I skate on the Kura, to the great stupor of many of the inhabitants, who have never seen skates in their lives. The last days of my stay are occupied with preparations for my drive of 400 versts to the Persian frontier. The postal authorities furnish me with a vehicle, a sort of *char-à-bancs*, supplied with the luxury of springs, covered in on three sides with leather curtains, and capable of containing myself and my baggage, and with a conducteur who can understand and speak a few phrases of German. A padarojna for four horses, and more in case of need, is procured for me, and I invest in huge felt boots and a portable bed weighing some ten pounds. Commissariat supplies, in the shape of tongues, chickens, preserved meats, bread, butter, wine, brandy, tea, and sugar—everything, indeed, that a man may want for four or five days—are laid in, and, on the morning of the 15th January, after wishing all my Tiflis friends good-by, and seeing my traps secured by ropes in the front part of my *char-à-bancs*, I take my seat beside them near the door, and we move slowly and regretfully through the roughly-paved streets and out of the town.

CHAPTER V.

The Plain of the Kura and Valley of the Akstaf — Snow — Pass of Dilijan — Lake of Goutche — Legend about its Trout — Erivan.

ONCE out of the hills which surround Tiflis, we get down on to the river bank, and the road being flat, keep up the *ventre-à-terre* pace during most of the day, and at eight in the evening come to a halt at a pretty good post-house called Nawo Akstaf. It is a monotonous and melancholy drive of 107 versts over a vast plain, traversed by the Kura and bounded by arid brown hills running parallel therewith; there is an utter want of vegetation, except when, at rare intervals, a belt of scraggy poplars, or a plot of scrubby brushwood, denote the existence of a stream, and an equally sparse exhibition of animal life in the shape of a string or two of camels, a herd or two of sheep and goats, and a native or two " pricking o'er the plain." At each post-house there are apparently a few inhabitants, and now and then we pass a Tartar village, composed of reed and mud-built hovels, like molehills, and guarded by a troop of huge white mastiffs, or a Mahometan cemetery, a mere jumble of broken headstones, sticking up in the desert plain, and unprotected by wall or mound, intensely expressive of the surrounding desolation.

After twelve hours of this sort of scenery, and of rattling and shaking, the bare walls of the post-room and the wooden tressel have a cheery look, and one almost goes into ecstasies at the sight of the smoking samovar. The conducteur whips bed, bedding, and provisions out of the carriage, and in half an hour hot tea and supper are forthcoming.

By the display of much energy my conducteur contrived to have his team ready before daybreak next morning, and as the sun rose we were leaving the plain of the Kura and entering the hills on its south-eastern side by the valley of the Akstaf; catching a last view, at the same time, of the great Caucasian chain, ruby red in the clear morning air. The rough and stony road rises rapidly along the banks of the stream, an affluent of the Kura, amidst hills at first arid and barren, but as we get higher up, covered with scrubby brushwood, which, on nearing our third station, Euruslam, becomes worthy of the name of timber.

Hitherto there had been no difficulty in procuring horses, and beyond the unnecessarily long delays travellers always meet with in these post-houses, nothing had interrupted our onward progress. But before descending from my perch at Euruslam, I spied with misgivings a telega at the post-house door, and five minutes later, after a long altercation with the master, my conducteur announced that an officer, on his way to Tiflis, had just ordered the only four fresh horses in the stable, and that none of the others would be fit to start till next morning. It being then only noon, the prospect of passing the rest of the day and night in this solitary post-house was not cheerful. No help for it, however, for the master, perceiving from our looks and language that we were anything but resigned to our fate, shut himself up in his own part of the premises, and refused to have further communication with us. Luckily the station, apparently the only building in the neighbourhood, was beautifully situated. Bold, abrupt hills of the most varied forms, sprinkled with hardwood and juniper, and lofty rocks exhibiting the most fantastic formation in their horizontal, perpendicular, and curved strata, rise around it on all sides, and give the scene an air of wild grandeur, enhanced, at that moment, by a lot of vultures careering about their summits. So a solitary scramble in the hills with my gun on my shoulder, and a vain attempt to get a shot at the vultures, occupied, *tant bien que mal*, the vacant hours till, towards sunset, snow drove me back to the post-house.

Since leaving Tiflis the weather had been milder, and the snow had almost disappeared in the valleys of the Kura and Akstaf; now it again began to fall, bringing in its train a host of troubles and difficulties to the traveller.

What a charming variety is a fall of snow in Old England! How pretty the white mantle looks, sparkling and glittering in the sun, as on some bright Christmas morning you survey it from your cosy breakfast-table! How pleasing to your ears the crackling of its frozen particles under your boot! How exhilarating to your spirits the sharp frost that generally accompanies it! Those who have only this agreeable acquaintance with it cannot realize the inveterate hatred with which the traveller regards snow, his greatest torment. Give me mud, dust, wind, rain, and heat, but preserve me from snow.

From the Bosphorus to Poti, wherever land appeared, it was white, but there was always relief for the eyes in looking at the sea; from Poti to Tiflis it was white without relief; thence to Euruslam there was brown relief and no white; but from Euruslam to the gates of Tehran a great white pall covered the earth. Far as the eye could reach, o'er mountain, plain, and valley, spread one vast sheet of snow, bewildering from its vastness, painfully blinding in the sunshine from its intolerable glare, sickening, without it, from its lifeless monotony. Apart from the cold and the obstacles it opposes to progress, the moral depression produced in the mind of the traveller, journeying for days and weeks over some 2,000 miles of snow, by the deadly monotony of the sight of this earth-covering winding-sheet and his feeling of inability to escape from its huge and dreary folds, is not what a Samaritan would wish his best friend to experience.

A slight foretaste of my snowy difficulties awaited me soon after starting early next morning, for we had hardly proceeded a couple of versts when my team of six horses (two additional on account of the snow) with one consent jibbed on a steep hill. My yamtchik and two chapars used their usual arguments, but in vain; the horses, with their absurd Asiatic shoes, slipped and floundered, and eventually fell in a heap. I sent the chapars back to the post-house for more horses. These likewise proved useless. Here was an occasion for the display of Tapleyan virtue: a possibility of remaining on the slope till the snow melted; for if ten horses can't drag a carriage up hill, what will?

After brooding over the prospect for an hour or so, we spied a Tartar's waggon coming down towards us, and there being no room for him to pass without first moving our vehicle, for there was a precipice on one side of the narrow road and a wall of rock on the other, he likewise came to a standstill. To our infinite satisfaction we found that his three horses were shod in European fashion, and after some parley as to the price of their services, they were yoked to my vehicle and delivered us from our difficulty.

Though incidents of this nature threatened to recur at any moment, no extraordinary delay was experienced until reaching the village and post-house of Dilijan, at the foot of the pass of that name. This pass is between 5,000 and 6,000 feet above the sea-level, and divides Georgia from the mountainous district of Karadagh. Here fresh horses were refused, but after passing one afternoon and night at Euruslam, I was determined to employ every means to avoid passing another at Dilijan ; where, to judge from the aspect of the place, my sole amusement would have been a walk in a foot and a half depth of snow. So summoning the conducteur and the post-master, I caused the latter to be informed with much solemnity that I was an intimate friend of the Governor-General, and that unless horses were at once forthcoming, I should write, nay telegraph at once to his Imperial Highness and await the result."

This unsparing use of the Grand Ducal-name, accompanied by considerable vehemence of manner and gesture, had the desired effect ; the fellow bowed, protested that he had been misunderstood, that the horses were ready, and disappeared at once to see them harnessed. The steepness and length of the ascent necessitated eight, and it was only after toiling and struggling for near three hours through snow, sleet, and mist that we at last reached the summit of the pass, and commenced rattling down its southern slope to the great Goutche Lake.

This vast expanse of water, sixty or seventy miles long and about thirty broad, I was told, is situated 5,000 feet above the level of the sea, and surrounded by an amphitheatre of barren hills. In the best of seasons its scenery must be wild and melancholy, but at the moment at which I first saw it, both these features were enhanced by the state of the atmosphere. The hills were covered with snow and partially hidden by whitish masses of mist and vapour, making the tranquil waters of the lake appear, by contrast and in the dim twilight, of a deadly leaden hue; whilst, poised and stationary above, a huge canopy of inky black cloud hung over the whole, so heavy-looking in its blackness that I expected each moment it would descend and envelop all in its sable folds. Getting down to the shore of the lake we found the post-house so comfortless that, notwithstanding all the stories I had heard of accidents which had occurred on the next stage from snowdrifts and brigands, I determined to go on. All my Tiflis friends, who had traversed this route, had informed me that this was the most dangerous stage of my journey; that as it was the wildest and most remote from cities and the fixed habitations of men, so it was the most unsafe; that I must mind and take an escort, and that carriages and even heavy waggons had been swept bodily off the road into the lake by the fierce winds which sometimes prevail on its shores. Almost their last words to me, indeed, had been, "Don't pass the Goutche at night." All this, and many stories to the same intent, recurred to my mind; and my first view of the lake was not one of a nature to dispel the disagreeable impression they had produced on my imagination. But anything seemed preferable to passing the night in a half-frozen state in the solitary post-house of Tchibukli, and I determined to start, in spite of the opposition of both driver and escort; who, on learning my irrevocable decision, became so anxious to break the back of the stage before actual darkness should set in, that I here witnessed for the first and last time the almost impossible feat of changing horses in ten minutes.

After half-an-hour's gallop over level ground, we ascended to a high bluff, rising some seventy or eighty feet perpendicularly from the lake, and forming its south-western boundary. The road ran along its extreme edge, and was narrowed to the merest necessities of a carriage-way by the rising ground on the land side. Much snow had fallen in the morning; it had drifted in many places to a depth of two or three feet, and, not being yet frozen, it effectually concealed, without counteracting their natural effects, ruts, holes, and loose stones. Here and there, at the most dangerous spots, a frail post or two with a transverse had been stuck up, more for form's sake than anything else. My journey from Tiflis had not been wanting in opportunities for accustoming myself to precipices and reckless driving, but I confess that my experience of them was insufficient to give me fitting calmness on this occasion. My driver had evidently *le diable au corps*, and went dashing along the zigzag edge of the bluff with seemingly as much sangfroid as if he had been taking his team *ventre-à-terre* across a bowling-green, whilst the two Tartars of my escort, one before and the other behind the carriage, appeared, perhaps from the ill repute of the stage, more than usually intent on performing it in the shortest time possible. Sitting down with my back to the precipice and my eyes steadily fixed on my baggage, I remained for some ten minutes revolving in my mind the probabilities of our being shot bodily into the lake. But in turning a sharp corner, and passing within a foot of the edge of the precipice, I involuntarily caught sight of the black waters far below us, whilst at the same moment a stone or a rut seemed to send us completely out of our centre of gravity and at once to turn the scale of chances lakewards. My nerves could stand this no longer ; so, opening the carriage door, I descended to the footboard and there stood, ready to jump off at any moment in case of an upset, and fully expecting to see carriage and horses flying over the precipice, and myself sprawling in the snow on its brink. My Tartar seemed somewhat puzzled at this change of position, but I fancy soon attributed it to its real motive, for if I mistake not, a grim, and, perhaps, contemptuous smile, came over his features as, galloping along in the snow and darkening twilight behind me, he gesticulated that there was no danger. Happily, there was no wind; our chances of perdition seemed to me sufficiently numerous without it, and, notwithstanding the well-meant assurances of the Tartar, I can only ascribe our escaping all mishaps to luck or a miracle. This dangerous bit of road is of considerable length, as we were near half-an-hour in traversing it; in two hours more, and when night had set in, we reached Yelenawka, and entered a post-house, in which an English master of hounds would feel scruples of conscience in kennelling his pack.

Yelenawka, a miserable village, is, as I perceived next morning, situated on the lake. The bay on which it stands was unfortunately frozen, and I was thus unable to taste the delicious trout with which it is said to abound, and which had been strongly recommended by the epicures of Tiflis. Their delicacy was probably known to our friend above quoted, Marco Polo, who visited the lake in 1273-4, and who, as will be seen by the following extract, attributes to them a peculiarity which it is to be hoped they do not retain at the present day.

"Quivi si è lo Monastero di Santo Lionardo, ov' è tale maraviglia, che d' una montagna viene un lago dinanzi a questo monastero, e non mena niuno pesce di niuno tempo, se non di Quaresima, e comincia lo primo dì di Quaresima, e dura insino al Sabato Santo, e viene in grande abbondanza. Dal dì innanzi non vi se ne vede nè trova veruno per maraviglia infino all' altra Quaresima. E sappiate che il mare, che io v' ho contato, si chiama lo mare di Geluchelari." *

The legend, no doubt, came from the monastery which I had noticed the evening before on a small

---

* "There stands the Monastery of St. Leonard, a place so wondrous that before it, surrounded by mountains, is a lake which contains no fish except during the season of Lent. The fish come in great abundance on the first day of Lent and remain until holy Saturday. Previously not one is to be seen, and afterwards there is not one to be found until the following Lent. This lake is called, as I have stated, the Lake of Geluchelari."

island about a mile from the shore. Had not its inmates had a surfeit of fish during Lent, and did they not invent this story as a pretext for indulging in more succulent food during the rest of the year?

Having with difficulty procured some water from the frozen lake for my modest ablutions and swallowed some hot tea, I left the village soon after dawn, amidst snow and clouds: a small group of natives huddled in sheepskin mantles looked shiveringly at my departure. The descent to Erivan possesses none of the fine scenery of the Dilijan side of the pass. The road, the stoniest I ever drove over, runs down a series of bleak bare hills and arid slopes, but it is said, in clear weather, to afford the traveller magnificent views of the monarch mountain of these parts—Ararat. The state of the atmosphere deprived me of this "distraction," nor did anything occur to enliven my forty-five miles' drive; for villages there were none and no human beings were visible, except at the post-houses where we changed horses, until we got down into the plain and the streets of Erivan.

We drove up to what is pretentiously described as an hotel, but it seemed to me so comfortless and dirty that a glance indoors induced me to prefer taking up my quarters at the stanzia (post-house). There was just time before dark for a wade through the streets of the town. It contains some 15,000 souls, I believe, principally Armenians, and, since it became Russian in 1828, has been Russianized to the extent of having its streets made as wide as boulevards, and some of its houses painted green. Otherwise it is Asiatic. Its principal building is a fort, of Persian origin, situated on a stream called the Zengui, an affluent of the Araxes. Having a letter of introduction to the governor of the province of which Erivan is the capital, I went to pay my respects and to enjoy the luxury of conversing for a few minutes in a known language, after three days' almost total silence; for my conducteur's knowledge of German was of the slightest, and mine of Russian almost nil.

The governor, a military man of course and a perfect master of French, received me most hospitably with glasses of hot tea and cigarettes. Happening to mention, in the course of conversation, that the Grand Duke, in talking of the dangers of the road, had told me that the only instance of highway robbery of late had taken place near Erivan, his excellency seemed to become rather nervous. "What!" he seemed to be thinking, "has the Grand Duke heard of this little affair? And why does this fellow mention it to me? Am I going to get a rap over the knuckles?" He soon, however, resumed his calmness, talked of the flourishing state of his province, of the roads he was constructing, of his hopes of some day seeing a railway from Erivan to the Persian frontier, &c., and I was just beginning to hope that he had forgotten my indiscreet mention of the robbery, when he again reverted to it. He said it was a trifling affair: some clothes and a little money had been extorted from a traveller; it was nothing; an escapade: there were no brigands, and no danger; and then added, to my surprise, as I rose to depart,—" You must take an escort with you to the frontier, and I will send you some Cossacks to accompany you on your intended excursion to-morrow to Etchmiadzin."

CHAPTER VI.

ARMENIA AND ARMENIANS — ST. GREGORY THE ILLUMINATOR — ETCHMIADZIN — TRADITIONS RELATIVE TO THE ARK'S RESTING-PLACE — MOUNT ARARAT — NAKHITSHEVAN — JULFA — THE ARAXES.

IN the immediate vicinity of Erivan lay the original kernel of one of the oldest nations in the world and the capital of one of its most ancient kingdoms. Armenia in the days of its power extended from the Caucasus to the Kurdish Taurus, and from the Halys to the Lake of Ooroomiah. "Amidst the natural fastnesses of this district," says a modern writer, "in a country of lofty ridges, deep and narrow valleys, numerous and copious streams, and occasional broad plains—a country of rich pasture grounds, productive orchards, and abundant harvests—this (Armenian) interesting people has maintained itself almost unchanged from the time of the early Persian kings to the present day."*

As to their origin and the name of their country, I cannot do better than quote an extract from some

---

* Rawlinson's *Ancient Monarchies.*

Russian State-papers which have lately been translated into English:*

"Armenians themselves, relying on traditions still preserved among them, trace their origin up to Haïk, a grandson of Japhet, who lived at the time of the Tower of Babel, and who, after the confusion of tongues and the consequent dispersion of peoples, left the plains of Shinar for the foot of Ararat. There he established himself and his family, the parent stock of the people that called themselves Haïkans, after him their ancestor, and gave the name of Haïzdan, or Haïkstan (retained by Armenians to the present day), to the land in which they first settled. The sixth descendant in straight line from Haïk, by name Aram, a contemporary and ally of the great Assyrian Ninus, distinguished himself in so many ways, but especially by conquests and victories, that ever since the surrounding nations called all Haïkans, Armenians, and their land, the land of Haïk, Armenia."

The descendants of Haïk seem to have governed their country until the time of Alexander the Great, the last of them having died fighting against the Macedonian, as the ally of Darius Codomannus (B.C. 328). From that time Armenia has had its full share of vicissitudes, and been successively the prey of Greeks, Romans, Parthians, and Persians. To avoid the horrors of the Mahomedan invasion, it threw itself into the hands of the Byzantine emperors, and for

---

* *The Life and Times of St. Gregory the Illuminator.* Malan.

four centuries the land was disputed by the latter and the Caliphs, who in turn nominated as its governors the heads of its greatest and most ancient native families. Such were the Bagratidæ, one of whom attained to so much influence and power that he forced the Caliph of the day to grant him the title of king (A.D. 885). Internal dissensions and the invasion of the Seljuck Turks put an end to the Bagration dynasty, and its last remaining scion became King of Georgia. Georgians, Turks, Persians, and Russians have since in turn had partial possession of the country, until in 1828 its present subdivision was completed.

These events fully explain how it has come to pass that Armenians are to be found in so many different and distant regions of Europe and Asia, and that they almost monopolize the trade of the East. Intestine wars and foreign invasions drove them from their native land, and commerce thus became the natural occupation of those who no longer had land to cultivate, nor a country they could call their own. It is hardly necessary to mention the parallel between Armenians and Jews in these two respects; but there is a third which equally characterizes them both. Religious belief is the bond which has ever united and still unites the scattered members of both nations, and has preserved to them intact the type and characteristics of their remote ancestors.

As we are bound to Etchmiadzin, the seat of the primate of the Armenian Church, a few words on its founder and doctrine may not be without interest.

According to Armenian * traditions, their country, the first to receive the knowledge of the true God in the days of Noah, was also the first to hear the glad tidings of the Gospel; one of their kings, Abgarus, having been in epistolary intercourse with our Saviour, and having received from Him his portrait not painted by human hands. Two of the apostles, Thaddeus and Bartholomew, each bringing with him a wonder-working relic—the former the spear which pierced our Saviour's side, and the latter a painting of the Virgin by St. Luke—are said to have there preached the new faith and suffered martyrdom for it. But the results of their labours seem to have been lost in the mixture of Persian fire-worship and Greek idolatry, which then formed the religion of the surrounding people, and it was reserved to St. Gregory to sow the first permanent seeds of Christianity, and thus become, under the title of the "Illuminator," the founder and patron of the National Church.

The hand of Providence is clearly manifest to Armenians in the circumstances attending the birth of their patron saint. Anak, his father, a Parthian nobleman, had, on condition of receiving the sovereignty of Balkh, offered to Ardashir, king of Persia, to murder Chosroes, king of Armenia; on his journey to accomplish this object he was accompanied by his wife, who gave birth to Gregory (A.D. 258) at the very spot where Thaddeus had suffered martyrdom. Two years later Anak killed Chosroes while out hunt-

---

* *The Life and Times of St. Gregory the Illuminator.* Malan.

ing, and fled for his life. His family were all put to death, except Gregory, who was saved by a certain Sophia, the Christian wife of a Persian then tarrying in the city of Valarshabad, the capital of Armenia, and was by her carried to her home, Cæsarea of Cappadocia. There he was educated in the precepts of Christianity, and grew up to man's estate, perfect in bodily form and abounding in spiritual graces and mental gifts. Nor did Sophia's care stop here. She provided him with a well-born and virtuous wife, who bore him two sons, both superlatively precocious, it would seem; for, in the words of tradition, "while as yet their tongues only stammered in children's talk, they already made mention of the most Holy Trinity and of the unity of the Godhead." But domestic happiness and a life passed in the practice of good works were insufficient to smother in Gregory's breast the innate yearning of his heart, the early-conceived object of his life—viz. to atone for his father's crime by opening the gates of eternal life, through Christ's Gospel, to the son of him who had been thrust out of the portals of this world by that father's murderous hand. So after bestowing his worldly substance on his children, and placing his wife, at her own desire, in a convent, Gregory departed and became the slave of Tiridates, who had succeeded his father Chosroes on the throne of Armenia.

Gregory's intelligence and fidelity soon gained for him that monarch's esteem and affection. He rose so high in favour that his master at last entrusted to

St. Gregory the Illuminator.

him, as the most worthy of his subjects, the duty of bearing to Anahid, the protecting goddess of the country, the thank-offerings which he wished to present for the numerous victories he had gained over his enemies. Then first did the saint declare his mission. Refusing to bow to images of wood and stone, he boldly anathematized the idolatry of the Armenians, and proclaimed himself the apostle of Christ. At this the king was wroth, and commanded that Gregory should be put to the torture, and on his persisting in his refusal to recant, that he should be cast into a noisome black pit full of vipers and other reptiles.

About this period there arrived in Armenia two saints, Guiane and Rhipsime by name. They had been obliged to leave the convent near Rome, where they had taken vows of chastity, and to flee to the East in order to escape the addresses of the Emperor Diocletian; who, being anxious to take to himself a wife, had sent commissioners all over the empire to seek out the handsomest woman amongst his subjects. The commissioners gave the palm to Rhipsime, who received notification of the emperor's gracious intentions. Flight or acceptance of the imperial favour were the only courses open to the lady. She unhesitatingly chose the former, and attended by her foster-mother, Guiane, and several of her companions, she departed for the East, and, after long wanderings, by the express commands of the Blessed Virgin, finally fixed her residence, and built herself a convent, at Valarshabad.

"The pangs of despised love" struck deep into

the heart of Diocletian, and, in the hope of recovering his lost treasure, he sent letters patent to all his sovereign allies, requesting them to aid him in his search after the beautiful Rhipsime. Tiridates' high appreciation of female beauty seems to have been known to Diocletian, for the emperor, in his letter to his Armenian friend, recommends him, in case he should find the lady and take pleasure in her charms, to keep her for himself.

Tiridates was not long in discovering the retreat of Rhipsime, and, at once smitten by her beauty, employed fair means and foul to obtain possession of her. His efforts were, however, all in vain. Rhipsime not only resisted all his persuasive arts, but foiled and vanquished him in a bodily struggle.

> The king's heart, left thus desolate,
> Flew at last for ease—to hate.

He signed the death-warrant, and Rhipsime and her companions suffered martyrdom. Heaven speedily avenged their deaths. Tiridates was transformed into a wild boar, and, like a still greater monarch, "ate grass as the oxen, and his body was wet with the dew of heaven," whilst all those who had taken part in his crime were driven mad and took to gnawing their own bodies. In this emergency the king's sister, of whom Moses of Chorene writes that she was " modest and well-behaved, like one of the virgins of old, and that she did not, like other women, let loose her tongue,"—was warned in a vision to seek out the now almost-forgotten Gregory. He was drawn up out of the noisome pit, where he had been miraculously preserved during fourteen long years, and, being entreated by the people, he prayed for the king and his courtiers, and they recovered their human forms and their senses. The king's conversion to Christianity followed of course at once, and with the king, the whole Armenian nation adopted the new faith. Gregory spent a long life in preaching and teaching and baptizing. His first act, after his consecration as Patriarch of Armenia by the Bishop of Cæsarea, about A.D. 302, was to build a church in honour of Saint Rhipsime and her companions, and he called the church "Etchmiadzin —the descent of the Only-Begotten—in consequence of a divine vision he had, in which the Only-Begotten Son, descending from heaven to earth, marked the spot by smiting it with his hammer of gold, which resounded into the very depths of hell."

St. Gregory, in founding the Church of Armenia, adopted all the liturgies and ceremonies of the Eastern Church; and complete union would appear to have existed between the two until the Fourth Œcumenical Council, that of Chalcedon, in A.D. 451. Internal disorders and calamities prevented the Armenian Church from taking part in this Council, and a report was propagated and believed in Armenia, to the effect that the Council had deviated from the dogmas of the Universal Church by recognizing in our Saviour the existence of Two Persons. This report, artfully spread by the followers of Eutyches, received confirmation by an accidental mistake in the Armenian translation of Pope Leon I.'s letter concerning the results of the Council. In writing of our Saviour's two natures, the one divine, the other subject to human suffering, the words "the one and the other" were rendered by an expression which in Armenian is applicable only to persons and not to things; so that, whereas Pope Leon really spoke of two natures, he was understood by the Armenians to mean two persons.

On this supposition the then Armenian Patriarch called together a National Council, which, persuaded of the heterodoxy of the proceedings of the Council of Chalcedon, rejected its authority and annulled its decisions. The misunderstanding was afterwards explained, but National antipathy and political differences prevented any healing of the rupture, and the bond of union once broken could never be renewed.

The dogmatic difference between the Greek and Armenian churches turns upon the explanation of our Saviour's nature, a point much too abstruse for the pen of a traveller. The supreme head of the latter Church is styled Catholicos and resides at Etchmiadzin. He is elected, subject to confirmation by the Emperor of Russia, by the votes of the Armenian bishops of all lands there assembled in conclave, and alone possesses the right of episcopal consecration and of blessing the holy oil. There are Armenian communities and churches scattered over Persia, Turkey, and India. In

1842, the Armenian population of Russia amounted to 500,000 souls, and they had 955 churches within the limits of the empire.

But we must be off to Etchmiadzin; for after a delay as long as this digression, the governor's escort has arrived, in the shape of four Cossacks of the Don mounted on sturdy ugly ponies and armed with carbines and long wooden lances. An open country car, half filled with straw, conveyed myself and conducteur, and once out of the town, my Cossacks left me, and were replaced by two mounted Tatars, who at once commenced showing their appreciation of my importance by performing their usual eccentric and picturesque antics on the snow-covered plain, hanging with their feet from their saddles, whilst their lips almost licked the snow, firing blank cartridge at imaginary enemies from under their horses' bellies, &c. An hour and a half's drive through fog and sleet brought us to our destination.

Though originally only applied to the church founded by St. Gregory in commemoration of his vision, the term *Etchmiadzin* now comprehends two other churches, dedicated respectively to Saints Guiane and Rhipsime. Hence the Turkish name of the place, "Ütch Kilise," or the Three Churches. The principal edifice stands in the centre of an open oblong space enclosed on all sides by a high wall, on the inside of which the conventual buildings, the residence of the Catholicos, &c., abut. It dates from about the middle of the fifteenth century, when after an absence of more than 1,000 years, the Armenian Patriarch was at length allowed to return to the head-quarters of his religion. The church is in the form of an equi-brachiated cross, each arm terminating in a Byzantine portico of bright red stone adorned with Arabesque carving; and it is crowned by a lofty octagonal dome, on each façade of which is represented in brilliantly coloured and glazed tiles, on a white and green ground, the colossal head of a saint. Outside stand a few tombs, and amongst them I noticed one of an English envoy to Persia, Sir I. Macdonald. The whole of the interior is covered with frescoes of Biblical subjects and miracles, and with scroll and Arabesque work of elaborate delicacy. These decorations have been added within the last 200 years, and are probably the result of contact with Russia and the Greek rite, as Chardin states that, when he visited the church in 1671, it contained neither sculptured nor painted ornamentation. I was shown the mitre, robes, and crozier of the Patriarch, studded with pearls, rubies, emeralds, &c. &c.; also a New Testament 700 years old, and some beautifully illuminated Bibles of the fifteenth century. But I quite forgot to ask to look at the sacred relics said to be here preserved; the most revered of which are the spear-head of Calvary, the arm of St. Gregory, and the skull of St. Rhipsime.

A monk with long flowing beard, clad in ample black folds, and wearing a high peaked cowl, then conducted me over the Patriarch's residence, which is remarkable only for its simplicity, and an extensive library; the convent similar to other buildings of the sort; the college, where there are always above 100 young men studying for the church, and where most of the Armenian religious books are written and printed; and he landed me finally in the great refectory, in which about 200 monks, priests, and seminarists, seemed to be making a hearty midday meal off boiled beef and a pilau of grits. I did not find either of these dishes very good, but cannot speak too highly of the convent wine, very much resembling Sauterne, which stood in great abundance on the long tables, and seemed to be as much relished by my hosts as by myself.

Etchmiadzin is not many miles from the foot of Ararat, and an Archbishop, who did the honours, was so flattered by the expression of my regret that the mountain was still hidden from view by the clouds, and of my fear that I might possibly miss seeing what had been an object of interest to me from my childhood upwards, that he begged me to stay with him till the weather should clear. He and all his countrymen are very proud of their mountain, upon which many of them believe remnants of the Ark are still extant: of course they scout as heresy the tradition according to which that vessel first came to an anchor on Mount Judi, a peak of the Cardu Chain, to the north of the Mesopotamian plains of Shinar. The grounds on which this tradition rests are, however, at least plausible.

The history of the Ark, as contained in the Syriac version of the Old Testament, in the Targums and

Koran, is, I am told, in accordance with this tradition: Josephus and many ancient writers adopted it: Assemanni mentions a convent bearing the name of Ark, as having existed near the foot of Mount Judi in the third century: Marco Polo, in describing Armenia, says: "Ancora vi dico che in questa grande Ermenia è l'Arca di Noe, in su una grande montagna negli confini di mezzodì inverso lo levante, presso al reame che si chiama *Mosul:*"* and finally Arabs, Turks, Kurds, Jews, and most Eastern Christians, believe in it. Nor is it in contradiction with our Book of Genesis. It is there stated that "the Ark rested on the Mountains of Ararat." But this word Ararat is used indiscriminately with Armenia to denote a country—not a mountain; and the country so denoted included the Cardu Range. A further argument in its favour may be drawn from the fact that in the region around Mount Ararat the climate is now too rigorous for the olive-tree, and there is no reason to believe that it was milder in former days.

If, then, this tradition be the correct one, the two cradles of mankind were in close proximity, almost in sight of each other, and I confess that the version of the story which thus places them in juxtaposition has a charm for the imagination. Having, however, always associated the Ark with Ararat, and having heard much of the symmetrical proportions of the latter, it was with

---

* "I must also tell you that in this Great Armenia there is the Ark of Noah; it is on the top of a high mountain, near the south-eastern frontier and the country called Mosul."

feelings of disappointment at not having seen it, that I declined the Archbishop's invitation, and mounted my car to return to Erivan.

Having nothing further to see in that town, I at once set off again on my way to the Persian frontier. Fifty versts over a level plain, evidently well irrigated from the number of frozen runners we passed, were accomplished before evening set in. The mist still hung about and impeded all view. If our second ancestor had had weather like mine, he might possibly never have found his way down from the mountain, and he and his quadrupeds might have died of hunger.

The next morning much resembled its predecessor: the mist was somewhat heavier, and the snow so deep that six horses were requisite. Instead of artificial runners, too, we had now rivers to cross. They were all frozen, of course, but not very hardly, and I observed that in approaching them, my driver always lashed up his team to a gallop, in the hope of getting across without a smash. He was successful in this manœuvre until about mid-day, when we came to a stream a good deal broader than those we had already traversed. A more than usual amount of thong was applied, and we started across the ice as fast as our horses could go. But, alas, human calculations often fail, and when about to reach the further bank, smash goes the ice, down go the off-wheels through it, whilst team and driver fall confusedly in the heap so often mentioned. Jumping from my perch, it was some consolation to find that the ice did not seem likely to give way any further; so the horses were put on their legs again, and attempts were made to drag the carriage out of its difficulty. Its wheels were, however, so jammed, and the quadrupeds found so little purchase on the slippery surface, that these were soon abandoned. So here we were, stuck in the middle of a river miles away from any village, with the thermometer at about ten degrees (of Reaumur) below freezing-point, and no apparent probability of being able to move on until a thaw came.

My chapars took the matter very coolly : the occurrence seemed by no means extraordinary to them : one cantered leisurely off to the next village, whilst the other remained to guard the carriage and to stop all passers-by to assist in dragging us out. My attendants being thus employed, and there being nothing to do until the villagers arrived, or a sufficient number of passengers had been assembled, my conducteur and I sat down to our luncheon, neither of us in the best of tempers. But a benign providence here interfered to restore equanimity and contentment to one of the party at least. As we were eating our last morsel of *pâté-de-foie-gras*, out came the sun, a vast gap of blue showed itself in the misty curtain, and Ararat's conical summit appeared sharply cut on this clear background, towering aloft above a sea of clouds and vapour. In an hour's time the sky was cloudless, and the great mystic mountain stood before me in all its symmetrical beauty, rising solitarily from the plain in its giant pride (for the hills at its base are barely worthy of the name) and sloping away gradually and majestically up into two summits, Greater and Lesser Ararat, both perfectly conical in shape, and so gracefully and harmoniously blended together that the effect of the whole is perhaps more striking than if the mountain had terminated in a single peak. The two cones softened, to my eye, its huge masculine grandeur, and gave it the soft charm of feminine beauty : for the lesser one nestles in the bosom of the greater, like a beautiful flower in the breast of a fair lady. The extreme summit appeared slightly flattened, as if expressly designed for a resting-place for the ark. It is some 16,000 feet above the sea-level, and when the rains ceased and the waters of the deluge began to subside, must have been the first land in this part of the world to appear above the surrounding flood, and probably long remained an island in the watery waste.

In this, the scene of mankind's second birth, there was plenty of food for my imagination, which had time more than enough to lose itself in dreams of the remote past. Three hours elapsed before I was roused from my reveries by the arrival of villagers with axes and ropes, and the hubbub created by the forced stoppage of a caravan of camels and donkeys, whose drivers were being reluctantly pressed into my service. The carriage had meanwhile been lightened of the baggage, and by the united efforts of peasants, drivers, and chapars, was at last brought to terra firma. Two stages more—during which the glaring refraction of the sun's rays from the snow was so painful that I could not keep my eyes open, and the cold so intense after darkness set in that I felt almost frozen—and we reach Nakhitshevan at eleven P.M. To welcome us, we find a post-house without glass in its windows, and a postmaster most chary of his fuel; so cramming my baggage into the window, I seek warmth in my bed.

The orthography of the word Nakhitshevan is a subject of dispute between the partisans of the two traditions relative to the Ark's resting-place. Those who are in favour of the Ararat theory maintain that, written as above, it means "first abode or settlement," or "first descent;" whilst their opponents as persistently deny this signification. Assuming the former to be correct, we must suppose that here was about the spot where Noah planted the first vine, primary source of so much conviviality, cause of so much woe, and remote origin of the occupation of the authors of permissive bills. What would have been the lot of these gentlemen, had that little plant sickened and died, and left no offshoots? I presume there are still vineyards at Nakhitshevan, but have no proof of the fact, as two or three feet of snow covered the earth, and my postmaster did not offer me a stirrup-cup as I left the miserable-looking little town next morning.

A drive of four hours down a gradual descent most favourable to the *ventre-à-terre* pace, through some wild rocky defiles opening out towards the end of the stage into a plain surrounded by lofty mountains, brought us within sight of our last Russian post-house, by name Julfa, and of the Araxes, the boundary between Russia and Persia.

Two swarthy individuals, clothed in long boots, wide dark-blue knickerbockers and jackets of the same colour lined with fur, and wearing gaudy neckerchiefs bound tightly round their shaven heads and hanging down behind their necks and ears, armed too with huge knives and a brace of pistols a-piece, assisted me from my carriage. They turned out to be Gholam Abdul Rezah Beg and Lazar, a Nestorian servant, sent down by her Majesty's Consul-General at Tabreez to convoy me thither. Lazar spoke a few words of English, and forthwith handed me a letter from the Consul congratulating me on my safe arrival at the frontier and expressing the hope that, as the weather was very severe and there was much snow, the brigands and wild tribes who frequent this part of the country and find impunity for their crimes by continually transferring their residence from one side of the Araxes to the other, would prefer keeping themselves warm at home to molesting my passage. A polite hint to me to keep my powder dry.

The post-house of Julfa is the best on the road from Tiflis. A good substantial building, evidently meant to impress the Persians with a favourable idea of Russian power and civilization. A few surrounding huts, built of sun-dried bricks, the only other habitations in the place, bring out the dignity of its appearance. I found it well warmed too, and calculated on having at last a comfortable night.

Lazar and the Gholam, however, at once dispelled these illusions, by telling me I should be much more comfortable on the Persian side of the river, where all was prepared for my reception, and that we must cross at once in order to be ready for an early start next morning, &c. I yielded very much contrecœur, paid my Russian conducteur, bade adieu to wheeled vehicles of all descriptions and descended to the swift-flowing yellow Araxes.

CHAPTER VII.

ARRIVAL IN PERSIA—PERSIAN COOKERY, TOWNS, POST-HOUSES, AND CARAVANSARIES—ORIENTAL HOSPITALITY—FERINGHEE—TABREEZ—GENERAL FEATURES OF THE COUNTRY—POPULATION—HEIR-APPARENT TO THE THRONE—GOVERNMENT—VISIT FROM AN OFFICIAL PERSONAGE—CHARACTER OF PERSIANS—THE BÂB.

A SPECIES of rudely-constructed raft conveyed myself and chattels across the river, and my inquiries as to where we were to pass the night elicited from Lazar the reply, "Telgeraf." In order more clearly to indicate his meaning, he, at the same time, pointed with his hand to a low mud-built edifice about a quarter-of-a-mile off, with which I could see that the telegraph wires communicated. These wires form one of the three telegraphic lines which connect England with India. They had been my constant companions from Tiflis, and were to be the only traces of Western civilization up to the gates of Tehran; thence they are carried down to Ispahan, Shiraz, and Bushir, to meet the Persian Gulf cable which connects them with Kurachee. Of the other two lines, one proceeds through Asia Minor to Baghdad and Bussorah, and the other goes through Egypt, and thence by cable to Aden and Bombay.

On entering the Persian Telegraph office I found its solitary official, a native, in high-peaked lambswool cap, flowing jubbah, wide loose trousers, and ample girdle, seated cross-legged on his carpet, whiling away the long hours of fasting (it was the season of the Ramazan) by fondling a couple of apples and calling upon Allah. He rose, and, with the stately courtesy common to all Persians, bade me welcome with the most ceremonious of salāms. A carpet was spread for me, and at once became sacred ground, on which no one presumed to tread without first taking off his shoes. This universal national habit of leaving one's shoes at the door has many advantages, besides being, especially in hot weather, most agreeable. It prevents that frequently exasperating creaking noise one so often hears in Europe; it to a certain extent conduces to cleanliness, and banishes the smell of leather. A Persian noble generally wears white socks; the lower classes prefer coloured ones; many none at all, and these generally give their feet what is considered a coquettish appearance by dying the nails with henna.

To complete my welcome, my Persian friend now approached with great reverence and begged my acceptance of a pomegranate, which he presented to me on the joined palms of both hands, it being disrespectful to offer anything with one hand alone. He added that the Shah-in-Shah had expressly chosen him for this frontier station in consequence of his knowledge of foreigners and their habits, and in order that they might thus be sure of a good reception on entering his dominions. Having thanked this elect of the Centre of the Universe, I took up my gun and went for a stroll on the river's bank.

This portion of the valley of the Araxes is anything but cheerful in winter. The high hills, which shut it in, were covered with snow; where mother earth peeped through her white mantle, she looked volcanic and arid; a furious cutting wind was blowing, and, with the exception of some wild-fowl, at which it was impossible to get a shot, neither man nor beast enlivened the scene.

On returning, I found that Lazar's culinary efforts had resulted in producing a meal composed of rice-soup, pilau with curded milk, and a fowl, which had probably seasoned both the preceding dishes. All Persians, let me here remark, have a notion of cooking, and the dishes they prepare are wonderful considering the means at their disposal. The traveller ought always to be provided with a supply of rice, tea, coffee, salt, pepper, and brandy; for with these primary ingredients his servants will cater for his board pretty well along the road. The kitchen-range, which the cook generally erects in the open air, consists of three or four bricks or stones, so placed that there may be a thorough draught between them: on these the pots and pans are placed, whilst the servants keep on supplying the necessary fuel. Eggs and fowls are always to be found in the post-houses;

except in the desert and very high passes, fruit likewise; and in most of the villages lamb and mutton. There is nothing better than a kebab of the latter. The Persian sheep is the fat-tailed one, *i. e.* its tail is enveloped in such a ponderous mass of fat that the animal always looks as if he had immense difficulty in carrying it all behind him, and old Chardin, somewhat of a *blagueur*, I fancy, affirms that in his time each sheep was furnished with a small platform on wheels to support this abnormal weight. The fat is very delicate, and a kebab is made by spitting alternate layers of fat and lean on a skewer, or oftener a ramrod, and after sprinkling with salt and pepper, and rubbing gently with a bit of garlic, broiling them over a wood fire. Of the merits of a pilau it is unnecessary to say anything further than that all European cooks ought to be sent to the East in order to learn how to boil rice. These two dishes afford a very fair meal; they can be procured almost everywhere; and I found my table much better furnished in Persia than in the Caucasian provinces of Russia, where the only certain thing is the samovar.

After partaking of Lazar's viands, and unpacking my English saddle, holsters, and revolver, I was left in solitary possession of the telegraph office; my bed being pitched between the two instruments which it contained. It was so piercingly cold when we left next morning that, even in fur coat and huge felt over-boots, it was difficult to keep the circulation going. My caravan consisted of self, two servants, three baggage-horses, and the post-boy. The horses (we should call them ponies) seemed strong and fresh, and after calling at a village a mile or two beyond our last bivouac for an escort of wild-looking fellows fairly mounted and armed with native muskets, we began the ascent of the Dara Diz—a pass which leads up from the valley of the Araxes, through abrupt barren mountains, to the great Persian table-land, and is notorious for the robberies and murders of which it has been the scene. As we wound slowly up the narrow path, Lazar failed not to point out the fatal spots and to expatiate, as far as his English would allow him to do so, on the lawlessness and cruelty of the neighbouring Kurdish tribes. The snow and cold seemed, however, to have kept them at home; though all the party were evidently relieved when, after an ascent of three hours, we reached the top of the pass and began cantering away over level ground and hard snow to our first Persian post-house (chapar khaneh) in the village of Irandibbi.

Most Persian villages and towns have certain general features in common. They are for the most part surrounded with walls of sun-dried bricks; the houses are principally of the same material, flat-roofed, and windowless towards the street; which is always very narrow, full of holes and ruts, and the receptacle of refuse. The mosques are distinguished by domes, but minarets are not, as in Turkey, very prevalent: the Persian generally goes up on to the house-top to pray; thence, too, the muezzin chaunts his summons to the faithful. In the capital and larger towns some of the mosques are covered with glazed tiles, and the bazaars and houses of the great are of stone or kiln-burnt bricks, but elsewhere there is seldom any colouring to break the brown monotony of the mud walls and roofs. Post-houses are invariably built on the same plan : they are square, enclosed by high walls, have a turret at each corner, and one entrance. Right and left, and sometimes above this, are post-master's and travellers' rooms, the latter devoid of all furniture but a carpet, and sometimes undivided by wall or curtain from the stables, which range round three sides of the enclosure. On arrival the traveller is offered a kalian (hubble-bubble), whilst fresh horses are being got ready ; if he intends to pass the night he establishes himself and his belongings in the most convenient corner. Caravansaries, too, are all uniform in shape and construction, differing from each other only in size and state of repair. Their external appearance is that of four blank walls surmounted with parapets. A single arched doorway admits to a large court-yard, from 50 to 100 yards square, as the case may be, in the centre of which is a raised stone platform for the deposit of merchandise, and sometimes a well. Around the court, and looking on to it, are vaulted cells, lighted only from the front, which is generally completely open. The doorways have no doors, and if there be any windows they are devoid of frames and glass. The stables are frequently under the cells. Many of these buildings, especially in the southern provinces, are substantial and handsome, and are always preferable to the accommodation afforded by the post-houses or villages.

As the towns, villages, post-houses, and caravansaries resemble each other, so do the stages. They vary in length from twelve to twenty-five miles, and go through a repetition of the same scenery: for Persia is a succession of mountains and plains, and after a series of mountain stages one is certain to come to a series of level ones, and *vice-versâ*. I need not, therefore, do more than mention one or two incidents illustrative of travelling post—chapar, in the native tongue —during my eighty miles' ride to Tabreez.

First of all, I found that my horses were exceedingly fresh, a phenomenon which later experience has proved to be a most exceptional state of things. The steed I myself rode carried me two long stages, some forty odd miles, the first day, and ran away with me at the end of the journey. Then my baggage-horses, always allowed to run loose, were continually bolting off the path at full gallop, and attempting, sometimes successfully, to kick their loads off into the snow, thus affording us some exciting runs of two or three miles, our object being to catch them before they succeeded in their intent. Whenever, too, we came to an unfrozen stream, great was the difficulty in counteracting their constant desire to lie down, baggage and all, in the water.

The whole country, mountain and plain, was covered with snow, and the sky was very very blue. We halted in two flourishing villages, by name Marande and Sofian. We passed some large ruinous caravansaries, dating from the reign of Shah Abbas the Great, and speaking of more prosperous times, but now tenanted by miserable lepers, who are banished here to the frontiers from the interior of the country, and who rushed out at us to gain our charity by the exposure of their hideous malady. On arriving at the gates of Tabreez all my luggage was impounded, on the pretext that I was smuggling gold lace, and only rescued from the hands of the customs officers by the aid of H.M.'s able Consul-General.

One hears a great deal about Oriental hospitality. Anything very profuse or splendid in this line in Europe is sure to be termed Oriental, and one might almost imagine that Easterns pass their lives in giving magnificent *fêtes* to the strangers who visit them. As far as Persians are concerned, this idea is certainly erroneous; if they receive at all, they do so, it is true, with admirable courtesy of manner, great professions of friendship, and much apparent cordiality: as in Spain, everything is *á la disposicion de usted*. But behind all this there is little, if anything, genuine and solid; so little, indeed, that on being asked to dine in a Persian house, I have often found I was only doing the proper thing in taking half the dinner with me, and have not unfrequently received hints through the servants of my host, a few hours previous to the meal, that a supply of wine or spirits would be most welcome. The hospitality known to us as Eastern, and so agreeable to the traveller, is that afforded by Europeans established in the East. In their houses he is sure of the warmest welcome, can come in and go out as he listeth, stay as long as he likes, and live as if he were in his own abode. There being no hotels in the country, he quarters himself, as a matter of course, on any European he may find, and the latter would look upon it as a slight were he to do otherwise. This arrangement is agreeable to both host and guest, for whilst the latter feels himself at home, the former cannot but find pleasure in seeing a new face and exchanging ideas in a Western tongue. I felt, therefore, no scruples on my arrival at Tabreez in quartering myself for a few days on the amiable family of the Queen's Consul-General.

In his *Decline and Fall of the Roman Empire*, Gibbon relates at some length the origin of the once famous Varangian Guard. The term Varangians, or Corsairs, was, he says, first given to bands of adventurers from Denmark, Sweden, and Norway, living by pillage and rapine, who, in the ninth century, offered their services to the descendants of Ruric, and maintained by their valour and ferocity the princes of that house on the throne of Russia. Wladimir the First, finding he no longer required their services, and was not in a position to satisfy their exorbitant demands, persuaded them to seek more remunerative service under a richer master. They accordingly assembled at Constantinople, recruited by a numerous band of English and Danes, who fled from the yoke of the Norman Conqueror, and were incorporated as a body-guard of the

Byzantine emperor. They preserved, he adds, to the last age of the Empire the inheritance of spotless loyalty and the use of the Danish or English tongue.

The reader will probably here pitch my book into the fire, and think my wits have indeed gone a-wool-gathering. What on earth, he will ask, have the Varangians to do with Tabreez? He may never have heard of the famous guard, and perhaps be as ignorant of their existence as were the Persian urchins who brought their deeds to my memory. But I would beg him to have just one moment's patience and to read on. Riding through the bazaar the morning after my arrival, ever and anon as I passed along, I heard, amongst the babel of sounds and street cries, the words "Feringhee," "Feringhee;" and as the term seemed connected with my person, and was the only one which, in my ignorance of the language of the country, had the definite form of a word to my ear, I naturally asked my companion the Consul what it meant. "Stranger," was the reply. "All Europeans are included in the term." As I afterwards found, this is the case all over Persia. The educated man has indeed some vague ideas that there are other countries and nations in the world besides his beloved and glorious Iran; he knows something of Turkey, of India, and Arabia; has heard of England, France, Germany, and Russia, and, if his studies have been deep, even of Yengidunya—the young world—America; but for the masses there is in Europe, or rather westwards of Constantinople, but one land, "Feringhistan," and one race, that of the "Feringhee." The Varangians came from that land, and their prowess or notoriety was so great that in this ultra-conservative of countries all foreigners are still designated by a corruption of their name.

Tabreez is a very ancient city. Persians tell us it was founded by Zobeida, the wife of Haroun el Reschid, who delighted in its shady and well-watered gardens, and made it his favourite residence. European geographers, however, place its origin at a much more remote period, and suppose it to be identical with Gansaca or Gaza, the capital of Atropatene—a part of Media, so called from Atropates, who after the death of Alexander made himself its independent ruler. For ages it has been a place of great importance, both commercially and politically. Under Hoolaloo Khan it became the capital of Persia. Marco Polo, writing of his visit to what he calls "La nobile città di Toris," in 1272-73, says,* "Gli uomini di Toris vivono di mercanzia e d'arti, cioé di lavorare drappi a seta e ad oro, ed é il luogo si buono che d' India e di Baudat e di Mosul e di Cremeser (Gherm-i-sir) vi vengono gli mercatanti, e gli mercatanti Latini vanno quivi e molto vi guadagnano." And again: "Intorno

---

* "The people of Tabreez are traders and artists, *i.e.*, makers of silk and cloth of gold, and their town is such a good mart that merchants go there from India, Baghdad, Mosul, and the warm region. Latin merchants go there also and make much money." "Around the city are beautiful gardens full of all sorts of pleasant fruits. The Saracens (Mahometans) of Tabreez are very malevolent and false."

alla città ha begli giardini e dilettevoli d'ogni frutta. Gli Sarraceni di Toris sono molto malvagi e disleali."

It is still a great emporium for the trade of Persia with the West, the principal halting-place of all the caravans going down to Trebizonde, capital of the rich province of Azerbaijan, residence of the heir-apparent to the throne, and contains 120,000 inhabitants. Though some 3,800 feet above the sea-level, it is situated towards the eastern end of a wide open valley, through which runs a river whose waters irrigate the girdle of gardens which surround the town; beyond this girdle all is barren and arid. Such is the case with nine-tenths of the Persian portion of that enormous table-land which, commencing in Asia Minor, near the sources of the Halys, or Kizil Irmak as it is now called, extends, with few depressions, south-eastward to the banks of the Indus. This region will be the scene of my travels for some time, and I shall be followed more easily if I here indicate in general terms its physical appearance, and give some data and general remarks as to its population.

A reference to the map will show that Persia extends from the Caspian to the Persian Gulf, a distance of 700 miles from north to south, and from the frontiers of Turkey to Affghanistan, Seistan, and Beloochistan, or, in round numbers, 850 miles from west to east, and that it contains within these limits a space about equal to France and Great Britain. Along the shores of the Persian Gulf there runs a strip of plain, varying in breadth from ten to fifty miles, which is little above the sea-level, and which, from its temperature, is called the gherm-i-sir, or warm region. Along the shores of the Caspian there is another strip of country of about the same breadth, equally low and flat. But there is this difference between the two—the southern one is, except in early spring, rainless, almost riverless, and generally arid and burnt, whilst the northern one is watered by continual rains and several considerable rivers, and is covered with magnificent forests, almost tropical vegetation, and dense jungles in which the tiger roams at will. The rest of Persia comes under the name of Sirhad (cold region), and forms part of the great Asian plateau above mentioned, which varies in altitude above the sea-level from 3,000 to 4,000 feet, and from which arise chains of mountains in all directions. The two principal chains are the Zagros, running along the western frontier of the kingdom, and the Elburz, which separates the plateau from the low land towards the Caspian Sea, rises to an average height of 9,000 or 10,000 feet, culminates in Mount Demavend, some sixty miles to the north-east of Tehran, and subsides again east of Meshed into the deserts of Kharazm. Spurs from these chains traverse the adjacent country, and in the vastest of Persian plains one is never out of sight of mountains.

In the eastern portion of the country there are enormous deserts of sand and salt which no effort of man could render productive, and it has been calculated that two-thirds of this elevated region are absolutely and entirely sterile. The soil of the remainder is good, and only requires water to make it excessively fertile. The rainfall is, however, very small; the rivers, which in general are only fed by the melting of the snow accumulated on the mountains, lose themselves, with few exceptions, in the sands and salt lakes; and the consequence is that, unless where artificial irrigation is employed, the eye in vain seeks relief on mountain or plain from the uniform and monotonous brown and grey colouring of the whole country. In early spring, it is true, herbs, generally of an aromatic nature, spring up and give a faint green tinge to the more favoured regions; but in a month or two they are burnt up, and their withered stalks and leaves seem to render the brownness more brown and the aridity more arid. Such are the general features of Persian scenery; though, as we shall see later, there are exceptions to the rule, and we shall find, especially towards the southern and south-western termination of the plateau, certain plains and valleys almost as green as those of Erin.

Vegetation, then, depends on artificial irrigation, *i.e.* on manual labour. Now a gentleman, who has been long resident in the country and has traversed it in every direction, states that the total number of inhabitants falls short of 5,000,000 souls. We may divide them into three classes—townspeople, nomads, and villagers. There are five Persian towns which contain more than 30,000 souls. They are Tehran, 120,000; Tabreez, 120,000; Meshed, 70,000; Ispahan, 60,000; and Shiraz, 40,000. Thĕre are further twenty or thirty other places, which may be dignified with the name of town, and have populations varying from 5,000 to 25,000. I shall therefore probably not be far wrong in allotting 1,000,000 to the first class; though, as a census is unknown, this and all other calculations are only approximative. The Eelkhanee of the Kaskäi, the most powerful and numerous tribe in Persia, has 25,000 or 30,000 black tents; the Kelhor of Kermanshah have 11,000; the Zengeneh, 10,000; the ₊Sheghaghee of Azerbaijan, 15,000 tents and houses. Besides these there are at least 100 other tribes of lesser importance, and at the rate of five or six persons to each tent the total number of Nomads may be set down at 1,500,000.

There would then remain 2,500,000 villagers, tillers of the soil and producers of vegetation. From personal observation, I should say that few villages contain more than 2,000 inhabitants; many of them are very small, and an average of 300 may be fairly given to each. At this rate we should have some 8,000 villages, scattered over a country equalling in extent France and Great Britain; and it will thus be easily understood how the traveller may frequently ride for scores of miles without seeing either an atom of verdure or a single human being. The environs of Madrid present on a small scale the natural features of the greater portion of Persia.

But I must hark back to Tabreez and its girdle of gardens, or, rather, orchards; for cool shade, fruit, and running water are the great objects of Eastern horticulture. The fruit-gardens are still very extensive, and celebrated for their peaches and apricots; which, if I mistake not, were introduced from Persia to Europe. January was not, however, the month to appreciate their beauties and products, nor indeed to enjoy any out-door sight-seeing, for from the altitude of its position the winters are very severe and long. Luckily, beyond the novelty which a European must find in his first visit to a Persian town, there is not much to be seen. A fine mosque, called the Blue Mosque, from the colour of the varnished tiles in which it is cased, built by Abbas the Great early in the seventeenth century, but much injured by neglect and the earthquakes * with which Tabreez has from time immemorial been continually visited; the ark or residence of the heir-apparent, a large frowning building situated in a commanding position near the centre of the town; the Great Maidan, a species of open square, in its front; and the spacious and well-filled bazaars: that is about all.

The life of an heir-apparent to an Eastern throne is not a bed of roses. He is always regarded with the utmost jealousy by the reigning sovereign, and in Persia is banished as far as possible from the capital. For many years it has been the custom to send him

---

* Azerbaijan, of which Tabreez is the centre and capital, signifies "*The Country of Fire*," perhaps from this circumstance; though its meaning has generally been explained by the number of fire-temples which are said to have existed there.

off when yet a child to Tabreez, as governor of the province of Azerbaijan, and there he generally remains until called to the throne. The Tabreezis (malvagi in Marco Polo's time) are ever a fierce and unruly set of people, exceptionally impatient under taxation, the sole aim and object of government in the East, and he can have no very quiet times with them; then his civil list is often in arrear or not forthcoming, so much so that he is often at a loss how to raise funds for his household expenses. He must avoid making himself too popular, for his popularity would diminish that of the sovereign. He must pay up exactly to the royal treasury the revenue due from his province, and yet abstain from over-violence in its exaction, for fear of rousing revolt, or of being accused of encroaching upon the prerogatives of the crown. Altogether his best policy seems to be to efface himself during his sovereign's reign.

The present system of government in Persia is very much what it was under the great kings. The country is divided into provinces, to each of which a governor (we may call him satrap) is deputed, removable of course at the will of the sovereign. Large sums are often paid for these satrapies. A fixed revenue is due from each; and provided this be punctually paid, and the people be kept from open insurrection, the satrap may do pretty much as he likes, and grind as much money out of his province as he can. It is thus that he recoups the amount he has paid for his appointment and the sums he must now and then disburse to keep himself in favour at court, where he is always certain of having rivals anxious to replace him. He has almost absolute power over the subordinate authorities in his province, who in turn must pay up a fixed annual quota; over and above which they also squeeze out from those below them further sums for themselves. These exactions are called in Persian, mudākl; and from the Shah down to the meanest subordinate, mudākl is the aim and object of life: dearer far to the Persian's heart than would be the free gift of an equal sum, for in the process of squeezing it out of his inferiors he finds satisfaction for two of his most cherished passions—avarice and the unbridled exercise of power.

The day after my arrival at Tabreez was devoted to receiving visits from the few Europeans in the place, and from a Persian official, who here represents the Minister for Foreign Affairs. Early in the morning there arrived from him a large circular tray, on which were four huge sugar-loaves, sugar-candy, and bon-bons, with a message to the effect that at two o'clock he would call on me. At the appointed hour I saw his Excellency enter the courtyard, preceded and followed by twenty servants in tall hats and long broad-cloth robes, marching solemnly two deep. On approaching the door the upper servants doffed their shoes and entered to announce their master—a lively-looking gentleman, with sparkling, cunning black eyes and long black beard, wearing a tall, brimless, lamb-skin hat, and dressed in a white abba,* lined with fur

---

* Abba, a species of burnous or long loose mantle.

and embroidered with shawl lace and gold braid, drab trousers and varnished leather boots. He made me a stately salaam, bade me welcome to Persia, and made a flattering speech to me about England, which was duly translated by the Consul-General. Then tea, coffee, and pipes were introduced; and the visit terminated by an exchange of many ceremonious phrases, and by my remunerating—unknown to their master, of course—the bearers of the sugar and sugar-plums with the usual *buona mano*.

In Persia—more than in any other country, perhaps—a man's rank is indicated by his *train de maison*, the number of his wives, and especially by the number of servants who accompany him when he walks or rides abroad. The Shah travels about and goes on hunting excursions accompanied by thousands; the great nobles have their hundreds, the lesser ones their scores, and so on. Many of these servants are unpaid; they pick up crumbs about the house, receive cloth for a jubbah each new year, and eke out their livelihood by perquisites of the nature of the *buona mano* I gave. I can't say much for their honesty: in ancient times the Persian was taught to shoot with the bow and speak the truth; these two acquisitions may possibly have been so closely associated in the national mind, that when the one was disused the other was considered superfluous. However this may be, truthfulness is not now much cultivated: indeed, I remember a great noble, an educated man too, once asking me, somewhat after the manner of Pontius Pilate, "What is the use of speaking the truth.?" With mendacity, cunning goes hand in hand in the Persian's character. He seems to derive so much occupation and amusement from their united practice, that he never is dishonest in a straightforward manner. He does not commit burglary, he seldom steals an article directly from your house, but he makes you pay double for whatever he has to buy for you, being in league with those with whom you personally bargain; he tells you your house and stable gear has been stolen, and must be replaced, and is intoxicated with pleasure if he can smuggle back the article thus said to be lost as a bran new one. In short, his lively imagination must be gratified at the same time that his pocket is filled.

He has, however, two good qualities, if not more, in a very remarkable degree—aptitude for almost any employment, and great powers of endurance. Evidence of this is visible, after a very short acquaintance with the country, amongst all classes. For instance, my head servant (a very handsome fellow, and a dandy in his way), when at home, had little else to do than to prepare my toilette, be smartly dressed, serve tea, coffee and pipes to visitors, and look after my household. On a journey this fellow was everything—valet, groom, and cook. More than once I was obliged to ride post 250 miles at a stretch, never taking off my clothes, and only snatching a few winks of sleep whilst fresh horses were being procured at the post-houses. My servant, of course, never had time for a moment's rest, but he never seemed fatigued; and after three days' and two nights' continuous travelling would, on reaching the end of our journey, take a bath and reappear as fresh as when we started. He had, however, the faculty of making up for lost time, by sleeping as often and as long as he pleased when he had nothing better to do. Most Persians seem to have complete command over sleep. As we should say, "I'm going for a walk," they say, "I'm off to sleep;" and off they go at any hour of the day or night. Riding about the capital, I have frequently met cassids (letter-carriers) coming in from far-distant towns: these fellows had frequently been walking sixty or seventy miles a day for several consecutive days, but bore no traces of great fatigue. These are fair proofs of endurance; and I am inclined to attribute the universality of this quality amongst Persians to the fact that their infants are so little cared for and so much exposed, that the strongest ones alone arrive at the age of manhood. As to their capacity for turning their hands to almost anything, I need only give another instance, that of the present Minister for Foreign Affairs, who was, I believe, originally a kawagee, or preparer of coffee, in this very town of Tabreez, whence I have made such unpardonable digressions. I must add one more to their number, and then journey on eastwards.

Some twenty years ago—in 1850, I think—there was brought out one morning from the State prison a prisoner well bound with ropes and well guarded by soldiers. He was led to the Great Maidan, and there securely attached to a stout stake. A platoon of soldiers fired a volley at him; but when the smoke cleared away, instead of a lifeless corpse, the prisoner was seen scampering away over the open space to the nearest shelter. The musket-balls had cut his bonds, but left his person untouched. The bazaar was not far distant: had he once gained its labyrinths, he would in all probability have found friends to assist in hiding him, and thus have escaped; but bewildered, no doubt, by his critical position, he turned in an opposite direction, to a building nearer to him. It was a guard-house; and there he was at once recaptured, once more led to execution, and shot down by a second volley.

By name Mirza Ali Mahommed, this individual was a native of Shiraz, who, after passing the earlier years of his manhood as a dervish, had, some time previously to the date above mentioned, given himself out to be a prophet, assumed the name of Bâb, a gate,— or Bâb Eddin, the Gate of Faith,—and propounded doctrines * as alluring to the minds of certain classes in Persia as those of the Communists were to the Sans-Culottes of Paris. There was nothing very original or new in these doctrines, even in Persia; and it is probable that a perusal of the history of his own country first introduced them to the notice of the Bâb, for

---

* This is the account, current in the country, of the doctrines of the Bâb. A very different light is thrown on them by M. de Gobineau in his interesting work, *Les Religions et Philosophies de l'Asie Centrale.*

they appear to be more or less analogous to the tenets of the "Assassins" (of whom more later), and the means employed to render them popular were somewhat similar to those used by the founder of that sect. The emancipation of women, and the equal distribution of all the property of non-Bâbees amongst the followers of the Bâb, were the chief inducements held out by the new prophet. To attain them he inculcated, as far as I could learn, the necessity of renouncing the Koran, and believing in the universality of God and the unreality of death. God was in everything, he said, and everything was God. Virtue and vice had therefore no existence, since all actions, moral and physical, were emanations of the Deity. Death was simply the immediate passage of the soul and body to a better state. The Bâbees, however, I need hardly add, were alone entitled to the privileges of thus enjoying total irresponsibility for their actions in this world, and of feeling perfect security as to their happiness in the next.

Imprisoned and bastinadoed for doctrines so subversive of Oriental despotism, the Bâb had several times recanted his errors, and as often reverted to them. His teaching found favour in many parts of the kingdom, especially with the Seyeds and women; and his adherents, as they increased in numbers, were emboldened to declare themselves openly, to raise the standard of the Bâb—*i.e.* revolt, and to seize upon several towns and villages. Zenjan became their headquarters, and there, after all their other conquests had been retaken by the royal troops, and for months after the execution of their chief, they defended themselves with a courage which in a better cause would be called heroic, and only succumbed at last to famine and quasi-extermination.

That the Bâb had great influence with his followers is proved by the fact that most of them fell fighting, and that the few who were taken prisoners refused their pardon at the price of recantation. If then he had not taken that, for him and them, unlucky turn towards the guard-house, all Tabreez would at once have attributed his escape through the bazaar to divine interposition, and having thus seen his claim to be a prophet substantiated by a miracle patent to all, would have been converted to his doctrines. It is, perhaps, futile now to speculate upon the consequences which the conversion of one of the most populous towns of the kingdom might have had upon an imaginative nation like the Persian.

After the fall of Zenjan a fierce persecution ensued against all suspected of Bâbeeism, and for a time it was thought that the sect had been utterly destroyed. But in 1852 it again reappeared, and an attempt was made on the life of the Shah by a band of its adherents. Four of them lay in wait for him as he was riding out from his country palace, near Tehran; they threw him from his horse, and, but for the bravery of his attendants, would have murdered him. One of the assassins was killed on the spot, the others were taken prisoners; and terrible indeed was the fate of the latter, and of those who were inculpated as the confederates of their crime and sharers of their belief. Some were blown from mortars, some hewn to pieces; one was horse-shod and danced to death, and several had lighted candles inserted in holes drilled in their flesh, and were thus dragged by the neck through the bazaars of the capital until life became extinct. But notwithstanding these examples, so dreaded had the sect become and so fearful was the prime minister of the day of its future vengeance, that he shrank from bearing alone the responsibility of these executions, and with a view to distribute it over as many heads as possible, had recourse to the expedient of causing one victim to be killed by a superior employé of each of the chief government offices.

A second general persecution followed, resulting in the death and flight of many guilty, and, I dare say, as many innocent persons. For Persians have no scruples and covet each other's property; and much was, no doubt, made of this golden opportunity for those in power to enrich themselves with the goods of their enemies. But still Bábeeism is not extinct; twenty years after these events, I have frequently heard such and such a one denominated a Bábee, and there are still not a few persons who believe that the Báb did really escape death and will shortly reappear.

CHAPTER VIII.

Departure from Tabreez—Some of the Discomforts of Posting—Turkmanchai—Mianeh—Lost in the Snow—Zenjan—Sultania—Kasvin—The Assassins—First Impressions of Tehran.

At dawn, on the 28th of January, 1866, my six post-horses appeared at the door of the Consul-General's house. It was a bleak, cold, snowy morning, anything but inviting for the commencement of a ride of 370 odd miles, and with much reluctance I buried my legs in huge felt boots, and my body in a fur coat, and wished good-by to my comfortable quarters and hospitable friends. Due care had been taken to renew my stock of provisions, and as a last welcome attention my hostess had, I found, furnished me with some loaves of English-made bread. The word loaf does not, I presume, exist in the Persian language, unless in its reference to sugar, for it certainly cannot be applied to the bread of the country. A Persian baker rolls out his dough into large thin flat cakes, pitches them for a few minutes into a heated oven, or in default of this on a heap of charcoal embers, and then throwing them over his shoulder, as we should a coat or a cloak, marches off to distribute them to his customers. Being only half-baked, the bread always remains flexible, and, besides being the staff of life, serves the purpose of platter and napkin at a native meal. A few English loaves were therefore a treasure.

Issuing from the gates of Tabreez we began to ascend the acclivities which approach it from the east, and for a mile or so our way lay through a quantity of ruins, which attest the former size of the town. To the left and on the heights were visible the remains of a large fortress built of huge quarried stones—anomalies in a country of mud and sun-dried brick-buildings, which almost tempt me to stop and indulge in speculations as to their origin ; but I have dallied too long already, and in order to get over the ground more quickly, I shall henceforward confine myself as strictly as possible to transcripts of the notes which I generally found time to jot down, under considerable difficulties, each night in my diary.

January 28*th.* — Passing more than the usual number of villages, we began to ascend gradually, and after traversing a plain bounded by mountains, as usual, reached Washmich, or Bosmeech, a lone post-house at the entrance of a wild gorge, at noon. After breakfast there, we crossed a short steep pass and emerged on another plain, over which we cantered to Hadjivava, our night quarters. There was constant bother with the luggage, in ridding themselves of which post-horses show great ingenuity. The deep snow on the road had been beaten by the passage of caravans into furrows whose regularity and depth would have rejoiced the eyes of a north-country ploughman; our pace was very slow in consequence: we only got over twenty-eight miles. Hadjivava, typical of many other Persian villages, may be described as consisting of a lot of mud-hovels, a few poplars and a brook. The traveller's-room at the post-house opened on a stable, but was not uncomfortable, as the chimney did not smoke.

29th.—If the Irishman houses with his pig, the Persian litters with his horse. After a long ride of twenty-four miles, my only place of repose for breakfast was a chakoo, or raised dais of dried mud, in the stable. A few small holes in the roof admitted just enough light to eat by, and see the horses feeding or kicking each other, the two chief occupations of Persian post-horses: I should rather say the latter is the chief one, for they never get many opportunities of indulging in the former.

Bitterly cold. First stage across a plain, alarmingly furrowed with snow furrows. Second, up hill and down dale, and at last, down a very steep hill into Turkmanchai, a considerable town: here a treaty, fixing the boundaries of Russia and Persia as they at present exist, was signed in 1828. In the post-house outside the town, a door once separated the traveller's-room from the stables; its absence afforded me a view of an immediate foreground of servants and post-boys eating garlic and bread and smoking hubble-bubbles. Horses filled the rest of the picture; they are clever, spirited little brutes and trot and canter over the furrows with hardly a stumble. I found my lump-sugar reduced to very fine powder. The gurgling sound of the pipes and the champing of bits sent me off to sleep in an atmosphere reeking with tobacco-smoke and ammonia.

30*th*.—Through fog and a succession of rugged defiles to Mianeh, a village said to be situated on the ancient boundary line of Media and Parthia: hence its name, which in English means "between." The place is notorious for its bugs, whose bite is exceedingly dangerous, and sometimes even fatal, to all except Mianese. I was shown some of these insects, which appeared to me larger and of a deeper colour than their European brethren. To avoid making acquaintance with their poison, I breakfasted on a heap of rubbish at the post-house door, the only spot free from snow. Hence we ascended the Koflan Kuh, or Leopard Mountain, part of a lofty range separating the province of Azerbaijan from that of Irak. Arrived at the summit of the pass, the mist cleared and the sun shone warmly out of Persia's clear blue sky. The view towards the east was grand from its extent, and the air so astonishingly pure that I could hear the voices of my servants, who had lagged near half a mile behind, as if they had been close to me. The descent was difficult and dangerous from the slippery state of the road. At its foot we found a large caravansary dating from the time of Abbas the Great, and a post-house; but hearing that the poison of its insects was almost as deadly as that of the denizens of Mianeh, I determined to go on another stage. It was only twelve miles over a plain, and we did it in two hours, trotting along the whole way without intermission. There being proper doors to the post-room, I enjoyed unusual privacy. Three stages to-day—forty-eight miles.

31st.—Snow fell during the night and our first stage of sixteen miles. The road followed pretty closely the course of a river—the Deerzy, I believe, by name—which has worn itself a deep bed in the plain. My horse fell at the extreme edge of a perpendicular cliff, overhanging the stream, and if he had rolled, or I had come off, these lines would never have been written, I presume; for I don't know any one who has lived to describe his sensations during a fall of some sixty or seventy feet. Second stage, twelve miles, performed in one hour and forty minutes: very warm work, as the sun came out. Our third stage of twenty-four miles was to take us into Zenjan, and we started on it at 3 P.M. The fresh-fallen snow was very deep, frequently reaching to our girths, and we made slow progress. When about five miles distant from our destination, it being nearly dark, an icy hurricane came on, freezing one's blood, one's brain, too, almost; driving the snow with blinding fury in one's face, and obliterating all footprints of man or beast. The post-boy, whose duty it is to ride ahead and lead the way, confessed himself uncertain as to our whereabouts, and led us first to the right and then to the left in a vain search after some landmark which might indicate our route. Thus we wandered up and down for hours in the darkness and snow and biting wind, and an occurrence which had happened two or three years previously to an acquaintance of mine presented itself with disagreeable vividness to my mind. Travelling along this very same road on his way to Europe, he was overtaken by one of these hurricanes, lost his way, and remained thirty-six hours in the snow. He had some brandy and bread with him, and with these and constant movement managed to keep himself awake and alive; but two of his attendants, Persians, preferring death to the agonies of such extreme cold, took opium and never awoke again. The wretched horses ate each others' tails off, but survived.

Though I of course hoped to get out of our ugly difficulties better than my friend, the probability of passing the night in the snow seemed each moment to increase, and weary and frozen I had almost made up my mind to it, when a blast of wind, more violent and icy than its fellows, wafted the welcome sound of a tinkling mule-bell to our ears. It at once woke me up from that despairing numbness, physical and moral, which extreme cold produces on the human frame, and sent up the thermometer of hope very high indeed. Making towards the spot whence the sound proceeded, we came upon a caravan of mules. A parley ensued between their drivers and my attendants, which lasted so long that, though I understood no Persian, I soon perceived that our neighbours were in the same plight as ourselves. There was much shrieking and yelling, but as it seemed to lead to no result, I got tired of it, and so did my very sagacious baggage-horses; each day since my arrival in Persia they had shown signs of irrepressibility, and now attempted to execute their usual freak of bolting. They moved along slowly at first, and we spurred and whipt after them as close as we could, fearing lest in the darkness we should lose sight of them for ever; but the nearer we got to them, the faster they went: we were soon all galloping along as hard as we could go, and, once in a gallop, Persian post-horses will follow their leader till they drop, rather than be left alone in the desert. It was a wild careering ride in the snow and darkness, but it warmed our blood, and eventually saved us from horrors of which we had already had a sufficient foretaste; for the way we sped, turned out to be the right one, and led us straight to the gates of Zenjan. Indulgence to the freaks of a baggage-horse is the moral.

Threading a long bazaar, where pitchy darkness was rendered visible by the feeble light of a tallow dip here and there, we at last reached the posthouse between ten and eleven o'clock. The chimney of my room had no vent; until the wood fire burnt itself out, door and window were opened, but sufficed not to draw off the dense canopy of smoke which filled the room to within three feet of the floor. To escape the torments which it caused to my bloodshot eyes and burning cheeks, I crept into my bed, which even under these circumstances, was paradise after what I had gone through.

February 1st.—Zenjan is a considerable town; fortified according to Persian fashion, by a mud wall. This was all I saw, as I left as early as possible. A three-hours' ride brought us to Sultania, residence of Sultans, and capital of the country in former days when Persia's sovereigns still styled themselves by that title. It is now a mass of ruins, tenanted by a few hundred inhabitants, but famous for the salubrity of its air and the excellence of the pasture which its magnificent plain affords. The Shah has a modern palace and large breeding stud here. Of the former glories of the place there remains but one monument, a large mosque tomb, built by Sultan Mahomed Khodabund, the first Persian monarch who publicly proclaimed the doctrine held by the Shiah sect of Mahometans (of which more later). With a view probably to establish it more firmly in the minds of his subjects, he entertained the project of transporting hither the remains of Ali and Hossein, and accordingly spent large sums in rendering the tomb worthy to receive them. Its dome is one of the largest in Persia—150 feet high—and was entirely covered with yellow porcelain tiles of great beauty: few of them remain at present. On the inside walls was written the whole of the Koran, only a few verses of which are still legible.

Easterns possess in the written character of their

languages a source of architectural decoration which fails us completely. The German character might perhaps be introduced on certain buildings with effect, but who ever thought of ornamenting the walls of St. Paul's with verses from the Bible in Latin letters! The sun was very powerful all day, and, notwithstanding green spectacles, my eyes suffered dreadfully from the refraction. Our second stage was most laborious: we wallowed through snow so deep that our horses' hoofs never reached the ground, and did not arrive at our night quarters until after seven, having been ten and a half hours in performing forty-four miles. The changes of temperature are most trying. Morning and evening are intensely cold: my breath then congeals and freezes my vashlik, or hood, to my mustachios and whiskers. At noon, when there is sun, one swelters in fur clothing.

2nd.—A bright sunny clear day. Road eastwards, over a long plain with a low line of hills to the north. Snow less troublesome than yesterday. Got over two stages, of twenty miles each, in less than eight hours. The post-house being in ruins, put up in a villager's house. My room was vaulted, whitewashed, and clean. In all the walls were square niches, where, in the absence of tables and cupboards, the household goods and chattels were stowed away. There was no fireplace or chimney, provision for ventilation being made by three holes pierced in the arched ceiling. Underneath these, and in the centre of the room, was the "kourci," a heating apparatus much in use all over Persia. It consists of a large jar filled with charred fuel, half buried in the floor. During the day it serves the purpose of a kitchen-range; at night it is covered with a wooden frame and thick wadded quilt, under which the members of the household insert their persons as far as their shoulders, whilst cushions, beyond the limits of the quilt, support their heads. Persians are not in the habit of undressing at night, and therefore this species of promiscuous bed-going is less shocking to our ideas than it would be in European countries. But though economical, it is a nasty method of procuring warmth; somewhat dangerous too, for if the sleeper draws the quilt over his head, suffocation from the fumes of the charcoal ensues. Had a great treat to-day in the shape of some grapes : in this dry atmosphere they can be kept, it seems, for almost any length of time.

3rd.—Where quadrupeds are the only means of locomotion, the time occupied in traversing a given distance must depend a good deal on the state of the moon. For even in summer and autumn, when the roads are at their best, one makes slow progress without it, even with the lantern which the post-boy then bears as its substitute. In winter there is, as we have seen, nothing to be gained and much to be risked by venturing forth on a moonless night. This morning the Nestorian Lazar awoke me at three with the words, "Moon, sir, moon." It was full and very bright as we left our quarters an hour later, after a bowl of hot tea, and rode over the long snow-covered plain of

Kasvin towards the town of that name. As the rosy dawn appeared in the east it declined westwards in receding folds of violet blue, but was still above the horizon when the sun shot his first rays into our eyes. No words of mine would do justice to the colouring at sunrise and sunset in this limpid atmosphere. Still less can I attempt to describe to those who have not experienced it the peculiar effect on the mind and feelings of the contemporaneous presence of these two full orbs in a cloudless sky on a windless morning. I almost hesitate at adding the latter condition, as whenever I have been up early enough to witness the phenomenon there never has been any wind : perhaps the two great lights take special measures to prevent interference, by any disturbing element of this nature, with the universal silence which so enhances the awing charm they, may be consciously, inspire.

However that may be, my speculations on the subject were abruptly put an end to by a headlong fall. The previous day's sun had melted the snow, and our path was simply a sheet of ice, on which the horses slipped at each step and often came to grief. None of our mishaps were serious, for the snow on each side almost reached the girths, and the beaten track was so narrow that when our horses fell in the latter we were invariably landed on the former. As I was gathering myself together from one of these falls a horseman, wrapped in furs, galloped up. His face was almost black from the combined action of the bitter winds and burning refraction, and so swollen that he could scarcely see out of his eyes: features he seemed to have none. My surprise was therefore considerable, and my pleasure not less when he accosted me with "Bon-jour," pronounced with a very German accent. Since quitting Tabreez I had had neither the opportunity nor the means of exchanging many ideas. On the road we had met but one solitary traveller, a Russian courier galloping westwards with despatches, and a few caravans of mules and asses. At our halting-places I had seen only post-boys and grooms. Had my knowledge of Persian been greater than it was it would not have availed much, as in most of the districts we had traversed Turkish is the language spoken. Lazar's knowledge of English was so limited that, after one day's experience of it, I had given up all attempts at conversation with him; and, in default of a companion to whom I could express my sentiments, had taken the telegraph poles and wires into my confidence. These were the only objects with which I felt any sympathy, and they alone seemed to connect me in any way with the many nice people and things I had left behind me in Europe. They had been, too, of great service in other respects, for they had shown me the road when every other indication of it was hidden by the snow: indeed I looked upon them as friends; but as they were deaf and dumb, I was heartily glad of an opportunity of unsealing my lips to a human ear. My fellow-traveller turned out to be a German commercial man going up to his place of business, Tehran. He had ridden hard and fast to catch me up, for company's sake, and we performed the rest of our long stage of twenty-four miles into Kasvin together. There he was so knocked up that I was forced to proceed onwards without him.

Kasvin, too, is a very ancient town (what Persian town is not?), and was, previous to the reign of Abbas the Great, long the capital of the country. It is situated on a plain, which extends far away to the south-east of Tehran, and is probably 200 miles in length, and being on the high-roads from the capital to Tabreez and to the Caspian Sea, is a place of considerable traffic. From the number of its Medrassehs or Colleges it has the reputation of being a learned and scientific city. Its neighbourhood is comparatively well watered, fertile and very productive, amongst other things, of the best grapes I have ever eaten: the cheapest too, for a mule-load costs three shillings. About twenty miles to the north of the town, hidden away amongst the Elburz mountains, lived the founder of a sect which for near 200 years was the terror and dread of kings and peoples, but of which, as Gibbon observes, "no vestige is left, except the word Assassin, which, in the most odious sense, has been adopted in the languages of Europe." Hossein, hence the word, was his name, and his doctrines and the deeds of his emissaries are too well known for me to think of describing them. I can't help, however, here inserting an extract from our friend Marco Polo, who visited Kasvin very shortly after the extermination of the sect by Hoolaloo Khan about 1260, and whose account of the means employed by the Old Man of the Mountain, as he calls him, to secure implicit obedience from his followers, is most graphic :—

"*Del Veglio della Montagna, e come fece il Paradiso, e gli Assassini.*

"Milice è una contrada dove il Veglio della Montagna soleva dimorare anticamente. Or vi conteremo l' affare, secondo che Messer Marco intese da più uomini. Lo Veglio è chiamato in lor lingua Aloodin. Egli avea fatto fare fra due montagne in una valle lo più bello giardino e 'l più grande del mondo : quivi avea tutti frutti, e li più belli palagi del mondo, tutti dipinti ad oro, e a bestie, e a uccelli : quivi era condotti : per tale veniva acqua, e per tale mele, e per tale vino. Quivi era donzelli e donzelle gli più belli del mondo, e che meglio sapevano cantare e sonare e ballare : e faceva lo Veglio credere a costoro che quello era lo paradiso. E perciò il fece, perchè Malcometto disse, che chi andasse in paradiso avrebbe di belle femine tante quante volesse, e quivi troverebbe fiume di latte e di miele e di vino. E gli Saracini di quella contrada credevano veramente che quello fosse lo paradiso ; e in questo giardino non entrava se non colui, cui egli voleva fare assassino. Lo Veglio teneva in sua corte tutti giovani di dodici anni, li quali gli paressero di diventare prodi uomini. Quando lo Veglio ne faceva mettere nel giardino, a quatro, a dieci, a venti egli faceva loro dare a bere opio, e quegli dormivano bene tre dì, e faceva gli portare nel giardino, e al tempo gli faceva ispogliare. Quando gli giovani si svegliavano, egli si trovano là dentro, e vedendo tutte queste cose, veramente si credevano essere in paradiso, e queste donzelle sempre istavano con loro in canti e in grandi sollazzi : donde egli aveano sì quello che volevano ; che mai per lo volere non si sarebbono partiti di quello giardino. Il Veglio tiene bella corte e ricca, e fa credere a quegli di quella montagna, che così sia com' io v' ho detto ; e quando egli ne vuole mandare alcuno di quelli giovani in alcuno luogo, li fa loro dare beveraggio che dormono, e fagli recare fuori del giardino in sul suo palagio. Quando coloro si svegliono trovansi quivi, molto si maravigliano, e sono molto tristi, che si trovano fuori del paradiso. Egli se ne vanno incontanente dinanzi al Veglio, credendo che sia un gran profeta, e inginochiansi. Egli gli domanda : ' Onde venite ?' Rispondono : ' Dal paradiso,' e contangli quello che v' hanno veduto entro, e hanno gran voglia di tornarvi : e quando il Veglio vuole fare uccidere alcuna persona, egli fa torre quello lo quale sia più vigoroso, e fagli uccidere quello cui egli vuole : e coloro lo fanno volontieri per ritornare nel paradiso. Se scampano, ritornano al loro signore ; se è preso, vuole morire, credendo ritornare al paradiso. E quando lo Veglio vuole fare uccidere alcuno, egli lo prende e dice : ' Va, fa tal cosa, e questo ti fo perchè ti voglio fare ritornare al paradiso:' e gli assassini vanno e fannolo molto volentieri. E in questa maniera non campò

The Old Man of the Mountain. 123

niuno uomo dinanzi al Veglio della Montagna, a cui egli lo vuole fare; e sì vi dico che più rè li fanno tributo per quella paura. Egli è vero che negli anni 1260, Alan, signore dei Tarteri del Levante, che sapeva tutte queste malvagità, egli pensò tra se medesimo di volerlo distruggere, e mandò de' suoi Baroni a questo giardino, e istettonvi tre anni attorno al castello prima che l' avessero : nè mai non lo avrebbero avuto, se non per fame. Allotta per fame fu preso, e fu morto lo Veglio, e sua gente tutta : e d' allora in qua non vi fu più Veglio niuno; in lui fu finita tutta la signoria."*

---

* "*Of the Old Man of the Mountain, and how he created Paradise, and the Assassins.*

"Milice is the place where the Old Man of the Mountain used formerly to dwell. We will now tell his story as Marco heard it related by several persons. In their language he is called Aloodin. In a valley between two mountains, he had caused to be made the largest and most beautiful garden in the world. In it were all sorts of fruits : the most beautiful palaces, covered with paintings, in gold, of beasts and birds : conduits running, some with water, some with honey, and some with wine : and the fairest youths and maidens, who excelled in singing, playing and dancing. The Old Man persuaded them that this garden was Paradise, and he succeeded in this because Mahomet said that he, who entered Paradise, would find there as many beautiful women as he desired, and rivers of milk, honey and wine. The Saracens of the country really believed it was Paradise, and no one was allowed to enter it but those whom the Old Man wished to make assassins. He kept at his court all the youths of twelve years of age who, he thought, would become valiant men, and when he sent them, by fours or tens or scores, into the garden, he made them take opium and they slept for three days, and then he caused them to be carried into it and undressed. On waking, the youths found themselves in the garden, and seeing all these things, really thought themselves in Paradise : and the maidens remained

After breakfasting at Kasvin, got over two more stages before dark—fifty-two miles in all.

4th.—Started at three A.M. The first stage over snow and ice, took me five and a half hours. During the second we passed close under a spur of the Elburz; the third was to be my last, and as we cantered over

---

with them always, singing and giving them many pleasures : so that they had everything they desired and, of their own accord, would never have quitted the garden. The Old Man holds a rich and brilliant court and he persuades the people of the mountain that it is as I have said : and when he wishes to send any of the youths anywhere, he causes a beverage to be given them which makes them sleep, and has them brought out of the garden to his palace. There they find themselves when they awake, and are surprised and sad to be outside Paradise. They go at once to the Old Man, whom they believe to be a great prophet, and kneel before him. He asks them : ' Whence do you come ? ' They answer : ' From Paradise,' and tell him what they have seen there and that they much desire to return ; and when the Old Man wishes to kill any one, he chooses the most vigorous of the youths and makes him kill him. This they do willingly in order to return to Paradise : if they escape, they return to their master : if they are taken, they court death in the belief that they will thus re-enter Paradise. And when the Old Man wishes to kill any one, he calls a youth and says : ' Go, do this, I give thee this commission, because I wish thee to return to Paradise,' and the assassins go and do it with great alacrity. And in this manner, no one whom he wishes to kill can escape the Old Man of the Mountain ; so that many kings, I tell you, pay him tribute from fear. It is true that in the year 1260, Hoolaloo, the Lord of the Tartars of the east, who knew all these iniquities, thought within himself to destroy the Old Man, and sent his barons to this garden, and they besieged the Castle three years before they took it ; nor would they ever have taken it, but for famine. Then they took it by famine, and the Old Man was killed with his people : and since then there is no other Old Man : with the first the whole brood was destroyed."

the plain, I kept straining my eyes to catch a glimpse of the capital of him who styles himself King of Kings and Centre of the Universe, expecting of course to see something worthy of containing a being rejoicing in such sonorous titles. But neither this modest expectation, nor another one in which I had often indulged during the miseries of my long ride, were to be satisfied. Arrived within sight of Tehran, I could perceive but a long low line of brown mud wall, capped here and there by the brown domes, very like ant-hills, of some insignificant mosques, rising above the snow-covered plain and backed by huge snow-covered mountains. Inside its gates I had to traverse bazaars as ruinous, and streets, or rather lanes, as squalid as any I had seen in any other Persian town; and on dismounting at sunset at the gates of her Majesty's Legation, I was shown to a room painfully similar to my quarters of the last week, the only apparent difference being that there were some panes of glass in the window-frames, a carpet on the floor, and a chimney which did not smoke. Thus are fancy's creations frequently dissolved: I had dreamt of tall minarets, gilded domes, and lofty bazaars; I found what I have just sketched. I had dreamt of a warm comfortably-furnished apartment, or at least of something like civilized accommodation; I found that I must camp on still. "Lazar, bring in my bed and go and see if you can buy me a chair."

After passing the best part of eight days and nights in the saddle, and riding sixty miles on the last of them, there is no greater luxury than a Persian bath. As the bathman shampoos each muscle and joint one feels new life instilled into one's members, whilst the damp warm atmosphere produces a delicious feeling of soothing relaxation in every vein.

Thus refreshed, and after a late dinner at the table of the English Envoy, or Yasir Muchtar as he is here called, even my dismal quarters appeared less dismal. For though comfort was wanting, I could at least congratulate myself on being out of the snow; which, as has been seen, had been my *bête noir* from the shores of the Euxine to the gates of my new home, and which had left painful marks on my person in the shape of swollen features, burnt skin, bloodshot eyes, and cracked lips.

CHAPTER IX.

SITUATION AND GENERAL APPEARANCE OF TEHRAN—A PERSIAN HOUSE—EUROPEAN COLONY—THE TELEGRAPH—FOOD—WINE—SKATING—THE SHAH'S PRACTICAL JOKES—THE PERSIAN ARMY—HUNTING AND HAWKING—HORSES.

SUN-DRIED bricks and mud mixed with straw—the latter now, and probably ever since the days of Moses, as much a subject of contention and haggling as at the time of the Exodus—have often been mentioned in the preceding pages as the materials generally used in Persian buildings. They are sufficiently hard to resist the dissolving influence of the very small amount of rainfall; they are cheap and always at hand. A further reason, however, for their use exists in a prejudice, entertained by every Persian, against inhabiting the house in which his parents have died. This prejudice is not counterbalanced by the ties of family affection, which in polygamous countries are much less strong than with us, and the consequence is that an incoming heir, whenever he can afford to do so, abandons the paternal mansion, and builds himself a new abode. A somewhat similar feeling must, I think, have animated the founders of the numerous dynasties, which have succeeded each other in the long cycle of Persian history, and caused each of them to abandon the capital of its predecessor, and set up its regal penates on a fresh site. Thus in ancient times, under the Kaianian, Parthian, and Sassanian dynasties, the metropolis of the empire was moved from Persepolis to Pasargadæ, and thence to Susa, and thus in modern ones the Soofee, Zend, and Kajar reigning families have successively chosen as their respective capitals Ispahan, Shiraz, and Tehran. The latter, however, owes its present distinction perhaps less to this feeling than to the fact of its being within a few days' march of the native districts of the Kajar Tribe, near Astrabad. For when, in 1788, Agar Mahomed Khan, the founder of the present dynasty, first got possession of the throne, his position was too precarious to admit of his fixing his court at a distance from his own clan.

His choice has turned out a prudent one from another point of view. Russia, as far as any one can see at present, is the only power which can cherish annexationist designs against Persia, and whenever attempts are made to put those designs into execution, they can be more advantageously resisted from Tehran than from any other point. Hence, too, the wild Turcomans, who infest the north-eastern frontiers of the kingdom, can be best held in check and their incursions best repelled.

The capital stands on a vast plain, on which to the west and south there is nothing to intercept the view except the faint outline of some hills which rise from its uniform level, like islets from the ocean, far away on the borders of the Great Salt Desert. Looking northwards from its walls, the Elburz mountains are seen raising, from advanced spurs some three or four miles off, their abrupt and picturesque heads to a height of 10,000 feet, and stretching out eastwards their massive limbs in gradual and jagged descent to the plain, whilst their loftiest peak, Demavend, its base hidden by intermediate ranges, and distant about fifty miles, towers high over all, 20,000 feet and more, into the sky.

Amidst natural scenery of these proportions, the most imposing architecture would lose half its effect; Tehran, which can hardly be said to contain any architectural building at all, is simply insignificant. It is built in the form of an irregular square, each side of which measures about an English mile, and is enclosed by a deep dry ditch and a thick mud wall, flanked at intervals with semicircular projections, and pierced by gates which are always guarded, and closed one hour after sunset. Outside the walls there are suburbs of considerable extent, several large caravansaries, and many enclosed gardens. Inside, the principal object is the Ark or Royal Palace, which occupies a large space of ground adjoining the northern wall, and is completely cut off from the rest of the town by its own circle of bulwarks. At all its issues sentinels keep guard, and at night no one can traverse the streets which skirt it without the password.

High walls impede all view of the interior; which will be described when we go to see the Shah.

There is little to be said about other buildings. The mosques, into which no Christian is allowed to enter, are all small, and, with the exception of one or two partially cased with coloured tiles, are all of sombre sun-dried brick; the baths, which play such a part in Oriental life, are of the same material and equally unworthy of notice. Some of the bazaars are spacious and lofty, especially those in the neighbourhood of the Palace, and, besides containing the best shops, are the principal thoroughfares of the city. As to the streets, if such they can be called, only three or four of them are broad and even enough to allow of the passage of wheeled vehicles; all the others run between blank brown walls, are very narrow, ill paved, or not paved at all, and full of holes and pitfalls; they are dusty in dry weather, muddy in wet, and filthy at all times. One of the best houses is that built by the Russian Government for its representative; it is of stone and kiln-dried bricks. The premises of the English Legation * were, at the time of which I am speaking, in a half ruinous state; but they had attached to them a large garden planted with huge cypresses and plane-trees, which somewhat compensated for their internal discomfort.

Persian houses, though varying in size according

---

* Parliament has since voted a large sum for the construction of a new Mission House, not before it was wanted, and H.M.'s Legation will soon be properly lodged.

to the means of their occupants, are generally built on pretty much the same plan : a description of my own dwelling during the winter months of my residence at Tehran will suffice to give a fair idea of their internal arrangement. Entering from a narrow lane, through a doorway just large enough for the passage of one person, a small corridor leads into an open paved court some forty yards square, in the centre of which is an oblong tank of water, surrounded with a border of garden soil for shrubs and plants at the proper season. Blank walls, rising high enough above the flat roofs to prevent my inquisitive eyes from invading the privacy of my neighbours, enclose two sides of the court; on the others, and *vis-à-vis*, are two buildings, each consisting of a large centre saloon and two smaller rooms on the ground-floor, and a bala-khaneh (hence our word balcony) or upper chamber. The windows of the saloons, filled with diminutive panes of stained glass, descend from the roof to the floor, and are furnished with an awning to keep out the sun; those of the other rooms are small, and all, as well as the doors, open on the court. An uncovered flight of very steep steps leads up to the flat roof of each building—always an agreeable place at dawn and sunset, and much used by Persians for prayer—and to the upper chamber.

This division of a house into two separate compartments, "biroon" and "anderoon," literally "outside" and "inside," is necessitated by polygamy. In the former are lodged all the males of the household, and there the master transacts his business, receives his visitors, &c. The latter is exclusively reserved for his harem; which is his *sanctum sanctorum*, and is inviolable, even to royalty.

The Mahometan law, as is well known, limits the number of a man's wives to four, but allows him as many concubines and slaves as he likes; and love, as understood in the East, being still one of the great ruling passions amongst Persians, they are as much addicted to its pleasures as ever, and, when they can afford it, fully avail themselves of the privileges accorded to them by their religion. There are, however, comparatively few who can do so, and thus it may be said of polygamy, as well as, to a certain extent, of monogamy, that it's all a question of money. If such be the case, it stands to reason that most Mahometans have only one wife. As to female slaves, I have only heard of their existence, and there can be but few in the country at present. Males are still, it would seem, smuggled into the southern provinces, for I have seen several eunuchs whose features bore unmistakable traces of their African origin.

Tehran contains, as far as can be ascertained, about 100,000 inhabitants, more than nine-tenths of whom are Persians, and the rest Armenians, Jews, Affghans, and Europeans. The latter formed a very small community in 1866, consisting only of the members of the English, French, and Russian Legations, of a couple of officers and some men of the Royal Engineers employed in superintending the telegraph, one

Austrian and three Italian officers, a French doctor and two English civil engineers in the Shah's service, and the representatives of three or four commercial houses: in all, about fifty persons. Scattered about in different parts of the country, there may have been a hundred more Europeans.

The entire staff of Royal Engineers then consisted of fifty men, principally sergeants and corporals, four officers and two medical men; in the society of the latter were passed my most agreeable hours, to their knowledge of the country and people I am much indebted, and their hospitality and kindness I shall never forget. Their duties are of a very arduous nature, comprising the maintenance in working order of the telegraph wires from the Caucasian frontier to Tehran, from thence to Bushire, and again from Tehran to the Turkish frontier in the direction of Baghdad, the transmission along them of European and Indian messages, and the settlement of accounts: a very knotty question with Persians. The description of my ride from Tabreez will give some idea of what these men are frequently exposed to; for interruptions in communication, caused by atmospherical influences, storms, lightning, snow, &c.—but more frequently by the mischievous wantonness of the numerous pilgrims who are constantly traversing the country on their way to the shrines, or for the purpose of transporting their dead relations to Kerbelah, Meshed and Koom—are of common occurrence, and as soon as they are signalled, away some one must gallop to repair them. I don't know what may be the opinion of their employers as to the manner in which they have discharged these duties, but this I can vouch for—the Royal Engineers are regarded with feelings of the highest respect and esteem by all classes of society with which they have come in contact, and they have certainly enhanced the prestige of the English name in Persia.

The Shah is a frequent visitor at the Telegraph Office, which is close to the Palace, and exceedingly fond of conversing directly through the wires with the governors of the provinces through which they pass. As the day approaches for the payment of their annual tribute, the governors have an uneasy time of it, and often, no doubt, curse this invention of the "Christian dogs;" for then his Majesty's visits are redoubled, and questions as to the amount of tribute and the time of its arrival become the burden of his messages. The Persian language is naturally deficient in words descriptive of most of our late inventions, and it is consequently difficult to make even educated men understand the theory and working of the telegraph. Thus, on one occasion, much of the time of one of our officers was occupied during several weeks in attempting to enlighten the mind of a provincial governor, who had got it into his head that the wires were hollow tubes, and that messages were transmitted through them, as in the pneumatic post. In vain was the whole apparatus shown to his highness, in vain were all its parts explained and re-explained; he stuck to his idea; and it was only by the suggestion of the following simile that he was, at last, induced to relinquish it and declare himself satisfied : " Imagine," said the officer, " a dog whose tail is here at Tehran, and his muzzle in London; tread on his tail here and he will bark there." Similar difficulties were experienced, it seems, in conveying to the mind of Ferrukh Khan a correct idea of the machinery of the steamer which was to convey him from Trebizonde on his mission to the courts of Paris and London ; for when, on going on board, he was told that the machine was of 500-horse power, his face beamed with pleasure at the prospect of seeing so many horses, and he at once asked permission to visit the stables!

It did not take me long to establish myself in my Persian house. Where every one seems to lead a sort of camp life, it is useless to indulge one's European.ideas as to the necessity of furniture : it is, indeed, an impossibility where every one sits, eats, and sleeps on the floor, and uses his knee as his writing-table. The bazaars did, however, manage to supply me with a few chairs and tables ; carpets, divans, and cushions did the rest. My household consisted of a peeshkedmet or body servant, Hassan Beg by name, who was much addicted to adorning his person with gold and shawl embroidery, of three farrashes or sweepers, and a groom and helper, to look after the four horses which were deemed necessary for my service. This may seem rather an extravagant establishment for a single man, but if you live at Rome you must do as the Romans, and in Persia custom forbids a European official to stir from his house, either on foot or on horseback, without two attendants at least; not so much by way of protection as to show and clear the road. Servants, moreover, are not expensive: their wages average about twenty-five shillings a month, and the keep of a horse is about the same. In other respects, living is decidedly cheap, if one can accommodate one's taste to the products of the country.

As to food, the markets in most towns are generally well supplied with mutton, lamb, fowls, rice, &c.; beef is rarer; fruit, eggs, chickens, and bread can be had everywhere. The other essential of life—drink—is a more difficult question. Water throughout the country is generally bad, being often so impregnated with nitre that neither man nor beast can touch it except in the direst straits. Wine and spirits are not always to be had. They are both much appreciated by many of the higher classes, more for their intoxicating than their cheering effects, but can only be indulged in secretly; and no Mussulman can disregard the precepts of the Koran to the extent of himself becoming a vendor or maker of either. The liquor-trade is consequently in the hands of Armenians and Jews, and, being illicit, is entirely dependent on the venal connivance of the local authorities. Even when thus winked at for a consideration, it must always be a precarious business, for, though a governor may have no religious scruples about its permission—nay, may derive a considerable income therefrom, and himself be a hard drinker—he is sometimes obliged to yield to the remonstrances of mollahs and priests, and put a stop to a traffic which threatens to become a public scandal, by destroying the contents of the wine-shops. More frequently, however, when a clerical storm is impending, he will smooth down matters by imposing a good round fine on the vendors, and thus extract from his goose another golden egg without endangering his future harvest. The best native wines are those of Hamadan—which are light and agreeable, somewhat resembling the cheaper qualities of Rhine wine—and Shiraz; which last is full-bodied and powerful, with a strong astringent taste: they are to be had on the spot for sixpence a bottle. As to wines introduced from Europe, they are only to be found, I think, in Tehran, and as they generally hail from Cette, and are sold at about double the price of the purest Bordeaux, I cannot recommend them. English beer and porter may be had, but only at four shillings per bottle.

The elevation of Tehran, 3,300 feet above the sea, and its proximity to the Elburz mountains, render its short winter exceedingly severe. The cold weather lasted some days after my arrival, and skating on yakchals—long shallow ponds, excavated for the purpose of procuring a supply of ice, and, to this end, completely protected from the sun's rays by high mud walls—was still the amusement of the Europeans. A fortnight previously, the Shah, who was desirous of witnessing their performances, had been graciously pleased to invite the skaters to breakfast and a display of their skill at one of his country palaces, Kasr-

Kajar, the castle of the Kajars, which Persians delight to compare with Windsor. It is a large lofty building, situated on a commanding hill about three miles to the north of the town, and, from a distance, has an imposing effect, which is much increased by a series of terraces connecting it with some spacious gardens. On the highest of these terraces, and in front of the castle—which, I need hardly say, on near approach, bears about as much resemblance to Windsor as a blank mud-wall does to a Gothic cathedral façade—is a large tank, on which the skating took place.

His Majesty, surrounded by his Court and some of his Ministers, stately long-bearded gentlemen in flowing robes and tall hats, took much interest in it, and highly applauded the performances of the two English engineers in his service. After a time, however, his interest flagged, and urged no doubt by the *espièglerie* inherent in the character of all Persians, he expressed a wish to see his courtiers try their feet on the ice. Now stateliness and dignity of movement have, by education, become an Oriental's second nature. Hence it is that, of all our European customs and accomplishments, none astonishes him more than dancing. At the sight of a number of ladies and gentlemen whirling about in a ball-room—or, as he would put it, giving themselves infinite trouble for a ridiculous result—his first impression is that they are mad, his second that they are foolish. For, dancing being, according to his ideas, a pleasure to be seen, he so little understands the charms it has for the dancers that, if called upon to give expression to his thoughts on the subject, he would probably do so by asking them, "Why don't you pay people to dance for you?" Skating is, I suppose, regarded much in the same light, and the dignitaries of the Court cast deprecating looks at their Sovereign when his wish was made known to them. But the more reluctance they showed, the more the idea seemed to tickle his Majesty, and the more he insisted; so the skates were attached to their feet, and they were launched on the ice. I refrain from attempting a description of the scene that ensued; its counterpart might perhaps be imagined by conceiving several Lord Chancellors in their state robes taking their first skating lesson on Virginia Water.

Practical jokes of this nature are, it would seem, not unfrequently indulged in at the Persian Court. Not long after this incident, the Shah took such a fancy to a portable india-rubber boat, that its owner, one of our officers, who had got it out from England with a view to exploring some of the rivers, begged, and of course obtained, permission to present it to him. It was at once transported to the Palace, and, when inflated, my friend had there the honour of paddling royalty about on one of the tanks. The amusement pleased his Majesty, and he took to paddling himself; the courtiers followed suit, and eventually the King caused a throne to be erected near the tank, in order that he might at his ease watch their progress in this new accomplishment. It was probably too slow to afford him satisfaction, for one day he announced that he should like to see how many persons his boat was capable of carrying. Three could sit comfortably in it, but there was room for a dozen, and accordingly a dozen A.D.C.'s and Chamberlains, in their handsome shawl dresses and gold brocade, stepped in. Meanwhile, some one in the royal confidence had secretly opened the valves; the boat was shoved off towards the middle of the tank, and, as the air escaped, gradually sank lower and lower, and finally disappeared with its gorgeous and unsuspecting freight in the water. For a moment there was nothing visible on the surface of the tank but lambswool hats and linen skull-caps: for a moment, too, there was silence. Then a dozen shaven heads were seen wagging their tufts and side-locks, and a dozen mouths and noses were heard puffing, blowing, and snorting as their owners struggled slowly to the side. The Shah laughed long and loudly, and was so much pleased with the success of his stratagem that, when his victims emerged, all dripping and draggled from their bath, and stood shivering and crest-fallen before him, he deigned to inquire, "What news of the fish?" Persians can take a joke, as it is meant; and, though the courtiers no doubt wished the boat and its donor a speedy descent to a warmer climate, I daresay they all ultimately joined in their sovereign's laughter.

When the snow had disappeared, and the mud which it had left behind it began to dry up, I began to ride about a good deal, and one morning went out to see the garrison on parade. Four regiments of infantry, each about 600 men strong, were assembled on the plain about a quarter of a mile from the town—hardy, wiry-looking men, but bearing evident marks of ill-treatment and scanty rations. Their uniform was semi-European—*i.e.* they had all of them European-cut coats (the rank and file dark blue, the pioneers red) and cross-belts; the rest of their costume was decidedly Persian, consisting of black lambswool caps, wide white trousers, and shoes of untanned hide. They were armed with muskets, a good many of them flint-locks, which about the time of the battle of Waterloo were probably in the hands of the French or the Allies, and have since then been slowly driven eastwards by the flood of new inventions. The Italian officers, who commanded, were in plain clothes, and, instead of swords, carried stout sticks, which they used both frequently and mercilessly on the heads and shoulders of their men, as they put them through some of the simplest manœuvres, such as marching in line and column, forming in hollow squares, &c. On inquiry I was told that this, to me, novel proceeding on the part of commissioned officers, was the only means of impressing the science of military tactics on the minds of the troops. When parade was over, a band of music, the only one in the kingdom furnished with European instruments, struck up a terrible discord, and the garrison returned to barracks.

While riding home, my friend the Austrian officer gave me a good deal of promiscuous information about the Persian army. Up to the commencement of the present century irregular troops, militia and cavalry, furnished by the different tribes and commanded by their chiefs, sufficed to maintain order and repel the inroads of the Turcomans, the only foes Persia had then to fear; but about 1820, the formation of a regular army in Turkey, the gradual approach of Russia, and the frequent struggles which ensued on the death of the sovereign between rival pretenders to the throne, induced Abbas Mirza, the eldest son of the then reigning monarch, Futteh Ali Shah, to attempt the organization of a regular standing army. For this purpose he obtained the services of several English officers for a number of years, and though it is long since they all left the country, what remains of organization is their work. The army at present consists of ninety regiments of the line, each regiment being 800 strong; of three squadrons of regular cavalry and 200 camel artillerymen, forming the Shah's body-guard; 5,000 artillerymen; and 30,000 irregular cavalry, which are only called out in cases of emergency. The infantry is armed chiefly with English percussion muskets, and one-half of it is always on furlough. There are barracks, if four bare walls and a roof can be so termed, in the capital and principal towns, but no hospitals; nor is there any code of punishments, these matters being left entirely to the discretion of the commanding officer. The bastinado, generally on the soles of the feet, abscission of ears, noses and hands, strangulation and decapitation, are the usual penalties inflicted. On a march, asses are the means of transport employed, one of these animals being allotted to three soldiers.

There is no fixed age for entrance into the army, and boys of fifteen are often seen in the ranks by the side of greybeards; the men are enlisted for life, but can leave the service on producing a substitute. As a rule, the commander of each regiment is the chief of the tribe from which it is raised and recruited: he consequently has the interests of his clan much more at heart than those of the army or the Shah, and it thus frequently happens that he is openly hostile to the Government. To obtain his command he must give bribes to the amount of 200*l*. or 300*l*., which he reimburses to himself with interest by the sale of the subordinate commands in his regiment, and by retaining and investing at usurious interest the pay of his men. Under this, the worst of all purchase systems, merit is seldom—or, rather, never —rewarded; hence efficiency cannot be looked for in any rank. As to army administration, no such thing is known; and contracts for clothing and commissariat are given to the highest bidder. The servants of the Persian crown, military as well as civil, receive their salaries at the end of each year's service; to obtain a portion of them earlier, they must submit to considerable deductions in the way of discount. The Paymaster of the Forces must therefore have a very lucrative post: if he discounts, his profits must be large; if not called on to do so, they are perhaps still larger, as in a country where money is very scarce, he can always invest the sums in his hands for very high interest.

Altogether, the lot of the Persian soldier is a very hard one: he is fleeced in every direction; and it is only the respect which he bears to his commanding officer, as chief of his tribe, which keeps him from revolt or desertion. His clothing reaches him in scanty proportions, he is mulcted of his pay, and is obliged to seek his livelihood when off duty as best he can. Thus in the capital all the butchery is done by soldiers; and they are continually to be seen where the hardest work is going on, staggering through the bazaars under huge loads, digging watercourses, or building walls. But in spite of all this, I have generally found them willing and obedient, sober and enduring, and capable of gratitude—that rarest of feelings in the East—for the smallest kindness; if properly cared for, they would, no doubt, make excellent troops. In the capital they are fairly equipped and armed, and a guard of honour of ten or twelve men is furnished from their ranks to each of the foreign Legations. The men then receive some additional pay (from the Legations, of course), as they have to mount guard day and night at the gates and escort the head of the Mission in his walks. In the provinces their uniforms are often in rags, and I once witnessed the eccentric spectacle of a sentinel on duty shouldering a stockless musket.

Towards the end of February hunting and hawking became our amusements. The English Minister,[*] who

---

[*] The late Charles Alison, Esq., C.B.

was a most liberal patron of these sports, supplied the pack and hawks, as well as a capital breakfast; so the meet generally took place at 8 A.M. in front of his house. We formed a goodly cavalcade, consisting of ten or twelve Europeans, each accompanied by a couple of mounted servants, the huntsmen and falconers ; and after threading our way, in Indian file, through the narrow streets and bazaars, and getting clear of the walls and suburbs, we spread ourselves over the ground, as do the beaters at an English coursing meeting. Our best coverts for hares and foxes were to the south of the town, on a large tract of the cultivated part of the plain, which, though from a distance apparently flat, is a good deal cut up by the open shafts of khanats or subterranean conduits, watercourses, deep and abrupt chasms and gullies only visible when one is within a few yards of them, and rotten ground caused by the burrowings of the jerboa, a large species of rat, which abounds throughout the country, and is the pest of the husbandman at seed-time. The huntsmen, with their hooded hawks on their wrists, or holding the pack in leash, rode a little in front of the line of sportsmen until a find was announced, when either the one or the other was let loose in pursuit of the quarry. The hawk swooped down on its prey, and, if successful, alighted on its head and held it pinned to the ground till the huntsman came up. We generally found, however, that if he failed in his first flight he seldom attempted a second one, and that hawking was more a spectacle to be looked at than a sport full of active excitement. It was otherwise with the pack, composed of several couples of Persian greyhounds. They have feathered ears and tails, and are much slower than our English ones. Puss, too, is more timid in Persia than with us, and contrives to get more law, so we had frequent runs of three and four miles, in which the whole field, servants and all, took part, and which, from the nature of the ground and the emulation existing between Persians and Europeans, were often most exciting. If a kill took place, the huntsman jumped from his horse and fulfilled the Prophet's orders relative to the slaughtering of animals destined for the table by cutting the hare's throat; but we were often baulked of our prey, for Persian hares are very fond of running to earth, and were often able to indulge this taste before we could catch them. After a couple of runs a halt was called, and we breakfasted by the side of a water-course or under the trees of an enclosed orchard, continuing our sport afterwards till late in the afternoon.

Pure Arab horses are only found in the stables of the wealthiest Persians. They are very expensive, and require much care during the severe winter season. Persian-bred horses are much better adapted to the climate. They have a good deal of Arab blood, are very hardy, and have plenty of pluck and courage. An average horse of this breed costs about 20*l*. Turcoman horses, larger and stronger in every way than the above, are highly esteemed for their staying powers, which are so great that journeys of 500 or 600 miles are sometimes performed on them in five or six days. They have no manes, and this peculiarity, the result of being from their youth covered up to their ears with heavy clothing, considerably detracts from their appearance.

All Persians are justly proud of their riding. From childhood they are accustomed to the saddle, and their belief in fatalism no doubt conduces to render them fearless in it. They are as bold and daring horsemen as I have seen, and delight in showing off their dexterity. One of their great amusements is shooting from horseback, and they show wonderful skill in thus bringing down ground game at full gallop. This is the more remarkable, as they have no idea of shooting at a bird on the wing—indeed, never attempt it, but wait until they can get a shot on the ground. They are excessively fond of their horses, and though unsparing of their powers in the field, take much care of them in the stable; where, strange to say, a pig is often kept for their protection, on the supposition that should an evil spirit pass the threshold it will take up its quarters in the soul of a beast so loathsome to the nostrils of a true son of the Prophet, and leave the horses unmolested. Much faith is, likewise, laid in the efficacy of charms, and the favourite animal of the stable has generally a turquoise, which is held to bring luck, strung to his tail. Oats and hay being almost unknown, the horses are fed on barley and chopped straw, and a course of green food in the spring.

CHAPTER X.

Rhé — The Guebres — Religion of Zoroaster — The Ramazan and Bairam — Bazaars — Persian Women — New Year's Day — The Shah — His Palace — Reception of the Diplomatic Body and Grand Salaam — A Debt of Honour.

On one of our hunting excursions we breakfasted amongst the ruins of Rhé, which are about five miles south-east of the town, under a prolonged spur of the Elburz. Of this place, the Rhages of the Apocrypha—the last halting-place of Alexander the Great in his pursuit of Darius—the capital of the proud Arsacidæ—the city which, if we are to believe ancient writers, once rivalled Babylon and Nineveh in size and luxury, and was hence called the market and spouse of the world—there remain but two lofty towers rising solitarily out of acres of unshapely masses of crumbling brick ruins, and the half-effaced lineaments of a colossal bas-relief. The towers are both circular, and round the top of each there runs a broad frieze of Cufic inscriptions executed in brick. The base of one of them is of stone. The bas-relief is sculptured on the smoothed surface of a rock, at the foot of which there is now a spring and some weeping willows—a romantic spot for our meal. The sculpture represents a horseman in full charge, with couched spear, wearing long flowing robes and a globular crown. It is said to be of Sassanian origin, and may therefore possibly be 1600 years old.

To the north of these ruins is a wild, secluded, desert valley, shut in on all sides, except towards Rhé, by high ridges of barren rock, and thither we proceeded after breakfast in search of game. The afternoon turned out a blank, however, and we were about to retrace our steps homewards, when a proposal was made by one of the party to ride up a steep hill-side and examine a low round tower, perched high amongst some desolate crags; we had previously noticed it, and now learnt that this was the cemetery of the Guebres. After a rough climb we reached the foot of a circular building about forty feet high and sixty in diameter, having neither doors nor windows. Looking down from a neighbouring elevation, we saw that on the top there was a platform of open iron grating, whereon lay exposed the body of a recently deceased disciple of Zoroaster and late gardener to the British Mission. There he was to lie until his bones had been denuded of their covering of flesh by the vultures, and fell through the grating to their last resting-place in the base of the tower. Such is the system of burial prescribed by the Guebre religion; a sketch of which (taken from Parsee authors), together with some remarks on its adherents, will occupy the time as we ride home.

Considerable mystery envelops the origin and birth of the great Persian Lawgiver, and various are the theories and hypotheses which have been put forward by those who have written on the subject. The modern Parsees, however, seem to have arrived at the conclusion that Zerdusht, or Zoroaster, first saw the light at Rhé, and that he flourished in the reign of Darius Hystaspes, in the sixth century before Christ. Prodigies and miracles were not wanting in connection with the appearance of the author of the new faith. Thus it is reported in Pehlvi works, compiled, it is supposed, by his disciples, that his father Poroshusp received a glass of wine from an angel; and that thereupon his wife Doghdo conceived and bore the son destined to create a new era in Eastern history. The governor of the district, informed of the descent of the celestial messenger and his wine, and dreading, instinctively, the consequences of such a portentous event, sought to destroy the infant; who, it would appear, was only preserved from death by Divine agency. Many were his miraculous escapes from the machinations of those in authority; until, in his fortieth year, he appeared at the court of Darius, and by a series of miracles convinced that monarch of the divinity of his mission and the excellency of his doctrines. It was then that he produced the sacred books—the Zendavesta—written in a language which is supposed to have prevailed in a great part of Persia some thirty or thirty-five centuries ago. The majority of these books—twenty-one in number—were probably burnt by Alexander in the great conflagration at Persepolis, or at the time of the Arab invasion, and one entire book—the Vendidad—and some scattered fragments of others alone remain extant.

The new faith was soon accepted by the whole empire, and continued to be the religion of the country until the Mahometan conquest. The purity of Zoroaster's doctrines seems, however, to have been, in the course of time, more than once corrupted by superstitious additions. The Magi (hence the English word magic) engrafted on it, "Fire-worship." Mithra, the sun, became an object of actual worship, and during the five centuries which succeeded the subversion of the Persian dynasty by Alexander, a certain species of idolatry had mingled itself with Zoroastrianism. At the expiration of this period (A.D. 226) arose Ardeshir Babegan, a religious enthusiast and founder of the Sassanian dynasty, and restored to the faith its primitive purity. In his reign the sacred books were collected and translated from the original Zend into Pehlvi, the current language of the country, and the fruits of this reformation seem to have lasted until the religion and monarchy of Persia were overthrown by the Arabs, A.D. 641.

What was the religion of Zoroaster? Now I think the Parsees, as we call the Guebres, must themselves be allowed to answer this question; more especially as their answer has been endorsed by the most distinguished European authors who have devoted their attention to the subject.

Their religion, they say, is a simple form of monotheism, recognizing but one God, the creator, ruler, and preserver of the universe, without form, invisible, omnipotent, without beginning or end. He is above all, and to him every praise must be given for the blessings enjoyed in this world. He is an immense light, from which all glory, bounty, and goodness flow; his mercies are as boundless as his being. In the government of this world he has allowed two principles to prevail:—Ormuzd, the principle of all good, the inspirer of purity of thought, word, and action; Ahriman, the author of all evil, the cause of the temptation to which man succumbs, to be hated and combated by enfeebling, as far as possible, the tyranny which he is permitted to exercise for a time over mankind. The belief in these two principles is one of the distinguishing features of their faith, and it was symbolically represented in their sculptures; though this symbolism must not be confounded with idolatry, to which the spirit of the Zendavesta is wholly adverse.

Prayer is one of the duties most strongly enjoined, because man, continually exposed to the assaults of Ahriman, stands in need of the succour which it procures. The Parsee priest prays for himself, and for all his brethren; he unites his prayers to those of all the Parsees, of all the souls acceptable to Ormuzd which have ever existed or shall exist until the resurrection. The whole fabric of their sacred works is built upon three injunctions, termed in the Avesta, Homuté, Hookté, and Varusté, purity of speech, purity of action, and purity of thought. Truth is the basis of all excellence; virtue alone is happiness in this world; its path is the path of peace. Good actions are the most acceptable sacrifices to God. Industry is a guard to innocence and a bar to temptation. Hospitality, philanthropy, and benevolence are strongly inculcated. Untruth is the worst of sins; wickedness is a garment of shame; idleness, the parent of want. At the resurrection, God will judge mankind: the good will be rewarded in Paradise for their good actions, whilst the wicked will undergo punishment for their misdeeds in a place of torture.

The Parsees maintain that the worship or adoration of any other object than God is blasphemy, and was so considered by Zoroaster, and they therefore strongly protest against the term "Fire-worshippers," which is so generally applied to them. Fire, it is true, is kept constantly burning on the altars of their temples; all public and private prayers are offered up before it, and it is a sin to pollute or extinguish it wherever found. But their veneration for this element is not worship. Light is the truest symbol of the great Governor of the Universe; the sun, the most perfect fire, produces the most perfect light; before it and before fire, He must be worshipped, being the cause of light. The sun is the fairest creation of God, and the sacred fire is a perpetual monitor, ever warning them to aspire to the purity symbolized by its pure flame. " My light," said God to Zoroaster, " is under all that shines."

This is what the modern Parsees tell us of the origin and purity of their religion. It is, however, more than probable that Zoroaster was not its founder, but rather the reformer of a much older faith, which he found tainted with idolatry and superstition; and which, no doubt, subsequently to his reformation, frequently relapsed into their practice. But though it has thus often fallen from its pristine purity, its precepts have always retained much that is admirable and sublime, and I therefore hope that no apology is necessary for the following quotations from the *Revelation of Ardai Veraf*—a code of morality drawn up for the use of the people at the time of the reformation of Ardeshir Babegan, and purporting to be an account of what was said to the author in a vision, in which he was transported into the other world.

"Recollect, O Ardai Veraf," said the angel, "that your body will return to dust, but that your soul, if rich in good works, will mount to immortality and partake of the happiness you have here witnessed. Take less care of your body and more of your soul; the pains and aches of the body are easily cured, but who can minister to the diseases of the soul? When you set out on a journey in the lower world, you provide yourselves with money, clothes, and provisions; but what do you provide yourselves with for your last journey of the soul from the lower to the upper world? Hear, and I will tell you what is requisite. In the first place, the friend who will assist you is God; but to attain His friendship you must walk in His ways, and place in Him the firmest reliance. The provisions must be faith, hope, and the remembrance of your good works. The body, O Ardai Veraf, may be likened to a horse, and the soul to its rider. Even in the world, the multitude would sneer at a man who took more care of his horse than of himself; for this reason, a man ought to take more care of his soul than of his body. God requires only two things from the sons of men: that they should not sin, and that they should be grateful for the blessings He continually bestows on them.

"Let not men be taught to set their hearts on the pleasures and vanities of life, as nothing can be carried away with them. In youth, and in the prime of manhood, when blessed with health and vigour, you suppose that your strength will never fail; that your riches, your lands, your houses, and your horses will remain for ever; that your gardens will be always green and your vineyards fruitful; but, O Ardai Veraf! teach them not to think so,—teach them the dangers of such a way of thinking. All, all will pass away as a dream. The flowers fade, and give lessons unto man that he is unwilling to profit by. Yea, the world itself will pass away, and nothing will remain but God."

The remote town of Yezd is now the head-quarters of the Guebres in Persia. In and around it there are still 7,000 or 8,000 of them. At Kerman there are about 1,000, and a few families are located at Shiraz, Cashan, and Tehran. They are everywhere subjected to much persecution at the hands of the Mahometans. They are not allowed to repair their long-ruined temples, to pray or celebrate in public their religious rites. As they are prohibited from having schools of their own, and no Mussulman would condescend to teach their children, they are plunged in the grossest ignorance. They cannot hold landed property, and prolong their wretched existence by hiring themselves out as agricultural labourers; the hardness of their fate may be imagined from the fact that no Guebre is permitted to appear mounted on a quadruped, an ass being considered too great a luxury for him. Under these circumstances their number is fast decreasing, and they would, probably, all at once emigrate to India, if they were not prevented from doing so by the Persian authorities and their own poverty. Many are assisted out of the country by the Parsee merchants of Bombay. All Persian Guebres are either agriculturists or gardeners, perhaps because amongst the good works which Zoroaster recommended as entitling to future rewards was the planting of trees, a recommendation which goes far to prove that Persia was always a comparatively treeless country.

On arriving at home this same evening, we found the town in a state of great excitement. The streets were crowded with men, women, and children; there was shouting and screaming in every note, from bass to highest tenor; guns were being fired off and drums beaten, and from the housetops the praises of Allah were being sung. The feast of the Bairam had begun, putting an end to the thirty days' fast of the Ramazan, and preparations were being made to celebrate it by junketing and banquets which were to last late into the night. This fast of the Ramazan is very strictly observed: from sunrise to sunset neither food nor drink must enter the Mussulman's mouth, not a whiff of his beloved Kalian can he inhale. When it falls in the summer months it causes a great deal of suffering, and, in general, at whatever time of year it may occur, completely upsets the ordinary course of life. Night is turned into day. The rich and those who have little to do pass the weary hours of abstention from worldly comforts in prayer and sleep; but the poor, who must work while there is light, are obliged to devote a portion of the night to the nourishment of their bodies—thus depriving themselves of sleep—and yet work during the day to obtain the means of doing so. Towards the end of the month they contract a hungry, half-famished look, business of all sorts comes near to a standstill, and life in general verges on a state of coma. The day had been a long one, but, according to my practice, I took my usual stroll at sunset in the garden of the Legation, and there found the Guebre gardeners prostrate before the setting orb, and amidst their prayers and ejaculations, ever and anon placing their hands—as if to assure themselves of its presence—on the mystic girdle which must never leave them from manhood till death.

The best bazaars at Tehran are some twenty feet broad and thirty high, arched over with the favourite Persian arch, something between an ogive and a horseshoe. Some of them are a quarter of a mile long, and open, at intervals, into large courts; caravansaries and minor bazaars intersecting them at right angles. On each side are the shops with their raised counters, on which the owners sit cross-legged amongst their goods. As a rule, each particular branch of trade has its own quarter, though vendors of provisions and *smoke*, as well as barbers, establish themselves wherever they find the best market and most customers. Bazaars are the stages on which public life in the East is concentrated, and the favourite resorts of all classes of society. They are the centres of all business, news, and gossip, and during the day are ever crowded with men, women, and beasts. Camels, mules, and asses are continually passing and repassing with their loads; great men on horseback with their scores of servants, mollahs on their milk-white donkeys, and ladies on their ambling mules and followed by their guardians, are constantly seen threading their way through the dense crowds of foot-passengers.

Women never lose an opportunity of visiting the bazaars, in order to escape from the dulness of the Harem, to have a chat and a look at the outer world. Their out-door costume is one of the ugliest imaginable, consisting of a dark blue mantle, covering head and shoulders and descending to the knees, a white veil sewn on to the mantle round the forehead and temples but loose below, and very wide trowsers, also dark blue, terminating in tight-fitting socks and slippers. Thus the feet are the only parts of a lady's figure of which one can form a definite notion. Very pretty feet they often are too, and, as ladies in Persia ride after the fashion of men, their owners have frequent opportunities of showing them to advantage : these they do not lose, and when circumstances permit it, the beauties sometimes go a little further and gratify the legitimate curiosity of a European by lifting their veils aside. On Thursday afternoons it is their habit to visit the graves of their deceased relatives, and especially those in the cemetery of Shah Abdul Azim, a village about four miles from the capital ; it is so called from the son of the seventh Imaum who there lies buried, and whose saintliness was so great in life that the precincts of his tomb are the favourite burial-grounds of Tehranese. On these days, therefore, the road thither becomes the fashionable promenade, and the ladies contrive sometimes to keep their attendants at a distance behind them and to uncover for a moment charms which elsewhere are so jealously hidden from view. Some of those I saw, when riding to meet them on their return home, were decidedly pretty ; having oval faces, to which rouge was not always a stranger, dark brown or black eyes, thick eyebrows joining each other above the nose (often, I fear, by the aid of antimony) and cherry lips. They seemed smiling and happy for the moment, at least; conscious, no doubt, of the admiration they were exciting and the pleasure they were giving.

The lot of Eastern women is a hard one. As a rule they are totally uneducated, very few being taught even to read. Amongst the lower classes they must work and labour harder than their sisters in the West, with very few of the home comforts which solace the latter. In the higher ranks a woman is, perhaps, happy as long as she retains her beauty, almost her only means of keeping her lord's affections. When this begins to fade, she has recourse to all sorts of stratagems to protract for a brief space longer her waning empire. Charms and incantations are then much used; she tries the effect of amulets supposed to have the power of softening the heart, or has recourse to more material measures by mixing in her husband's food ingredients having a similar reputation. Then comes a time when these no longer avail, and with it a jealousy which does not subside in resignation, but lasts till some new beauty has erased all traces of her influence, and premature ugliness destroys the last hope of regaining it. Henceforward, if she has children, attention and kindness may be shown her on their account; but if childless, she is generally considered and treated as a burden to the household. A lady's amusements consist in going often to the bath and paying visits to her friends. In the harem itself a good deal of time is devoted to dress, costumes similar to those of our opera-dancers being most in vogue; sweetmeat-making, frequently productive of very palatable results, and other household occupations of a similar nature, fill up the rest of her day. She takes little exercise, and her figure is consequently seldom fully developed. On the whole, from what I have heard and seen, I should say that few Persian women can rival European beauties either in face or form.

A Persian school is a very funny affair. The room is generally open to the street. Looking in, one sees a lot of boys squatted on their heels on the floor round a Mollah, all rocking themselves to and fro, and all repeating aloud the tasks they have to commit to memory. The result is a little babel of sounds,—a jumble, to those who understand the language, of verses from the Koran, drinking and love songs from Hafiz, and heroic lines from Firdousi. These are the books most studied; and a Persian's education is pretty well complete when he can quote freely from them and talk a little Arabic. Hafiz is the favourite poet, and he is quoted and recited by all classes, as was Tasso some years ago by the gondoleers of Venice.

Winter generally departs about the middle of February, but this year we had a fall of snow as late as the 2nd of March, and spring weather only set in a few days before the Persian New Year, the 21st of that month. Custom has reconciled us Europeans to the celebration of New Year's day at the gloomiest season of the year; and, as we have always been told so, we must believe that our arrangement is the most convenient; but there is much to be said in favour of the old calculation which Easterns, whose time is not money, have retained. At the vernal equinox all nature revives and celebrates a general resurrection; springing grass, sprouting buds, milder breezes, and sunnier days, make us feel that we are entering on a new season; spring creates new life around us and arouses new hope within us; it is only in its verdant freshness that we fully and inwardly realize to ourselves that we have left the old year behind us and entered upon the new one.

The Nowrooz, new day, is a great festival in Persia. The Shah then receives his annual tribute and presents from his ministers and governors, and distributes dresses of honour amongst the punctual payers; the army and civil service get their salaries, retainers and servants their suits of new clothes. Presents are exchanged on all sides, the houses are decked with flowers, the people wear their holiday attire, and on all sides there are signs of rejoicing and gladness.

Early in the morning a score of the Shah's servants arrived at our Legation charged with his Majesty's compliments to the Minister, and bearing, in token thereof, several large wooden trays sparsely sprinkled with sweetmeats and little silken bags containing diminutive silver coins about the thickness and size of ordinary wafers. We soon afterwards started to present our congratulations to the monarch and witness the royal salaam.

Four soldiers, carrying stout sticks in addition to their side-arms, headed our procession. Behind them strode the Ferrash Bashee, or head servant of the mission, and about three-score of ferrashes in their tall hats and new broad-cloth jubbahs; the British Minister, in full uniform and mounted on a richly caparisoned horse, came next; and behind him rode his secretaries, according to their rank, surrounded and followed by more ferrashes. Thus marshalled, we marched at a slow and stately pace through the bazaars, which were crowded with courtiers hurrying to the palace and a more than ordinary number of sight-seers. Our soldiers' sticks were in constant requisition to clear the way, and the assistance of the entire troop of ferrashes was necessary to procure space for our passage through the Maidan to the Palace gates. There we left our horses, and taking off our goloshes—the proper use of which, in official visits to his Majesty of Persia, is minutely defined in the stipulations of several solemn treaties—were ushered into an antechamber and received with much stateliness by the Grand Master of the Ceremonies, the Minister for Foreign Affairs, and some A. D. C.'s, all wearing gay-coloured vestments embroidered with gold brocade, jewelled belts and scabbards, rich Cashmere or Kerman shawls wound turban-fashion round their hats, and long scarlet stockings. The usual inquiries after our health having been made, and the answers thereto received with the usual number of Alhamdellillahs (praises to God), coffee and tea were served, smoke was inhaled from jewel-headed kalians, and then, the whole diplomatic body having arrived, the Grand Master and Minister for Foreign Affairs called for their enamelled wands of office, and led the way to the presence of "The Centre of the Universe."

After slipping into our goloshes, we traversed a large court, to be mentioned later, and entered a smaller one adjoining it, planted with plane-trees and cypresses, and laid out in flower-beds intersected with running streams and paved walks. Its walls were covered with brilliantly glazed tiles, and on three sides there were buildings having large saloons opening wide upon it. With measured tread we descended one of the walks until we arrived at a tank in the centre of the court. The Persians bowed low as we here came in sight of their sovereign, and we followed their example; with less decorum, I fear, most of us being at that moment intent on upholding the sacred character of treaties by again discarding our goloshes. A few steps more and we entered the presence chamber, a moderately-sized saloon, on three sides of which the walls were covered with paintings of birds and flowers,—the loves of nightingale and rose—on a blue ground; the fourth was occupied by a window fitted with carved wood and painted glass, looking on to the court, and now open. The ceiling was vaulted and honey-combed, and glittered with gilding alternated with small pieces of mirror-glass. In the centre of the room, which was richly carpeted, played a rock-crystal fountain, a present from the Empress

Catherine to a former Shah, and around it stood eighteen solidly gilded chairs. Near the window was a throne of sandal-wood thickly studded with large emeralds, and most incongruously cushioned with Manchester chintz; close to it, on a carpet sewn with pearls, stood Nasreddeen Shah.

He was then thirty-six years of age; he is a little above the average height, well proportioned, and has regular features, though his forehead is rather low and his nose somewhat too prominent. His eyes are dark, and overhung by thick black eyebrows, which give them a mistrustful expression. He wears a moustache and closely-cropped beard. Altogether he is a handsome man, and the magnificence of his dress added not a little to his appearance.

In his hat he wore an aigrette, the distinctive emblem of royalty, of diamonds and rubies; his tunic, cut square and descending to his knees, was a blaze of brilliants and pearls, and in his belt, from which hung a jewelled sword and scabbard, glittered the Darya-noor, or sea of light, a sister diamond of our Koh-i-noor. White trousers and socks completed his costume. At his feet lay another of the royal insignia, a large sceptre, completely studded over with precious stones. By the side of all these treasures, a pair of common cotton gloves of an ugly brown colour, over which he wore several sapphire and turquoise rings, looked as incongruous as the Manchester chintz.

Our audience was a short one. The senior of the envoys addressed, through an interpreter, a few complimentary phrases to his Majesty, who was pleased to return a gracious reply; some presentations were made, and we then backed out, and, once more putting on our goloshes, were conducted to an upper chamber looking out on the grand court of the Palace.

This court, of much larger proportions than the one we had just left, was of oblong shape, and had at its upper end a large hall, similar in form and arrangement to the saloon above described, opening on a tank, in the centre of which played a fountain, and around which were placed flowers and shrubs, trays of sweetmeats and silver coins, and large china bowls of sherbet; beyond it extended a broad paved avenue, flanked by tall plane-trees and poplars. On each side of the tank and avenue were ranged, according to their respective rank, the grandees and officers of the court: the men of the pen, civilians, mollahs, astrologers, &c., in scarlet jubbahs and stockings and conical turbans of varied colours, to the right; the men of the sword, in uniforms heavily embroidered with gold lace, and of such eccentricity of form and cut that a Persian imagination could alone have invented them, to the left. Reclining in the avenue were three chained lions, and behind them an elephant.

As the Shah entered the hall, the whole assemblage, elephant and all, bowed to the ground; and the military bands, stationed in different parts of the court, produced an outburst of the most discordant music. Deep silence ensued as his Majesty seated himself on the throne, and the highest dignitary of the court, advancing towards the edge of the tank, commenced reciting the glories, and eulogizing the qualities of the sovereign; at every mention of whose name the lowest of salaams was made by all. At the end of this oration the chief mollah took his place, and called down the blessings of Allah on his Majesty's head; the court poet followed, singing his praises in verse. Handfuls of coin and sweetmeats were then distributed amongst the courtiers; sherbets were handed round; the Shah descended from his throne, and deafening discord announced his departure and the conclusion of the ceremony.

The festivities of the day were not yet, however, at an end, and we adjourned to another room looking out on to the Maidan, where, on a space of ground thirty or forty yards square, which was kept clear with the utmost difficulty—only, indeed, by the constant application of stick to the heads and shoulders of the invading crowd—were collected half-naked wrestlers, dancing-boys and mummers, giants and dwarfs, fighting rams, their fleeces stained in all the colours of the rainbow, dancing bears and monkeys, and chained tigers. At a given signal, as soon as his Majesty entered the room adjoining our own, all this motley crew was set in motion amidst fresh outbursts of discord. The wrestlers wrestled; the boys, mummers, bears and monkeys, danced pellmell; the giants threw the dwarfs aloft, the rams fought and the tigers roared, whilst the crowd renewed its efforts to get a sight of the sports, and the sticks of the ferrashes descended thick as hail on their shoulders. The spectacle was anything but regal, and we were all glad when an end was put to it by the distribution of small coin amongst the performers and the departure of his Majesty.

The rest of the day was occupied in paying State visits, but illness prevented my leaving the house again. The climate of Persia is a treacherous one; its clear blue sky and limpid atmosphere look as healthy as they are beautiful, but they seldom agree with Europeans, who are almost always attacked either by fever or diarrhœa and dysentry. Weakened, probably, by my long journey in the snow, I had suffered, ever since my arrival at the capital, from the latter; and as they did not yield to the doctor's remedies, and threatened to take a chronic form, I was at last advised to try change of air, and eagerly availed myself of a proposal made to me by two of our Engineer officers, to accompany them in a journey to the southern provinces of the kingdom. The mere prospect of escaping from the monotonous life of an Eastern town seemed to abate the acuteness of my complaint, and in a few days I felt strong enough to mount my horse. Before starting, however, I must relate an anecdote illustrative of Persian habits and customs.

There was then but one European lady at Tehran, and our social resources were consequently very limited. The post from Europe only reached us once a month, and time often hung heavy on our hands, especially in the long winter evenings. There was a billiard-table at the English Mission, but one can't always play at billiards; and thus it came to pass, as it does so frequently when young men are deprived of ladies' society, that card-playing became one of our amusements, and games of hazard, restrained within certain limits, not the least agreeable of them. Gradually a few Persians, whose whole life is so much a question of luck and chance that they at once entered into the spirit of these games, joined our party, but turned out such bad payers that it was found necessary to adopt with them the rule of "money on the table." It was not, however, always very strictly observed; and one evening, the first time I ever played, I found that I had won some 10*l*. or 12*l*., which were not at once forthcoming, from Prince * *, the son of the Prime Minister. As I was a complete stranger in the country, my host informed me before leaving him that, in accordance with its customs, I must send my servant next morning to claim the money. He accordingly went to the house of the Prince, but was told to call again next day. The same answer was given on his second and all future visits, until the eve of my departure from Tehran, when, being disgusted with these attempts at evasion, and all the more determined to make his Highness pay, I put the matter in the hands of a mirza, who at once sent a mohassil, or armed bailiff, with orders to sit at his door until the debt was acquitted. And there he sat for three or four days, before shame, or the annoyance caused by his presence, induced the great man to open his purse-strings.

CHAPTER XI.

PREPARATIONS FOR A CARAVAN JOURNEY — START FOR ISPAHAN — VALLEY OF THE ANGEL OF DEATH — DEVILS — KOOM — KASHAN — THE GOOD EMIR — ISPAHAN — PALACES OF FORTY PILLARS AND EIGHT PARADISES — ARMENIAN QUARTER — SHAKING MINARETS — RIFLE-PRACTICE — MANNA.

THE preparations which must be made for a three-months' journey in Persia, where, as we have seen, inns and hotels are unknown, and, except in the sparsely-scattered towns, only the merest necessities of life are to be found, require some forethought; though much less than would be supposed by a complete stranger to the country. There is there no such thing as settling down for life; existence is always more or less nomadic; all classes of society are accustomed to being constantly on the move, and, either as a consequence of, or a reason for, this custom, none of them are encumbered with what is not easily portable in the way of furniture and household goods. The word "home" has much less connection with the idea of permanency than with us, and the inconveniences of going abroad are consequently much fewer.

I have already described a journey by post. We

were now about to undertake one by caravan, and the first thing to be done was to find the means of transport. After a good deal of preliminary haggling and bargaining as to the price of the beasts and the length of each day's march, we succeeded in hiring twenty mules, at the modest rate of 1s. 10d. per diem, and three muleteers. Then came the question of the quantity of baggage we should take with us : we had to make ourselves as comfortable as possible, and yet not overburden our mules. Had we been Persians we should at once have solved this problem by taking a Fal : *i.e.*, opening a book, the Koran or Hafiz for instance, at random, and interpreting, no matter how forcedly, the first line at the top of the page as decisive of the point in question one way or the other ; then, having thus made fate responsible for our future comfort or discomfort, we should have camped outside the town for a couple of days, in order to prove our gear and be ready to start at the moment which astrology might declare propitious. As we were still uncontaminated Englishmen, these matters were referred to common sense ; which decided that, in addition to beds, bedding, wardrobe, wine, washing, cooking and table apparatus, guns, rifles, ammunition, and a few books, we should each of us have a camp-stool, three saddle-horses, and three servants, together with one table and a cook for the party ; and that, as the stars might have quite enough work on hand in combining horoscopes and auguries for their numerous Persian readers, we should not add to their labours by requesting them to fix the hour of our departure, but remain quietly in our homes until all preparations were completed.

Our caravan finally consisted of twenty-nine quadrupeds and thirteen bipeds, besides ourselves— viz., an officer and doctor of the Telegraph Staff and myself: and, the bulk of it having been despatched on its way two days previously, we donned our pith helmets, boots and spurs, stuck our pistols and flasks into our holsters, and, accompanied by our three head servants, rode out of the gates of Tehran on the morning of the 27th of March.

As a preliminary canter to our long ride, we had a couple of hot runs—for the sun's rays were already becoming powerful—with the Legation hounds, and after partaking of a farewell breakfast, which was given us in a cool garden by the friends we were to leave behind us, mounted fresh horses, and proceeded on our way to the south. The cultivated portions of the plain were green with the fresh-springing corn, but as we advanced these disappeared from view, and we soon found ourselves amidst the usual characteristics of Persian scenery—aridity and brownness. A march of four hours, the latter part over a low ridge of hills running east and west, brought us to Kinarigerd, our first manzil or halting-place, twenty miles on the road to Ispahan.

We rose betimes next morning from our straw couches on the floor of the post-house, and started with the sun through the "Valley of the Angel of Death." No other name could better indicate the dreariness of this region. It is a succession of narrow gloomy glens, shut in by parched volcanic hills, through which the path runs over alternate patches of nitre and moveable sand. Not a blade of grass, not a solitary herb ever grows in its lifeless salt-sown soil, and no locality was ever better chosen for what Persians suppose it to be— the abode of Gins and Deeves, the satellites of Shaitan : the Devil. Emerging, after a three-hours' ride, from this weird scenery, we reached the plain of Houze Sultan, equally devoid of vegetation, but having its dun monotony relieved by large tracts of salt, cropping up, white as snow and a couple of inches thick, from the soil ; and by spiral dust columns, striding along and about like so many giant beings from the lower world. These phenomena are caused by whirlwinds; their base is generally about twenty feet in diameter, and they rise straight up into the sky, becoming broader and less dense as they get higher and the force of the air-current decreases. The natives call them devils, and as they move, without losing their original forms, at a pace as capricious as the wind, they look very much like animated beings. Curiosity induced me to ride through one of them, and I found the draught so strong that all my clothes flew upwards, and fancied that a slight addition to its strength would have carried myself and horse in the same direction: needless to say that I was blinded with dust and gravel. In the middle of the plain, which is unbounded except by some ranges of hills to the north and south, we came upon a large lake nearly a mile broad, which owed its ephemeral existence to the unusual quantity of snow which had fallen amongst the hills during the winter, and was now fast melting in the warmth of spring. So impregnated is this region with salt, that its water, three feet deep in many places, was more than brackish. Wading through it, with the telegraph-posts for our guide, we arrived in due time at the southern extremity of the plain, crossed the hills, and descended to the post-house of "Pool-i-Dellàk," "The Barber's Bridge," so-called from the bridge which a barber, either from patriotism or by way of atonement for past misdeeds, erected many years ago over the neighbouring river Konsar.

Fresh horses were here procured, and carried us over another dun plain in a few hours to the city of Koom, where green cornfields and glittering domes were a refreshing sight after the dreary scenery of our sixty-five miles' ride. Here we rejoined our caravan, and found comfortable quarters and a good dinner awaiting us.

Koom is a very holy place, second only in holiness to Meshed, and one of the most favourite burial-grounds in the country. All Persians like their bones to lie near those of some saintly personage, in the hope, probably, of gaining easy admittance to Paradise under the ægis of his sanctity, and Koom has within its walls the tomb of a saint—Fatima, a near descendant of the Prophet—whom they all especially revere. Such, indeed, is the reverence in which she is held that the dome of her tomb is covered with plates of gold, and an intercessionary influence is ascribed to her, as great, perhaps, as that which, in Catholic countries, is attributed to the Virgin. Two kings of Persia lie near her, besides many men of note in their day. Caravans of bodies, packed in the frailest of coffins and slung like merchandise on the backs of mules, are continually arriving from all parts of the country; and the only occupation of the inhabitants of the place seems to be interment. Seyeds who, as descendants of the Prophet, are alone authorised to wear his colour, green, in their turbans, and mollahs abound, and are as intolerant as they are numerous. We knew, of course, that it would be impossible to obtain admission to the tombs, and, therefore, refrained from attempting to obtain it; but the mere presence of " infidels " within the precincts of the holy place seemed to be viewed with disapprobation, and I was not sorry to ride away next morning through the ruins which surround it and still mark the ravages committed during the Affghan invasion of 1722.

We were now to march at caravan pace, and the order of our day was generally as follows. At sunrise we were called, and, after washing, where water was procurable, and dressing, had tea and bread; the mules had meantime been loaded, and, as soon as our bedding was packed, were sent off with our grooms and led horses; the cook trotted ahead as fast as he could go, with his pots and pans, in order to have time to prepare our meal at the end of the stage;

last of all, we started on our own horses, and with three servants carrying our breakfast, prepared the night before, and our guns. Between ten and eleven we halted to eat and rest for an hour or two, and rode on again in the afternoon. Now and then we left the road to get a shot from our horses, trained to stand fire from their backs, at red-legged partridges and wild pigeons; or, more rarely, to have a useless gallop after antelope. We generally reached our manzil by sunset: if the muleteers, who are fond of loitering and require some trusty servants to keep them up to time, had done their duty, we found our quarters ready to receive us, the table laid and dinner at once forthcoming; and the day closed by our going early to bed.

Notwithstanding the monotony of most Persian scenery, this species of travelling has a great charm : in fact, with agreeable companions, good health, and fine weather, I can imagine nothing pleasanter. The traveller has perfect freedom—he can go where he likes and halt where he likes. With a well-equipped caravan, he is as independent as man can be. There is always sufficient incident to drive away ennui, and the certainty, continually brought home to him, that his safety depends solely on himself, is productive of quite enough healthy excitement.

Our march on the 29th was a long one—twenty-eight miles. During the whole day we skirted, to our right, a range of volcanic-looking hills, showing strong indications of the existence in them of sulphur and iron, whilst to our left, *i.e.* eastwards, our view extended unimpeded over the flat arid confines of the Great Salt Desert. Not a single traveller did we meet, and only one solitary cultivated oasis did we see—a garden, where two fine firs overhung the remains of a ruined village, and the apricot and peach-trees were in full blossom—until we reached the caravansary of Sin-Sin, and took up our quarters, almost *à la belle étoile*, within its shattered and crumbling walls, fitting abodes of jackals and owls, which kept up their dismal screeching all night.

Longer still was our next day's journey, thirty-two miles, to Kashan, a town of about 15,000 inhabitants, famous for its silk brocades, copper kettles, and scorpions. Our morning's ride was through scenery similar to that of the previous day, but after breakfast we reached an open stoneless plain, and left the hills some distance to our right. At their foot, and about four miles from Kashan, are the villa and gardens of Feen, well known throughout Persia, not only for their beauty, but also as having been the scene of one of the saddest tragedies in its recent history.

Mirza Taghi, the son of a court cook, had raised himself by his talents and clear-headedness from a menial post in the household of Mahomed Shah to that of Persian consul at Erzeroum, and had there entered into commercial relations and gained much influence with the richest merchants of his own country. On the death of that sovereign, in 1848, he hastened to Tabreez, where the heir-apparent was living almost in a state of penury, and rendered such services in procuring money for the payment of his troops and other pressing wants, that, previous to his entry into the capital, the new Shah made him his Grand Vizir, with the title of Emir-i-Nizam. The whole kingdom was then in a most disordered state; the treasury was empty, the army undisciplined, the taxes unpaid, and revolt imminent in several of the provinces. Nasreddeen Shah was an inexperienced lad of eighteen, and it required all the sagacity and energy of a strong mind to overcome these difficulties and seat him firmly on his throne. The Emir showed himself equal to the occasion, and, after disarming the dangerous tribes, re-establishing order, and replenishing the State coffers, received as his reward the hand of the King's sister, a very pretty girl of fourteen, who, though at first averse to this forced marriage, afterwards became much attached to her husband. He was now at the zenith of his power, and, with the return of tranquillity, devoted all his attention to the regeneration of his country; which he foresaw could only be accomplished by a complete reform of the administration, and by ameliorating the condition of the agricultural population.

The measures he took for carrying out these projects resulted in his becoming hated by the numerous and powerful class of courtiers, khans, and governors who lived on the proceeds of extortion and abuses, and idolized by the still more numerous but weaker class which found protection under his just rule. The former determined on his ruin ; the Queen-Mother was gained over to their views, the King's mind was poisoned with calumnies, the Emir was represented as aiming at the throne, and his popularity was cited as a proof of his ambitious designs. For some time the King wavered, but finally the Palace intrigue succeeded, and in 1851 the Emir was banished to Feen. His young wife accompanied him in his exile ; she left him neither day nor night, herself attended to all his wants, and prepared all his food, with a sad but well-founded presentiment that her presence alone could shield him from further injury at the hands of his now triumphant enemies. Not content with his ruin, they soon afterwards demanded his death, and induced the King, in a moment of weakness, to sign the warrant. The man entrusted with its execution was a former *protégé* of the Emir. On his arrival at the villa, he gave himself out as the bearer of good news from court, and thus calmed the wife's fears, and induced her, though reluctantly, to leave him alone with his late benefactor. She never saw her husband again. He was taken to the bath, his veins were opened, and there he expired.

The widow's fate is illustrative of the treatment of a Persian royal princess. Some months later the Shah ordered her to marry the son of the new Prime Minister. Her compliance was signified by these words: "I give you permission to marry me to this man and to all future Grand Vizirs." As may be supposed, her second marriage was not a happy one. Her health failed; a European doctor was called to attend her, but in reply to his daily inquiries as to her malady, he got but one answer, "My heart is sore." She recovered, however, and on the disgrace of her father-in-law, which occurred a few years afterwards, was divorced by the King's order, and finally married to her cousin, "the Eye of the Kingdom."

The Garden of Feen is surrounded with high walls and planted with avenues of tall cypresses, through which run streams of water inclosed in canals of blue tiles. The villa consists of a number of pavilions, only one of which need be described. Its external form is that of a square kiosk, with a projecting portico in front; the ceilings of the interior being vaulted and decorated with minute arabesques in gold and brilliant colours. The walls of the kiosk are covered on three sides with paintings of a royal hunt, in which the king is represented as double the size of his sons and courtiers, and of combats between Persians and Turcomans, in which the latter are, of course, getting much the worst of it; whilst the fourth opens into the arched portico, which is, so to say, floored with a tank of clear bubbling water. The bath in which the good Emir, as he is still called, died, is fast falling to decay, but otherwise the place is well kept up, and may again become the abode of disgraced ministers. To us, after our long hot ride, its green shade and cool waters appeared a paradise, and we left it at sunset with regret.

No scorpions disturbed our dreams, and next day, after twenty miles' march, we reached the southern extremity of the plain of Kashan, and ascended a rugged steep path, which brought us before evening to a large and flourishing upland village, by name Kohrood, supplied with abundance of water and embedded in trees. Its elevation is about 6,000 feet above the sea, and we consequently again found ourselves for the night in a wintry temperature.

On the 1st of April we breakfasted on the summit of the pass we had been ascending. A boiling thermometer showed it to be 8,000 feet high. On its southern slope we found snow, several feet deep, and so soft that we were obliged to dismount and drive our horses before us for some hours. The mules had a sad time of it, often sinking up to their bellies and requiring the asistance of several men to put them on their legs again, and we did not reach our quarters in the caravansary of Sow till late in the evening. On the 2nd and morning of the 3rd, we marched fifty-two miles, through the village of Mourcha-Kar, and over an undulating brown plain, sparsely sprinkled with camel-thorn, where we had some vain gallops after antelope, to Gez. There we left our caravan to follow at its own pace, took post-horses for our last short stage of sixteen miles, and at noon reached the gates of the city of Ispahan.

ISFAHĀN
NISHFI JEHĀN.
(ISPAHAN IS HALF THE WORLD.)

Such was the proud title given to the capital of the Soofees. The name of the most distinguished king of this dynasty, Shah Abbas the Great, has already been often mentioned in connection with the finest caravansaries and mosques which we have seen during our journey, but it is here alone that a correct idea can be formed of his magnificence and of the prosperity of Persia during his reign. Since then (1585—1627) two centuries and a half have elapsed, time and neglect have done their work, and the city has been occupied by devastating hordes of Affghans; but it still possesses sufficient remains of its former splendour to prove that the adoption of its title was justifiable, and to confirm the description given us of it by the chroniclers of the time.

Ispahan is beautifully situated on the banks of the Zeinderood, a considerable stream which issues from the hills a few miles to the west of the city, and, after irrigating a large portion of the surrounding plain, finally loses itself, like so many other rivers in this country, in the sands of the desert. The climate is salubrious and the soil most fertile. In the time of its glory, it is said to have contained 1,000,000 inhabitants, who received their supplies from 1,400 neighbouring villages. There are now barely 60,000 of the former, and probably not 100 of the latter.

The river is spanned by three bridges, the finest of which is provided with arched and covered footpaths on each side of the roadway. From it a broad stately avenue of several rows of enormous chenars (a very fine species of plane-tree), with a canal of black marble and hewn stone (now waterless) in the centre, leads through the heart of the city to the Great Maidan, a large square, surrounded by handsome arcades, and formerly the scene of royal reviews and pageants. On each side of the avenue are the structures most worthy of note—the College of Hossein, and the Palaces of "Chehel Sitoon" (forty pillars) and of "Heshte Beheste" (eight paradises).

The college is a large imposing edifice, completely cased in tile-work, covered with the most exquisite tracery, like the finest lace, brilliantly coloured on a white ground. Its high arched doorway, supported by columns of white marble, gives admittance into a spacious court shaded by tall trees and planted with roses, and having a tank and fountain in the centre. Around three of its sides run double ranges of cloisters, one above the other; on the fourth, a noble horseshoe arch opens into a mosque, the interior of which was concealed from view by a heavy curtain. There was an atmosphere of coolness, serenity, and seclusion about the place which seemed peculiarly adapted to reverie and thought; and had it not been for the brilliant colouring of the walls and the excessive purity of the blue sky, I could have fancied myself inside some silent Catholic convent in Europe. Students there were none; nor, indeed, any living beings except the porter, who offered me a glass of sherbet and a kalian daintily decked with fresh roses : we saw a couple of white-turbaned mollahs on their way to mid-day prayer.

The Palace of Chehel Sitoon stands in a large shady garden, laid out, according to the usual fashion of the country, in parallel walks with running streams. Its forty pillars, ranged at intervals of a few yards, in five rows, rise forty feet high from sockets formed by the united backs of four couchant lions of white marble, and support the roof of a portico entirely open to the garden on three sides. Each pillar is covered with arabesques and patterns in gold colours, and innumerable pieces of mirror glass, so minute and intricate, and yet harmonious, that it were vain to attempt to unravel them. The ceiling is decorated in the same style, so that there are not only reflections on all sides of everything within sight, but likewise refracted reflections *ad infinitum*, and the eye is dazzled and bewildered amidst a blaze of the most lavish glitter and colour. Passing from this fairy hall through a lofty arched doorway, a saloon is entered still more gorgeous in its designs and colouring, gilding and glass. It was the throne-room, and all that Eastern fancy could invent and Eastern art execute has been expended in the labyrinths of its elaborate decoration, which my pen cannot describe, and the like of which I have only met with in the tales of the *Arabian Nights*. Close by is the banqueting-hall, the floor of which was still covered with a carpet, dating, I was told, from the time of Abbas. It is adorned with paintings representing scenes which probably often took place within its walls. In one of them the king reclines on carpets and cushions amidst goblets and flagons; around him sit his courtiers; in the foreground are girls in beautiful shawl dresses, dancing amongst jars of wine and dishes of pomegranates, whilst behind, pages and more dancing-girls play on guitars and tambourines, or hand pipes and bowls to the revellers. These paintings, though ridiculously defective in perspective and drawing, and completely wanting in effects of light and shade, are interesting studies of customs and costumes. It is evident from them, did we not know it from other sources, that the Soofee monarchs were much addicted to carousing, not to say debauchery of all sorts, in public, and that instead of the beards and ugly tall hats of the present generation, the men then wore turbans, moustaches, and had their chins shaven. Many of the paintings have been sadly spoilt by the subsequent introduction of would-be European figures, one of which is often repeated. It represents a youth in the costume of the reign of Charles I., who goes by the name of Mirza Istirgey, but is really a portrait of a Mr. Strachey, secretary to one of the English envoys to the Persian Court, where his handsome features and figure were very much admired. Chehel Sitoon is now the workshop of the Prince Governor's tent-makers.

The Palaces of Heshte Beheste are smaller, but in the same style as that which I have just sketched, and are surrounded by extensive gardens. The further sights of the town are: the stables of Abbas, ornamented with paintings of horsemanship and the chase; the bazaars, which are the handsomest in Persia, and extend for miles in different parts of the city; the Meshed-i-Shah or Shah's Mosque, with its dome of glazed tiles, ornamented with dark blue and green foliage and flowers on a pale turquoise ground; and the gate of Ali, a tall three-storied building some ninety or one hundred feet high. Beautiful as is the ornamentation of many of them, it was their proportions and solidity which most impressed me.

All the other Persian towns which I have seen previously or subsequently are cramped and confined, resembling assemblages of molehills intersected by narrow dirty lanes. But Ispahan is a city of stately broad avenues, handsome bridges, lofty and spacious bazaars, extensive squares and gardens, and palaces worthy of a great king. It was evidently designed by a master hand, and restoring, in my mind's eye, all that I had seen to its original splendour, I could well imagine that in the days of Persia's "Grand Monarque" it was one of the finest capitals in the world. The view from the top of the gate of Ali quite confirmed me in this opinion. Thence I saw a scene of devastation which surpassed anything I had yet witnessed in this country of ruins. I think I am not exaggerating in saying that, around the portion of the city just mentioned, there are square miles of tottering and crumbling walls. Ispahan has indeed fallen from its high estate. Since the terrible blow it received from the Affghan occupation in 1722, it has ever been going to destruction. Its beautiful gardens are deserted, its vast bazaars untenanted, and its streets empty. Decay is slowly but surely eating into the very entrails of the city, and, unless arrested, will soon have consumed all that now remains of its magnificence.

We were very comfortably lodged, during our stay of four days, in the house of the telegraph officer of the station, in the Armenian quarter of the town. In one of his wars with the Turks, Abbas the Great found it necessary to besiege and take Julfa, then a flourishing town inhabited principally by Armenians, but now the miserable place I have described on my first entrance into Persia. Well knowing the commercial talents of these people, he transported the whole of them to Ispahan, and settled them in one of its suburbs, which still bears the name of their native place. They had no reason to regret this treatment, for they always enjoyed the special protection of the Soofee kings and became exceedingly wealthy. But their day has likewise gone by : instead of thousands there are now only a few hundreds of them ; with their numbers, their wealth has decreased, and they are now not only poor, but oppressed. I paid a visit to their archbishop, who was delighted to hear news from Etchmiadzin, and to his church, St. Joseph ; its walls are covered with hideous paintings of martyrdoms and the last judgment, in which torture and torments are the prevailing features. No external signs of their religion are tolerated : the cross must not appear on their churches, and, as bells are prohibited, the sacristan announces the hour of service by beating a board with a species of drumstick.

The wonders of the world are now innumerable; but in the days of our childhood, books told us there were only seven, and that next to the Colossus of Rhodes, the shaking Minarets of Ispahan were the most marvellous of them. Mindful of this, we rode out one morning after breakfast, through four miles of ruins, to see them, and I confess that my expectations were so wofully disappointed when I first came in sight of them, that I felt inclined to turn tail and ride home again. Instead of graceful airy forms, of bright-coloured tiles and gilding, I saw two constructions exactly like the brick chimneys of an English foundry, rising some twenty or thirty feet high above the roof of a decayed and desecrated mosque. Their custodian, however, prevailed on us to dismount, and feel, if we could not see, the effect of these world-wide marvels. Narrow stairs, just capable of admitting one man, lead to their summits, which are surrounded by low parapets; he mounted one and I the other, and as soon as we were aloft, he signalled "attention" to me and commenced swaying his body slowly backwards and forwards. The Minarets at once followed his motions, and began to bend and sway like pliant willow-wands; in a few moments their oscillation became so great, and we got so far out of the perpendicular, that I quite repented of my first-disappointing impression, and was glad to descend again to *terra firma*. One can imagine a single tower so constructed that a man at its top can make it oscillate ; it is more difficult to discover how he can make a second tower, twelve or fourteen yards distant, participate in that oscillation. Therein lies the marvel. Its explanation might perhaps be found in a minute examination of the mosque roof which forms the base of the Minarets; but we had no time for this, as our departure was fixed for the next day.

We had set our minds upon enjoying once more the uncommon luxury of river scenery, and upon passing our last afternoon on the banks of the Zeinderood in the pleasant gardens of the " Haft Desht," or Seven Suites, and " Ayneh Khaneh," or House of Mirrors, formerly occupied by the royal harem, and similar in structure and decoration to the palaces we have already seen. Close to them is the two-storied bridge of Alaverdy Khan, a picturesque mixture of stone and brick arches. The day was hot, and we stopped for a few minutes near some groups of Persians who were sitting cross-legged in its shade, smoking their kalians and enjoying the cool breeze from the river. Whilst there, a messenger arrived to tell us that the Prince Governor, the King's eldest son, and then about sixteen years old, would be glad to see us. We found him in one of the neighbouring gardens, whiling away the time with rifle-practice. He welcomed us with great courtesy, invited us to sit on his carpet, and, after tea, pipes and compliments, to join in his amusement. The target was a brickbat on the opposite side of the river about eighty yards off, and to the Prince's great delight, we all missed it. When his turn came, a servant prostrated himself as a rest for the rifle, and the brickbat fell to his shot. This naturally increased his good-humour, for nothing pleases a Persian more than skill in the use of fire-arms, and we parted the best of friends; we well satisfied that the employment by his attendants (unknown to him, and of course winked at by us) of the very simple and transparent artifice of loading his rifle with slugs instead of ball, should have afforded his Highness the pleasure of supposing that he had beaten us with our own weapons.

On our way home, we passed several of the pigeon towers with which the neighbourhood of the town is thickly studded. They are very valuable property, being the deposits whence the manure is obtained for the cultivation of what is here an important article of food—the melon; a fruit which, as far as my experience goes, can only be eaten to perfection in Persia: perhaps, indeed, only at Ispahan, where so much attention is paid to maturing it that it is never pulled until, to use the people's language, the gallop of a horse near its bed would make it burst. Its mellowness and flavour are exquisite. Equally good are the peaches, apricots, and quinces, which are sent in a dried state all over the kingdom. Another of the products of this district is "gez," or manna, a fine white powder, having the cohesive qualities of gum and a mawkishly sweet taste; it accumulates from the contact of a diminutive insect with the leaves of a low shrub very common in the vicinity, and is collected by shaking the branches every third day into earthen vessels. In its origin and insipidity it thus strongly resembles the food which was provided for the children of Israel in the desert, and of which they so soon tired. Worked up into round cakes, it is much relished in the harems. The trade of Ispahan is very trifling. Its gold brocades and printed cottons have a certain reputation, but as hand-dies are the only implements used in printing, the quantity of the latter must necessarily be very limited.

CHAPTER XII.

FELLEK AND CHUB—PERSIAN DOCTORS—YEZDICAUST—ABADEH—ANTELOPES AND MOUFFLONS—PASARGADÆ—TOMB OF CYRUS—PLAIN OF MERDASHT—NAKSH-I-RUSTEM—TOMB OF DARIUS—SASSANIAN BAS-RELIEFS—BAHRAM GOUR AND HIS FAVOURITE WIFE—PERSEPOLIS—TRAGIC STORY OF A LUTEE BASHEE—BENDEMIR.

THE reasons which induce English schoolmasters of the Squeers category to give their rods the most prominent place in the schoolroom, likewise cause Persians of rank and authority to keep a "fellek" and "chub" always conspicuously in view. The first of these implements is a stout pole six or eight feet long with two rope nooses in the centre; the second, a bundle of the most pliable sticks that can be found; and when the wholesome fear their aspect inspires is unavailing, they are put in requisition as follows. The culprit is laid on his back with his legs in the air; his feet are inserted in the nooses and held immovable, with their soles in a horizontal position, by two men, one at each end of the pole; two others commence beating with all their might, supplying themselves, when necessary, with fresh sticks out of the bundle, until the number to which he has been sentenced is exhausted, when he is allowed to creep home if he can, or is carried off by his friends. This punishment is a cruel one, but often unavoidable, and we were very near being obliged to have it inflicted on our muleteer before we could proceed on our journey.

He naturally preferred the luxuries of dried peaches and apricots for himself, and those of green fodder and abundance of chopped straw for his mules, to the hard commons of the desert, and, under all sorts of pretexts, retarded our departure. At last, finding argument useless, we requested the kedkhoda or mayor of the district to try his means of persuasion, and he accordingly paid us a visit with his myrmidons and insignia of office; thus brought face to face with the fellek, the muleteer came to his senses and consented to fulfil his contract and proceed on his journey.

It was not, however, until late in the afternoon of the 7th of April that we could start, and our march was consequently a very short one of twelve miles, to Marg, a tumble-down post-house amongst the hills which form the southern boundary of the Ispahan plain. On the 8th, passing through rugged brown valleys and desert plains, we reached Mayar, 24 miles; and on the 9th, Koomeshah, about the same distance. On the 10th, our way lay for sixteen miles through an unusual number of villages and fields of corn, cotton, and castor-oil plants, where wild pigeon abounded. We managed to bag ten couples, and also a sand-grouse, a very pretty bird, resembling its own genus in the legs and lower part of the body, and a pigeon in the form of its head and neck: the belly is very dark brown, and the rest of the plumage of a beautiful fawn-colour, painted with black. It is found, scattered in small numbers, over almost the whole of the Persian table-land, but is very shy and difficult to approach.

After our sport, and whilst breakfasting in the shade of a ruined village wall, it became noised abroad that one of our party was a Hakim (doctor), and before we had eaten many mouthfuls, the blind, the halt, and the lame came out to us, in full expectation that a Feringhee would work wonders and at once cure them of their maladies. My companion had some medicines with him, and some of them were distributed, more with a view to get rid of importunity than in the hope of affording relief; for, unless the cure is instantaneous, these people generally throw the drugs to the dogs. The state of medical science in Persia is not indeed such as to inspire much confidence, being probably much below what it was in Italy when the barber added its practice to that of his own more lucrative profession; and the acquirement of sufficient skill to pursue it in the empirical manner in which it is commonly practised cannot, for one or two good reasons, present many difficulties. First of all, the practitioner is relieved from the necessity of any but the most superficial study of the human frame by the Koranic prohibition against dissection: under cover of which poison can be, and no doubt often is, administered with impunity, especially in the harems; and secondly, as all diseases, whatever their symptoms, are attributed to two causes—excess of heat or excess of cold—the doctor has little else to do than to decide between them, and apply a hot or a cold remedy in accordance with the results of his diagnosis. All classes, luckily for them, place little reliance in his skill, and are the more anxious, therefore, to get advice and medicine from a European doctor; who, wherever he goes, is besieged by scores of patients, and is regarded with such confidence that even the harem doors are open to his visits. His profession thus affords him opportunities of seeing much that is hidden to the eye of the ordinary traveller; and it is likewise, to some extent, a guarantee for his security. A little practical knowledge of medicine is, therefore, a great advantage in the East, and all who are intent on exploring its least-frequented parts, and cannot disguise themselves as Dervishes, will best consult their own safety by passing themselves off as doctors. Amongst the most prevalent diseases in Persia are blindness and all sorts of ophthalmia, especially cataract, which are due, no doubt, to the excessive glare and dust of a treeless, arid country. Great precautions should be taken by travellers for the protection of the eyes; even with the utmost care mine were always much affected by inflammation, for which I found a solution containing zinc the best remedy.

Leaving this subject, and the village, we had a ride of twelve miles of desert, during which I saw what I had never seen before, a dead donkey. The vultures had already found out their prey, and were sitting in solemn conclave around it, so gorged with their feast that we had shots at them with our revolvers. The powers of sight or scent, or the instinct (let ornithologists decide which) of these birds, are incredible. I have seen a horse fall dead in an almost boundless plain, on which no living thing was visible; in an hour or two black specks appeared on the distant horizon, or high up in the blue sky: they were the vultures, coming from afar, gathering together where the carcass was.

On the 11th, a couple of hours' march brought us suddenly to the precipitous edge of a huge chasm, about half-a-mile broad, worn deep below the surface of the surrounding plain by the action of a small stream, which here divides the province of Irak from that of Fars—ancient Media from ancient Persis. In the middle of this ravine, which was then green with corn, rises an isolated, perpendicular-sided mass of rock, some two hundred or three hundred feet high, surmounted by the picturesque village of Yezdicaust. At first sight it looks inaccessible, and one wonders how the villagers get up to their eyrie-dwellings; but on near approach we found that a drawbridge, thrown over a deep ditch, afforded communication with the foot of the rock, and that a steep zigzag path led up over its face to the village. This natural stronghold is often thronged with the inhabitants of the vicinity, who seek safety within its walls during the frequent incursions of the Baktiaries, a wild marauding tribe, which inhabits the high mountain-ranges on the border of Fars, and is the terror of traveller and peasant. After a short halt, we rode on to our manzil, in the dilapidated caravansary of Shulghistan (sixty-four miles from Koomeshah), which we found filled with a band of two hundred live pilgrims (besides a considerable number of dead ones) on their way to the shrine and cemetery of Kerbela. After dinner, their leader, a mollah, and their chief men, paid us a visit in our cell, and examined our camp-furniture and arms with the greatest curiosity. Pistols and penknives seemed to interest them most. They had come from Shiraz, many of them with their families, and were to be absent six or seven months. After they had left us, to unite in chanting a chorus of prayers before going to sleep, we discovered that several articles, such as napkins, gloves, &c. &c. were missing; and in order to be ready to resist further depredations during the night, we all went to bed with our revolvers under our pillows.

Next day, after a twenty-miles' ride, we reached Abadeh, a town of 10,000 inhabitants, fortified against attacks from the Baktiaries with high mud walls. My friends had business with the governor, and a halt of two days was the consequence; the first being devoted to selecting telegraph poles out of the adjacent gardens. His excellency, escorted by a large following of servants, accompanied us, and in the afternoon proposed rifle-practice; during which he was so much astonished at the accuracy of some of our shots at a four-hundred yards' range, that he at once offered several horses in exchange for our Westley Richards. In the evening he asked us to dinner; or rather, as his servants explained, to send our dinner, and especially wine and brandy, to his house, and mess with him; an arrangement which was so far advantageous to us that we thereby secured the use of our knives and forks. Our host's contribution to the feast consisted of excellent kebâbs of antelope, sun-dried shrimps from the Persian Gulf, and raki, a strong fiery spirit. It lasted several hours, pipes being handed round between each dish, and ended by the governor being carried off to bed by his servants. For the second day he had arranged a hunting excursion, and at 8 A.M. sent his horses to our door. Soon after leaving the town we spied a troop of twenty antelopes, and galloped off in different directions in the hope of getting within range of them. I was lucky enough, after a chase of three or four miles, to approach within sixty yards of a few of the herd, but finding my horse would not stand whilst I aimed over his head, was obliged to try the Persian method and fire at full gallop. I missed, of course, to my great regret, as neither before nor since have I ever been so near these shy fleet animals. The governor's chikaries (huntsmen) had, meanwhile, been sent to drive the neighbouring hills, and whilst we were breakfasting at their foot on his pilaus, we heard them hallooing with all their might. A wild sheep (moufflon) had been viewed, and, full of expectation, we all hastened to our posts. He broke away back through the line of beaters, and neither he nor any of his fellows was ever seen again; though, before starting, we had been assured we should have capital sport and come back laden with game. At sunset we returned to the town, mounted our own horses, and started in the dark on a sixteen-miles' ride to the village of Sormak, whither our caravan had preceded us.

Early on the morning of the 15th the muleteer came to tell us his brother was dying. The doctor succeeded in reviving him, and seeing that rest and quiet were the only means of saving him, recommended his being left where he was. To this the muleteer objected that he could not abandon him amongst strangers, that if it was Allah's will that he should die, die he would; and that he had better die, as he had lived, with his mules. So he started with us on one of them, but expired soon afterwards, and was carried back to the village; there his body was interred, according to the custom of the country, in a shroud inscribed with verses from the Koran, and with the face duly turned towards the sepulchre of Ali.

From Sormak we ascended gradually over a wide steppe, twenty-eight miles, to the solitary post-house and caravansary of Khonehkhorreh. There is no water of any sort between these two places, but there must be a considerable rainfall, for, as we neared the latter, we found the ground thickly sprinkled with wild-peach bushes, thyme, and a sort of furze which grows into the shape of a hedgehog. Here and there were crocuses, hyacinths, and scarlet tulips, like our English garden ones—the first wild-flowers we had seen. In the midst of so much desert they looked marvellously beautiful, and, though small and rare, were the causes of long reveries and much recollection of scenes in more favoured lands.

On the 16th we at last reached the southern extremity of the long sloping plain we had been marching over for five days. It terminates in a range of hills 7,800 feet high, where snow was still lying in large deep patches. When near the summit of the pass, a servant who had preceded us came galloping back with the news that a moufflon had been seen. As usual there was much excitement amongst us, and our ardour was shown in scaling the steep sides of mountain peaks and scrambling down precipices; as usual, too, the result was *nil:* none of us got even a sight of the animal we were all so ambitious of killing. In the afternoon we descended slowly to Dehbeed, the village of willows. Willows there were none, but there was something more joyous and grateful to an English eye—real genuine elastic green turf, clothing the banks of the numerous rills and streams which water the upland valley in which it stands. After traversing hundreds of miles of desert, and passing weeks in the saddle, a stroll on grass was most enjoyable.

We were still slumbering next morning when the English Legation courier arrived from Tehran on his way to the Persian Gulf, and brought us news from

England. It was six weeks or more old, to be sure, but then the last letter is always the best; so we retarded our start by an hour or two to read letters and papers, and forget for a while poor desert Persia.

The country was becoming at last a little less arid and desert as we proceeded southwards, and our march of twenty-eight miles on the 17th brought us to a plain where, around our manzil in the miserable village of Moorgâb, there were clumps of brushwood composed of wild almond and terebinth bushes, and ponds of water sufficiently deep and sweet for frogs to croak in. Next day the change was still more striking and agreeable; green had supplanted brown on the famous plain of Pasargadæ, which lay before us environed by the circle of hills which, like a girdle of bulwarks, surrounds the site of the capital of the great Cyrus. As we cantered towards its ruins, our horses seemed to rejoice as much in feeling the level velvety turf under their hoofs as we did in discarding our spectacles and veils to look at it.

The remains of Pasargadæ have been described so often and so accurately, that more than a very few words about them would seem superfluous. I therefore confine myself here, as well as later at Persepolis, to a very rapid sketch of the monuments which I examined. The first of them to attract the attention of the traveller coming from the north, is a terrace front about one hundred yards long, crowning the top of a mound; it is more than thirty feet high, and built of huge masses of white marble, beautifully chiselled and joined, and is supposed to have been the base of a building in which the immediate successors of Cyrus were crowned. About half a mile south-eastwards of this mound, and on the plain, a large rectangular platform may still be traced above the soil; of its superstructure, probably a temple, there is but a single relic, a square pillar of marble fifteen feet high, bearing on one of its faces this simple inscription in cuneiform character—" I am Cyrus, the king, the Achæmenian." Below it is a bas-relief, representing a human figure in profile, dressed in a tight-fitting robe which descends from the neck to the feet; on his head he wears a cap sitting close to the skull, and from it rise two horns, emblems of strength, supporting an ornament which—to use an irreverent simile—looks like three English decanters in a row, with balls in the place of stoppers; from his shoulders start four spreading wings, two on each side. The face is a good deal injured, but the feathers of the wings, a border of roses adorning the robe, and the carefully curled hair, all exquisitely chiselled, look as if they had left the sculptor's hands a few months instead of 2,400 years ago. The whole figure is very imposing and expressive of calm dignified ease, without any of the stiffness of Egyptian sculptures. As to the person represented, it is argued that it cannot be Cyrus, since the inscription above it has been found repeated on unsculptured stones; one traveller supposes it to be a Cherubim or Seraphim, and imagines that the idea of it was taken from the descriptions of these beings in the Old Testament; the learned in these matters seem now to concur in thinking it is the tutelary deity or guardian angel of the king.

Not far from it is the tomb of Cyrus, where we had ordered breakfast to be prepared. Arrian calls it " a house upon a pedestal," and this description gives the best idea of its form. The "pedestal," composed of immense blocks of white marble, rises like a pyramid, from a base forty-seven feet by forty-three, in seven steps of unequal height; the "house" is a huge sarcophagus, of large slabs of the same material, with a pent-house roof and low gable-ends in front and rear: the whole edifice is thirty-six feet high. Inside the "house" is the chamber, a little more than six feet high, eleven long, and six and half broad, in which the body of Cyrus, inclosed in a golden coffin, was deposited. His epitaph, as recorded by Strabo, is perhaps the simplest and grandest that ever was written, and tells us, I think, more of the great conqueror's character than all that we can learn about it from the history of his exploits: "O man! I am Cyrus, son of Cambyses, founder of the Persian empire, and sovereign of Asia; therefore grudge me not this sepulchre." For two hundred years no one grudged him his last home, but then came another great conqueror, whose serried phalanxes overcame the Persian hosts, and whose followers, insensible to the grand simplicity of these words, violated the tomb, carried off the body for the sake of the gold, and thus merited the stigmatic term of barbarian, which they applied to all the world but themselves. It is now empty, defaced with Arab inscriptions and blackened by the fires of wandering tribes; but as we sat at our meal on the marble steps, we all felt that it would yet endure when all other structures we had seen in the country were reduced to dust. Persians call it Meshed-i Mader-i Suleiman, the Mosque of the Mother of Solomon, and attribute its origin to the wisest of kings; an error which need create no surprise, since many of their fanciful historians have committed the still grosser one of converting Alexander into a Persian under the name of Iskander. At a short distance from its base, there runs round it a wall, in which ancient and modern Persia are significantly indicated; the former by the solid shafts of marble columns, the latter by the crumbling mud which fills the intervals between them. Beyond this is a caravansary, but otherwise the plain seemed uninhabited: complete solitude reigns around this the most ancient and interesting monument in Persia, and we were undisturbed in our comparisons between the past and the present, until the sun reached its meridian and gave us notice that it was time to move on.

In an hour we quitted the turf and reached the entrance to a pass, the only approach to Pasargadæ from the south, through which flows the Kurâb or Water of Cyrus. It is so narrow that in many places there is not room between its perpendicular cliffs for both river and road, and the latter is carried along galleries cut in the rock—works of such magnitude that they are attributed to the golden age of Cyrus, and certainly cannot have been executed in recent times. Perhaps Alexander caused them to be made for the passage of his army in pursuit of Darius?

Issuing from this formidable defile we entered one of the most beautiful valleys in Persia. Picturesque rocks rose in fantastic forms into the bluest and purest of skies on each side, enclosing a level space thickly covered with terebinth bushes and wild peach and almond trees in full blossom, whilst pale green willows fringed the river's banks : rollers (a species of jay) and gorgeously-plumed fly-catchers swarmed in the balmy air, chasing brilliantly-coloured dragon- and butter-flies. The scene teemed with vegetable and animal life : from the dreary wintry wilderness we found ourselves all at once transported into the midst of the freshest beauties of spring. The effect of this transition on our spirits and sensations was far too agreeable to be described, but was not destined to be of long duration ; for tamer scenery soon succeeded, the trees and bushes disappeared and the hills receded, though we had still the green turf to ride over until the end of our day's march at the village of Kawamabad. It is a miserable place; so having much of interest before us, we left it at dawn on the 18th, and following our river of yesterday through a second gorge in the hills to Sivend, thence crossed a steep stony pass little frequented by travellers, and descended to breakfast under a blossoming apple-tree in the garden of the hamlet of Hadjiabad. Some miles farther on we got out of the hills and debouched on the plain in which stand the far-famed ruins of Persepolis and the tombs of Darius and Xerxes.

The plain of Merdasht is about eighteen miles in breadth from north to south; its length it is impossible to state, as, though bounded to the west, it has no other limit towards the east than the flat Salt Desert. Two rivers, the Bendemir and Polvar, irrigate its soil, and in conjunction with its mild climate, render it the most productive district in the kingdom; thus, both from its extent and fertility, it is well adapted for the site of the capital of a great empire. It would seem that these natural advantages were duly appreciated in the very early days of this world, since it is here that the great mythical heroes and demigods of Persian lore, Jemsheed and Rustem, performed those wonderful exploits which are still the theme of discourse amongst the inhabitants of the plain, and are commemorated to this day in the Persian names of its principal monuments. The first of these monuments we visited is called Naksh-i-Rustem (Rustem's pictures), under which appellation are comprehended four royal tombs and several Sassanian bas-reliefs, situated in the north-western side of the plain near the point at which we entered upon it. The hills here rise in almost perpendicular masses of yellowish marble to a height of 300 yards, and it is on their faces that the monuments just mentioned are sculptured.

The tombs are all so much alike, that only one—that

of Darius—need be described. Placing myself at a convenient distance from the foot of the rock, I saw that its surface had been hewn into what may be described as the façade of a building in three compartments or stories, each about forty feet in height and fifty broad. The lowest or basement is simply a deeply and roughly-excavated surface. The first story, which is wider by several feet, represents a shallow portico, supported at each end by plain smooth pilasters and by four equidistant columns in high relief: their capitals are formed of two half-bulls, and upon them rests a horizontal cornice richly sculptured. Between the two centre columns is a doorway ornamented with mouldings and a fluted architrave; the upper half of the door is the rock sculptured into panels, the lower half alone having been excavated to give admittance to the tomb. Above the cornice of this story is the third compartment, representing a platform or throne raised on the heads of two tiers of captives in the posture of caryatides, fourteen in each tier. On the platform is the king standing before an altar on which burns the sacred fire, and above is an extraordinary figure in profile, like that of a man in a kilt, minus his legs and plus a pair of horizontal wings; he wears a crown on his head, and holds a large ring in his left hand, and is supposed to be what Persians call a Feroher —Divine intelligence, or ministering spirit. On this supposition my simile of the kilt and wings is very much out of place, and another, radiating sunbeams in a petrified state, on which he is floating towards his *protégé*, must be substituted. Above all there is a long inscription, repeated in three languages, and commencing in each with the words, "I am Darius." Having thus noted the exterior, we were of course anxious to see the inside, the object for which all this elaborate carving had been undertaken. This was no easy matter, and it was not until after several attempts that a peasant from one of the neighbouring villages succeeded in scrambling up over the flat surface of the basement to the entrance of the tomb. He had a rope with him, and, tying it round our waists, we followed one by one, with more ease. Creeping through the open part of the door, which is $4\frac{1}{2}$ feet high, we found ourselves in a dark chamber about 11 feet high and 20 or 30 long. In it, and hewn out of the rock, were three sarcophagi: one was open and empty; the others, covered with large slabs, are said to have never been used.

The figures on all these tombs, which are within a few yards of each other, express dignity and calm repose. The Sassanian bas-reliefs, on the contrary, on the lower parts of the cliffs, are full of action and impulse. In the one, stately etiquette, regulating every motion and ornament, is the principal characteristic; in the other, nature is predominant, and the movements of both horses and men are unconstrained and free. Their subjects are scenes from the lives of the two greatest monarchs of the Sassanian dynasty: one representing Sapor (A.D. 260) receiving the homage of the Roman Emperor Valerian; and the four others, various episodes in the romantic career of Bahram Gour (A.D. 420). This sovereign, who received the appellation of Gour, from his excessive fondness for the chase of the wild ass—Gour being the Persian name of that animal—and from his having lost his life in its pursuit, is stated to have been the best prince of his race; and, to judge from one of these bas-reliefs, he was certainly, in one respect, in advance of his age. It is now half buried in rubbish which has fallen from the cliffs, and only the upper portion of its principal figures is consequently visible. They are Bahram and his favourite wife; he is represented with an abundance of long streaming locks, a beard and moustache, and as wearing a high, balloon-shaped diadem and a loose tunic, fastened at the waist by a belt; she wears a crown likewise, has her hair arranged in long plaits falling over her shoulders, and a necklace of round stones on her breast, and is habited in a tight-fitting jacket attached with a single button, and a thin under-garment clinging to her limbs and secured at the waist by a girdle tied in a bow. With their right hands they hold between them a wreath, in token of the bond of love which united them; and which must indeed have been a strong one, since under its influence Bahram was induced so far to disregard the most deeply-rooted prejudice of his own and present times in the East, as to exhibit in effigy the charms of his own wife to the public gaze.

Illustrative of the origin of this bas-relief is the following story, which has often been related by writers on Persia, and is still current in the vicinity. Bahram was very proud of his skill in the chase, and, thinking his wife would like to witness his feats, one day took her out hunting. Arrived on the plain an antelope was descried at some distance asleep. The king drew his bow and fired; the antelope, awakened by the passage of his arrow close to its ear, put its hind hoof to the spot to drive away the fly which it thought had been the cause of disturbance to its slumbers; the king drew again, and pinned hoof and horns together. For this shot he naturally expected much praise from his wife, but to his inquiries as to her opinion, she quietly replied, "Practice makes perfect;" which so filled his soul with fury, jealousy, and disappointment, that he ordered her to be taken to the mountains and there abandoned to perish. Only half of this order was, however, obeyed, and, unknown to the king, she was allowed to retire to an obscure village, where she took up her abode in the upper chamber of a tower which could only be reached by ascending twenty steps. There she bought a young calf, and carried it daily up and down the stairs, in the hope that this exercise would increase her strength and beauty, which she still regarded as the property of the king. At the end of four years accident brought him one evening to the tower just as she was bearing the now full-grown cow in her arms. Astonished at such a display of strength on the part of a woman of apparently delicate form, he demanded to see her. She consented, on condition that he would come alone.

The gallant Bahram went at once, and began expressing his admiration of what he had seen, when she begged him to curtail his praise; "for," she added, raising her veil, "practice makes perfect." Recognition was immediate, explanation followed, and the king was so convinced that love for him could alone have induced her thus to spend the long interval since he had seen her, that his love returned and she became again, and ever afterwards remained, his favourite wife.

Most of the bas-reliefs bear inscriptions in Greek and Pehlvi, and it is not unlikely that some of them are the work of Greek artists. The other objects of interest at Naksh-i-Rustem are a so-called Magian fire-temple and two altars. The temple stands at a short distance from the base of one of the tombs, and is a tower twenty-four feet square and thirty-five high, built of immense blocks of marble; which, from the incisions running from one to the other, seem to have been originally clamped together with iron bars, though their size and weight are so great that this precaution might apparently have been dispensed with. Its lower half is solid. Above this, a door, to which there is at present no approach, admits into a small chamber just under the roof, which is composed of four enormous slabs. The great solidity of this building, and the smallness of its interior, are both in favour of the supposition that it was not a temple, but a sacristy or treasury, where the Magians kept the sacred fire and the vessels used in their sacrifices. Not many yards westwards are the altars, hewn out of a solid mass of rock projecting on to the plain, and approached by a low flight of steps. They are almost close together, and measure seven feet in height, and four and a half square at the base, tapering thence a little towards their tops, which are surrounded with parapets, and excavated in the form of fonts. There is every reason to believe that they date from the time of Ardashir, A.D. 223, if not from that of Darius.

A scramble to the summit of the cliffs which contain the tombs, terminated our sight-seeing for the day. On their brink stands a solitary column of marble, and around it are several squares, like the floors of rooms, cut out of the rock, and alleged to be the platforms on which the funeral rites of the dead monarchs were performed. The view from this point, over vast ranges of naked lifeless hills behind us and the great green plain at our feet, was very fine; but time to muse over the past glories and present solitude of the scene failed us, and at sunset we descended and rode away to our manzil, three miles eastwards, in the village of Kinareh.

Notwithstanding the fertility of the region in which we now were, its agricultural population is as sparse and poor as in the less-favoured districts of the north; a proof that other than natural causes are at work in bringing about the decline of Persia. Kinareh differed in no respect from our preceding quarters, and after a good night's sleep in one of its mud hovels, held out as little inducement to rest and be thankful as any of them. We were, therefore, early on our way next morning towards Takht-i-Jemsheed, the throne of Jemsheed, as Persians now call the ruins of Persepolis.

They are situated close under a high hill of naked brown marble, which projects considerably on to the plain from the range on its northern side, and, seen from a distance and measured by the surrounding scenery, are somewhat disappointing. On nearer approach, however, this feeling is obliterated, and, as soon as proportion and detail become visible, is succeeded by one of surprise and admiration. A terrace wall, nearly 500 yards long and thirty feet high, appears rising from the plain, and forms the western side of a large platform abutting on the hillside. The marble blocks of which it is built—larger, perhaps, than any used in our finest edifices—are beautifully fitted together, and chiselled perfectly smooth. About 150 yards from its northern end, a double staircase, of such magnificent proportions that ten or twelve horsemen abreast can ride up its gentle ascent and wheel with ease on its landing-places, leads to the platform. The mechanical resources of the builders must have been very considerable, for, though the steps are little more than three inches high, they are above twenty feet long, and I counted no less than eleven of them hewn out of one block. Arrived on the platform, we found ourselves confronted by the headless forms of two colossal bulls, supporting the remains of an enormous portal; they are admirably sculptured and proportioned and very similar to the Nineveh bulls in the British Museum. Their necks are adorned with collars of roses of elaborate execution, and their flanks defaced with the names of many well-known travellers, Malcolm, Morier, &c., who might have found close at hand a thousand harmless places for thus commemorating their visits. Opposite to this first portal is another of the same size, likewise ornamented with bulls, looking directly towards the mountain. Here they are winged, and have human faces, now much mutilated, and crowned heads: they are especially interesting as being the only specimens in Persia of the conjunction of man and beast in the same animal. It does not appear that the bull ever received from the Persians the divine honours paid to him in Egypt; but he was regarded by them as the truest symbol of power. In their mythology, he was the first animal created, and from his union with the moon, man and all other living creatures proceeded: hence, no doubt, the prominent position given him in these buildings.

About sixty yards south of the portals stand the remains of the palaces of Darius, Xerxes, Artaxerxes, and Chehel Minar, or Forty Pillars, each on a separate terrace. The three former seem to have been built almost on the same model, and a description of the first of the three, as given by a recent writer,* will

---

* Rawlinson's *Ancient Monarchies.*

suffice for all:—"It is a building about 135 feet in length, and in breadth a little short of 100. . . . It fronted towards the south, where it was approached by a double staircase, which led up to a deep portico of eight pillars, arranged in two rows. On either side of the portico were guard-rooms, which opened upon it. Behind the portico lay the main chamber, which was a square of fifty feet, having a roof supported by sixteen pillars, arranged in four rows of four, in line with the pillars of the portico. . . . The hall was surrounded on all sides by walls from four to five feet in thickness, in which were doors, windows, and recesses symmetrically arranged. The entrance from the portico was by a door in the exact centre of the front wall, on either side of which were two windows looking into the portico. . . . At the back of the hall and at either side were chambers of very moderate dimensions. . . . It seems probable that this palace was without any second story."

Such was the original form of one of the earliest palaces of the world, as reconstructed in the heads of wise men from long study of its remains : viz. broken portions of the wall of the great hall, and several doorways, windows, and recesses. The jambs of most of these are ornamented with bas-reliefs of elaborate execution, representing a king, much larger than life, either walking, and followed by two attendants, the one shading his Majesty's head with a parasol, and the other driving away the flies with a fly-chaser; or seated on a throne, placed on a lofty platform, which is raised on the heads of five tiers of warriors variously armed and costumed, ten in each tier ; or transfixing, with perfect nonchalance, a monster, half lion half bull, or half griffin half eagle, with a short two-edged sword. The features of many of the figures have been completely effaced, but in other respects time and weather seem to have had no effect on them. Indeed, except where man has taken the trouble to injure them, all the sculptures and bas-reliefs of these ruins look as if they had left the sculptor's hands a few years ago.

Chehel Minar, the prototype of Chehel Sitoon at Ispahan, was probably an open-air hall, having porticos on three sides, and being completely open on the fourth. Each portico was supported by twelve columns, in two rows of six, whilst the roof of the hall rested on thirty-six columns in six rows ; the area covered by the whole building being 50,000 square feet. Of this forest of pillars there remain standing only thirteen. They are sixty feet high, accurately fluted, and taper slightly upwards from bell-shaped bases, beautifully ornamented with pendent lotus-leaves, to capitals composed of two half bulls or two half griffins, with their heads looking in opposite directions.

The terrace on which the building stands is approached by the finest of the many fine staircases to be seen amongst these ruins. Its façades are covered with bas-reliefs so multitudinous and elaborate that drawings alone can give a correct idea of them. The principal subjects are gigantic Persian guards armed with spears and bucklers; combats between colossal lions and bulls; and long processions, interspersed with cypress-trees, of men, horses, camels, oxen, wild asses and rams, such as probably took place annually when the governors and satraps of the different provinces of the empire came up to the capital with their tribute and presents. A cuneiform inscription on one of its balustrades ascribes the building of this magnificent work to Xerxes.

Around and about all these upright ruins, in which the blue rock pigeons now nest, lie recumbent pillars, broken shafts, and hundreds of massive blocks of sculptured marble half imbedded in the soil and the grass. For hours we wandered up and down amongst these silent remains of departed grandeur,—our thoughts reverting to the days when the magnificent Xerxes here held his court, and half Asia bowed at his feet; or when the hardy veterans of Macedonia satiated their hatred of Persian arrogance by destroying his capital, and Alexander earned fresh favours from the beautiful Thais by burning his palace. At last we came to the three royal tombs, similar to those at Naksh-i-Rustem, which are cut on the surface of the hills overlooking the platform, and our wanderings were interrupted in the abode of death by a reminder from the cook that life must be sustained, and that breakfast was ready.

In the cool shade of the Great Bulls we lay down to our meal; pilaus and chilaus, and cups of the best wine of Shiraz, were there to refresh us; gentle zephyrs fanned us, and whilst between puffs of the fragrant tembeckee we sat gazing up into the deep blue sky, and over the emerald green plain towards the grotesquely weird heights of Istakr, a village greybeard regaled our ears with the history of the last of the many deeds of blood which these ruins have witnessed.

In Persian, as in European cities, there is a class of society whose members have no apparent profession, or at best a very precarious one; who live no one knows how, and are ever ready to create or take advantage of disorder and confusion for the purpose of satisfying their lusts by pillaging their neighbours. Rowdies, roughs, loafers, canaille, in the west; in the east they take the name of lutees. Their principal occupations, if they have any, are those of athletes, jugglers, dancers, or tamers of monkeys, bears, and lions. They are a lawless, riotous, unscrupulous, anti-koranic set of vagrants, who, from their organization and the obedience which they pay to their elected chief the Lutee Bashee, are a frequent source of anxiety and trouble to governors and mayors. Some twenty years ago the Lutee Bashee of Shiraz resigned his functions, though he still retained his title; and, by reforming his manner of life, and prudently investing in land and villages the money he had laid by, soon became respected and rich. After his retirement he lived as a loyal subject, a good Mussulman and a generous landlord, and became an influential personage in his native town; where he, no doubt, hoped to end his days in peace. The people of Shiraz are particularly unruly and excitable, and, as had frequently happened in previous years, broke out into open riot in the winter of 1864. When the news reached the King's ears, he sent for the Mushir or mayor of the town, who happened to be then in Tehran. This man had a private feud with the Lutee Bashee, partly on account of the latter's influence and partly because his daughter looked with favour on the Lutee's addresses; so, when questioned as to the cause of the riot, he at once attributed it to his enemy. Upon this his Majesty requested the attendance of his uncle, who was about to proceed to Shiraz as Governor of the province of Fars, and exacted from him a promise on oath that whenever or wherever he should first set eyes on the Lutee he would cause him to be strangled.

The Prince Governor and Mushir had hardly left the capital when the riot was put down. Arrived on the plain of Merdasht they were met, according to the custom of the country, by the chief men of the town of Shiraz, who came out on their best horses and in their gayest costumes to welcome their new ruler. Amongst them was the Lutee Bashee, now considerably past middle age, mounted on a horse of such beauty that it attracted all eyes. The Governor saw it, and admired its paces so much that the owner at once dismounted, and requested his Highness to accept it. The request was granted, and the cavalcade moved on to the terrace of Persepolis, where the great man's tents were pitched. Half an hour later the Lutee Bashee was summoned to his presence. Proud of the honour thus shown him, and having no reason to suspect any danger, he hastened to obey the summons. As he crossed the threshold of the tent, he heard his doom from the Prince's lips : " Seize him, and strangle him." The ferrashes fell on their victim and gagged him ; whilst the wretched man in vain made signs with his fingers that he would ransom his life with all his fortune. An oath had been sworn, and his worst enemy, the Mushir, was there to watch its performance ; a rope was cut from the tent fixings, and in another minute the Lutee was a corpse.

This story was afterwards confirmed to me at Shiraz ; but, in justice to the Governor, I must add that, on finding from the inquiries he made that the Lutee was innocent of all participation in the riot, he at once caused all the murdered man's property, which lapsed to himself and the Crown, to be restored to his children.

> There's a bower of roses by Bendemir's stream,
> And a nightingale sings round it all the day long :
> In the time of my childhood 'twas like a sweet dream,
> To sit in the roses and hear the bird's song ;
> That bower and its music I never forget,
> But oft when alone in the bloom of the year,
> I think—is the nightingale singing there yet ?
> Are the roses still bright by the calm Bendemir ?

It was not without some latent expectations of a pleasing nature that I thought of these queries, as, after leaving the ruins, we rode southwards towards the stream thus immortalized. I can answer them now with a negative, and honestly affirm my belief that neither roses nor nightingales have enlivened its banks for many a century: possibly never since the beauties of Persepolis came out to enjoy their perfume and song. The Bendemir is a river of considerable volume; and as I looked at its muddy, turbid waters, now swollen by melted snow, flowing through their loamy grass-grown banks, I almost fancied myself back by the side of old Tiber, in the silent campagna and within sight of the outlying ruins of Rome. We crossed the river over a dilapidated stone bridge and entered the hills which bound Merdasht on the south; after traversing, on a broken stone causeway, a swampy plain alive with thousands of wild duck and geese, white and blue herons and other aquatic birds, we reached Zergoon—a wretched village, situated in a narrow valley, amidst mountains of bare brown rock—where an execrable post-house, swarming with insects, was the only habitable dwelling.

Having felt hardly a drop of rain since leaving Tehran, a thorough wetting which we got next morning was almost an agreeable surprise. A ride of four hours over a very bad road and through rugged hills, brought us to the source of the Roknabad, a stream famous, as Hafiz tells us, for the sweetness of its waters and the beauty of the gardens on its banks. Since his time the gardens have been abandoned, and the stream now runs at will over the stony path. A mile further on and we arrived at a narrow opening in the hills, through which we looked down on the plain of Shiraz and across its now green corn-fields to snow-capped mountains on its southern side. A short descent ensued, and we then entered a broad straight avenue about a mile long, and bounded on either side by gardens filled with cypresses, pomegranate-trees and roses. At its end was the gate of the city, and we thence made our way to the house of my hospitable friend the English telegraph officer of the district.

CHAPTER XIII.

SHIRAZ — TOMBS OF HAFIZ AND SAADI — MARCH SOUTHWARDS — PARTRIDGE-SHOOTING — VALE OF WILD ALMONDS — ASYLUM — PASSES OF THE OLD AND YOUNG WOMAN — RUINS OF SHAPOOR — SCULPTURES — STATUE OF SAPOR — A GARDEN AT KAZEROON — ENVIRONS OF SHIRAZ — THE SWORD OF THE STATE — A NOMAD CHIEFTAIN — MIRZA MAHOMMED REZA.

SHIRAZ, the capital of Fars, or Persia Proper, the kernel of the empire founded by Cyrus, is situated in a valley plain some twelve miles broad and twenty-five or thirty long, well cultivated and dotted with gardens in the vicinity of the town. It has no unsightly suburbs, and though there are of course many ruins and much dilapidation within its walls, vegetation comes right up to them, while the fresh April foliage of numerous large chenars scattered about in its different quarters, and the glitter of its green and blue domes, give it a brighter and more cheerful appearance than that of most Persian cities. The finest buildings are the mosques, the ark or citadel, and the bazaars. They date from the time of Kerim Khan, the founder of the Zend dynasty, which ruled Persia from 1753 to 1788 and made Shiraz the capital of the country, and are much more solidly built than those of Tehran; stone and kiln-burnt brick being their principal materials. If a country's history is to be read in the greater or lesser degree of solidity of its buildings, the decline of Persia is plainly visible in those of its successive capitals which I had seen and have sketched. At Pasargadæ and Persepolis we saw nothing but huge blocks of marble; at Ispahan, marble in less profusion, stone and kiln-burnt bricks; at Shiraz, stone and a mixture of kiln-burnt and sun-dried bricks; at Tehran, kiln-burnt brick is the exception, sun-dried bricks and mud being the rule.

Founded soon after the Hegira (A.D. 622), there is little of note in the early history of Shiraz. It is principally interesting as having been the birthplace and residence of the poets Hafiz and Sheik Saadi, whose verses are in the mouths of all Persians. Hafiz sang much of the delights of love and wine, and described the beauties of nature in mellifluous strains. He was a man of soft words, and when Tamerlane besieged and took the town (A.D. 1380), so turned away the wrath of the fierce Mogul conqueror that the two became friends, and favourable conditions were granted to the townsmen. His tomb is about half a mile from the northern gate, in a neglected cemetery, where a large slab of semi-transparent alabaster, beautifully chiselled with extracts from his poems, covers his remains. Their custodian showed us an illuminated manuscript copy of his works, considerably dog-eared and soiled from being constantly handled by the Shirazees, who are wont to settle disputed points by a "fal" in its pages. Saadi lies buried three miles off, in a solitary romantic dell at the foot of the hills to the north of the plain, where a marble sarcophagus, in one corner of a garden of cypresses, contains his bones. His remains are carefully guarded by one of his descendants, who gains a sorry livelihood by cultivating vegetables around them, and by exacting a small fee for the exhibition of a copy, about one hundred years old, of his ancestor's writings. Close by is an underground chamber, traversed by a stream of deliciously clear water, — a cool, quiet retreat, in which Saadi, no doubt, imbibed many of his moral precepts from the purity of the fountain, and is said to have written his best compositions.

Excursions to these places, and a visit to the governor of the province, Sultan Ferhad Mirza, occupied the two days of our stay. It was beginning to get warm, and we thought it prudent to push on as fast as possible to Bushire, where my companions had telegraph business to transact, in order to be able to leave it again before the great heats set in. So, on the understanding that we should give ourselves several days' rest at Shiraz on our return journey, we set forth again southwards on the afternoon of the 24th of April, and had a moonlight ride of twelve miles to the village of Chenarahdar, and the latest of dinners, at 11 P.M., in its comfortless caravansary.

Next day our stage of twenty miles to Khonehseniou lay through a pretty country, a foreground of undulating slopes covered with wild almond and thorn trees and coarse grass, backed by high snow-capped mountains. About four miles before reaching our manzil we crossed the Karagatch, a swift stream of considerable volume. Sending on our horses with the servants, we here shouldered our guns and went in search of game. Hares and red-legged partridges abounded, and a fair bag was made. The afternoon was very hot, and, on arriving at the caravansary, a large bowl of the very best of Persia's dairy products was a most welcome sight. In the language of the country it is called Maust,* and is a species of curded milk, so light and delicately soured that large quantities of it can be indulged in without harm. Eaten with dates—not the hard indigestible fruit known in England by that name, but juicy masses which almost melt in one's mouth—it is the staple food of the inhabitants of the Gherm-i-sir (warm region) and most delicious; whilst mixed with water it forms a drink called dukh, which slakes thirst better perhaps than any other liquid, tea alone excepted.

Just as we were retiring to bed, our servants came to report that a regiment of soldiers had arrived and demanded admittance to the caravansary, informing us at the same time that if the demand were granted they could not be responsible for the safety of our effects. The porter was thereupon summoned and told to exclude the new comers; he declared his readiness to do so,

---

* Better known, perhaps, to travellers in the East under its Turkish name, Yaourt.

but observed that the sirteeb, or major of the regiment threatened to enter by force unless the doors were opened to him. Negotiation became necessary under these circumstances, and the major was invited to a parley. He was at first highly indignant at our entertaining suspicions as to the honesty of the Shah's soldiers, and swore by his beard and the head of Ali that his men were the most honest fellows in the world; but as he refused to be held responsible for any robbery or disorder which might take place during the night, it was impossible to yield to his demands. A compromise was finally agreed to by all parties, to the effect that the soldiers should bivouac elsewhere, but that he and his officers might take up their quarters within the building.

On the 26th we alternated our march between riding and shooting. The road lay through very hilly ground, much cut up with deep ravines, and covered with a low jungle of terebinth-trees. In their shade were gorgeous masses of lilies, white, yellow, and red, hyacinths and geraniums. Partridges swarmed, and in our walk of two or three hours some fifteen brace were bagged. Towards evening we ascended a steep pass, from the top of which there is a beautiful view southwards into the vale of wild almond-trees; Dasht-i-Arjeen (its Persian name) is about ten miles long and four or five broad, and is so shut in on all sides by perpendicular crags and lofty mountains, that the streams which descend into it find no exit, and form a lake of considerable size at its southern extremity. This abundance of water, which never fails even in seasons of drought, keeps the turf with which the basin of the valley is carpeted, perpetually green. "Iran hemeen est," such is Iran, travellers coming from the thirsty south are invariably told when they first come in sight of this verdant plain: if credulous enough to believe their guides for a moment, their expectations of seeing a continuation of this scenery will soon be wofully disappointed as they go northwards, and each step in that direction will teach them to accept Persian descriptions of their country, or indeed of anything else, with many grains of salt. At the foot of the pass we found our quarters prepared in the house of the Kedkhoda of the most miserable village I had yet seen. As a compensation for its discomfort, however, fresh-made butter, a luxury which none of us had enjoyed since leaving Europe, was laid before us by our host. He was a great sportsman, and told us many stories of his lion-hunts; showing us, in proof of his veracity, a terrible wound he had received in one of them. He had killed one male lion, he said, the previous year, and two others were known to be at that moment in the neighbourhood; he and his villagers, who, as usual, came in the evening to stare at us and our arms, pressed us much to stay and help them to kill them.

As we rode away next morning we passed at a short distance from the village, the source of one of the streams which water the valley. It issues from the base of a high perpendicular mass of rock, and is believed by the natives to have been confined within the bowels of the mountain until Moses visited the spot and there performed his well-known miracle. Above it is a cave which Ali is alleged to have frequented before his birth, and where a mark in the stone floor is shown as the print of his horse's hoof. The visits of two such exalted personages have naturally rendered the place a very sacred one, and, accordingly, a small square building which stands close by, shaded by weeping willows, is endowed with the privilege of "bust" or asylum. Once within its walls, the greatest of criminals is safe from all pursuit: his pursuers can of course surround the building, cut off all supplies, and thus force the fugitive to choose between death by famine or surrender, but on no account can they enter it. Thanks to this privilege, which is accorded to many places in Persia—to the principal mosques, for instance, and to the stables of the king and of men of distinction—many an innocent person escapes persecution, and many a guilty one, I dare say, death; for once in "bust," his friends have time to use their influence in his favour, to bribe a little here and promise more there: in short to save him, if he can be saved.

The plain was perfectly alive with wild-fowl of all sorts, amongst them great numbers of Brahmini ducks, and as we neared the lake, we saw a large wild-boar coming up across our path towards the cover on the hill-sides. Chase was at once given, and after a long gallop my companions had shots at him from their horses; he went away, however, unhurt, snapping like whipcord the telegraph wires, which happened to be on the ground. A terrible thunderstorm put a stop to further pursuit and obliged us to seek shelter in a solitary square building of mud, the only one visible. Having gained admittance within its walls, we found it was a sort of penfold in which the cattle and sheep were housed at night for protection against lions and panthers. Its inmates, several unveiled females, were most hospitable; one of them was very pretty, somewhat like an Italian peasant-girl. She wore a very peculiar ornament—an ancient silver coin attached, like a bit of white sticking-plaster, to the left side of her nose; in answer to my inquiries she said she had worn it ever since she was a child, and that it was the custom of the district so to do. A necklace of similar coins round her neck took my fancy very much, and whilst she served us with curds and honey, I spared neither complimentary words nor offers of gold to induce her to part with it; but she refused to sell what was evidently an heirloom, and when the storm cleared off we bade her good-by without coming to a bargain, and rode on to the end of the valley.

Hence a rough steep path ascends to the southernmost edge of the great table-land, which is here 7,200 feet above the sea-level, and from this point the road to the Persian Gulf is carried down a series of the most precipitous passes in the world. Looking from it we saw, 3,000 feet below us, a narrow valley bounded to the south by a range of hills parallel with those on which we were, and jagged like the teeth of a saw; beyond it was a second range lower than the first, and then another and another, until the eye lost itself in the hazy atmosphere of the flat region bordering the Gulf. An idea of the steepness of this descent may perhaps be best formed by imagining a gigantic staircase, the steps of which are from 1,800 to 3,000 feet high and half-a-mile broad. We were now on the edge of the first of them, and before descending its almost perpendicular face, halted a moment or two to look at the new region we were about to enter. The hill on which we stood, and all those to the south of us, were covered with trees; those on the same level with ourselves were completely leafless; a few hundred feet lower down they were budding; on the ridges opposite to us and in the valley at our feet they were luxuriantly green. And yet it was not a forest that we saw; for the trees, almost all gallnut-bearing oaks, were not in tangled confused masses, but stood separately at convenient distances from each other, as if they had been planted in measured rows or been thinned with constant care. Whether it be that the soil is unequal to producing thickets, or that these particular oaks are intolerant of greater mutual proximity, I know not; but there they stand in formal lines, like the olive-trees on the slopes of Fiesole or the mulberry-trees on the plains of Lombardy, and constitute the only semblance of a forest between Tehran and the Persian Gulf, a distance of 650 miles and more.

Kottel-i-pyr-i-zan, the Old Woman's Pass, is the name of the first of the giant steps. The roughest of paths, zigzagging amongst enormous boulders of detached rock, leads down its steep side to a platform 1,500 feet from the top, on which stands the solid caravansary of "Myan Kottel" (half the hill), where we were to pass the night. In the short space of one hour, the time occupied by our descent, we had passed from winter to summer. The trees around our quarters were in full foliage; the swallows, of which I counted no less than forty-one nests in the spacious gateway, were already hatching their eggs; the air was warm and balmy, and the sunset was resplendent with colours which even a Turner could not reproduce.

On the following morning we descended to the narrow valley, and rode along its level ground in a westerly direction through luxuriant crops of wheat, already bursting into ear, for about five miles; then turning southwards, through a chasm in the range of hills we had seen opposite to us the day before, and leaving behind us the strip of oak forest, we reached the edge of the second step, Kottel-i-duchter, the Daughter's Pass. Youth generally receives greater attention than age, and the young lady would seem to have been much more admired than her aged neighbour, for her Pass is actually graced with a made road, paved in the steepest places and protected in the dangerous ones by stone parapets: the first work of the sort I had seen outside a Persian town. It is, perhaps, even more precipitous than the Old Lady's Pass, being carried for 1,000 feet or more down the face of a rock as perpendicular as the Gemmi, and thence through a steep rugged ravine, studded at rare intervals with wild fig and almond trees, to the entrance of the plain of Kazeroon. The heat was becoming inconvenient, and on arriving at the bottom of the descent a clear babbling brook, issuing from the base of a roadside crag and filled with young watercresses, was a most refreshing sight. The crag is called Takht-i-Timur, the Throne of Timur, from a rough bas-relief sculptured on its face representing that individual, one of Futteh Ali Shah's numerous progeny, sitting apparently in amicable converse with a lion. In its shade, breakfast awaited us, at which cresses were a luxury highly appreciated; we then rode on for seven miles to the village of Kazeroon, a wretched place inhabited by a tribe called the Mâmaceni, who are said to be the most accomplished thieves in the country.

Although 2,800 feet above the sea, the plain of Kazeroon is within the limits of the Gherm-i-sir, or warm region. In form it is like hundreds of other Persian plains, long and narrow; the hills, too, which surround it are of the usual type, arid and brown; but the level ground, which is excessively fertile, being irrigated by natural streams and favoured by the most genial of climates, is covered with the most brilliant and luxurious vegetation. On its grassy prairies, the oleander, the myrtle and locust-tree grow wild; masses of variegated stocks and petunias, lupins, irises, geraniums, ranunculus and convolvulus mingle their bright glowing colours with the green of fennel, wild rhubarb, artichoke, and the liquorice-plant; whilst interspersed amongst fields of waving corn are patches of scarlet, lilac, and white poppies. Lighted up by the sun, the scene was like the richest of Persian carpets intensified in colouring and beauty, as we rode through it next morning for ten miles to the village of Direez. There we were to halt for a couple of days' shooting and a visit to the ruins of Shapoor, and there I was to part, for some time, with my companions. The heat continued increasing each step we took southwards, and I became afraid of a return of the illness from which I had been suffering if I ventured into the furnace-like temperature of Bushire; I therefore reluctantly abandoned my project of descending to the bottom of the Giant Staircase and having a look at the sea. The steps which I thus missed seeing were described to me as being quite as formidable as those we had descended. At their foot, a sandy plain some forty miles in breadth extends to the Persian Gulf, the whole distance from the point where we were being over seventy miles.

Direez is such an abominable place, and its inhabitants have such a reputation for lawlessness and villany, that to avoid entering its walls we had brought with us a comfortable double-walled tent, which we found pitched on the banks of a stream about a mile from the village. Half-a-dozen Tofengchees, men armed with long muskets and big knives—devil-me-care, wild-looking fellows, whose features entirely justified the reputation they have acquired from the frequency of robberies and murders on this portion of the king's highway—soon came out from it to offer their services as guards and guides to the best coverts. There were, they said, plenty of wild-boar in the neighbourhood, and we were sure to have good sport; so we each took a beat, and marched off with a couple of these gentry. Their promises, as usual, turned out illusory; for, on meeting again in the evening, the result of a hot afternoon's work was that one pig had been fired at, and that we had killed half-a-dozen francolins—derrâj in Persian, and known to Englishmen under the name of black partridges. They are a good deal larger than the ordinary partridge, and are only found in hot countries; on the banks of the Tigris and in the neighbourhood of Baghdad they are so plentiful that I have heard of eighty brace being shot in a day. The male bird is of a beautiful brown chocolate-colour, spotted, like a guinea-fowl, with white, and has a deep orange beak and legs, and a very peculiar call. Its flesh resembles in colour that of a grouse, and has a disagreeably aromatic taste.

Disappointed in my expectations of game, I determined to pass the next day in the ruins of Shapoor, and in visiting a cavern in the mountain, some eight or nine miles off, which contains the only statue in the country; and accordingly started at seven in the morning with a mounted servant and several Tofengchees, who, in keeping up with my horse, showed themselves as agile on their feet as Scotch gillies.

The city of Shapoor built by Sapor the First, in commemoration of the battle of Edessa (A.D. 260), in which he vanquished the armies of Rome and took the Emperor Valerian prisoner, covered a large space of ground on the banks of the river Tab, about four miles from our camp. A round arch, and a building, half buried in the soil, which my guides called "Sar-i-gaw," the bullock's head, from a sculptured stone representing the head of a horned animal on the top of one of its four walls, are the only remains still standing. To judge from their solid masonry and the hardness of their cement, it seems probable that Roman captives had a hand in their construction. In other respects the site of the city is only distinguishable by extensive mounds of loose stones and broken foundations; we threaded our way amongst them for a mile or two, until we reached a narrow gorge in the hills on the north-west side of the plain, where there is just sufficient space for river and road to pass between two tall cliffs. On these the exploits of Sapor are recorded in a number of bas-reliefs, four on one side of the river and two on the other, in the same style as the Sassanian reliefs of Naksh-i-Rustem, but more highly-finished. The submission of Valerian forms the subject of most of them: the Persian monarch, crowned and magnificently dressed, is mounted on a richly-caparisoned charger, which tramples on a corpse; above him a winged figure appears bearing towards him a crown of victory; the Roman emperor kneels before him, bareheaded and in the posture of a suppliant; and guards and soldiers carrying trophies fill up the sides and background. The fate of Valerian was a bitter one; for, though doubts may be entertained as to the truth of the tradition according to which Sapor used to place his foot on his prisoner's neck whenever he mounted his horse, and caused his skin after death to be stuffed with straw and exhibited in the most-frequented temple of the country, it is quite certain that the emperor lingered out the rest of his life in captivity.

Below the sculptures, and on the right bank of the stream, is a small aqueduct about two feet broad, hewn out of the rock, which formerly conveyed, probably to the king's palace, the waters of a copious spring which issues from the base of the cliffs about two hundred yards further up the gorge. This, too, is in all probability the result of Roman skill, since remains of aqueducts are seldom found amongst ruins of exclusively Persian origin of this date; and, in this instance, an abundant supply of water was procurable, without this artificial and expensive conduit, from the river which traversed the city from end to end.

Beyond the gorge is a circular valley, three or four miles in diameter, shut in by an amphitheatre of stupendous rocks; and high up in its north-western angle is the cavern I had come to visit. Leaving my horse at the foot of the ascent, I and my Tofengchees toiled up the steep hill-side, until after an hour's hard work we reached the base of a cliff so nearly perpendicular that further progress appeared almost impossible. My guides, however, intimated that up its nude slippery face we must go; and, after divesting myself of my boots, by their advice, up we clambered, holding on as much with our feet as with our hands, and, with some little risk and a good deal of difficulty, attained the object of my desires. Entering the cavern we found ourselves in a large natural hall, in the centre of which are two gigantic feet, a yard and a half in length, on a roughly-hewn pedestal; alongside, with its thighs resting on the pedestal and its head half buried in sand, is the equally gigantic statue of Sapor; the features, adorned with a close-cut beard and the abundance of flowing locks common to all Sassanian sculptures, are much defaced; round the neck is a necklace, and the body is clothed in a tight-fitting tunic, secured by a girdle and shoulder-belts; the legs, from above the knees, are wanting, and the arms are broken off at the elbows: in its present condition the statue is thirteen feet high, and seven feet in girth round the waist.

This, as I have said before, is the only known statue of ancient Persia, and is presumed to be Sapor from its resemblance in dress and detail to his figure on the bas-reliefs; it must have been chiselled on the spot where it now lies, and from a block of stone cut out of the cavern; but why it should have been hidden away in a place which is almost inaccessible, no one knows. Engraved on its legs are the names of Rawlinson 1831, and Hyde 1821, as well as two others which I could not make out.

The hall just described is only a vestibule; beyond it the cavern becomes enormous, and its dimensions and gloom were vastly increased by the flickering light of the tapers we had brought with us. In two or three places its sides have been worked into flat panels, and several tanks hewn out of the rocky floor prove that it was once made use of. After inspecting these, my guides offered to take me I don't know how far down into the bowels of the earth, to a deep lake which they said was full of fish; but the wildness of the place, its semi-obscurity, and the thought that, though I had a revolver, I was only one against three, who certainly looked as if they were capable of anything, induced me to decline their offer. Returning to the open air, I mounted my horse and cantered back to my friends, who were to start for Bushire the same evening. Soon after their departure a violent storm came on, and put my tent-ropes and pegs to a severe test. The circumstances attending the death of a grandson of Sapor, who was suffocated under the folds of his royal marquee, recurred to my mind; so to avoid a similar fate and be prepared as far as possible for all emergencies, I went to bed with a large knife under my pillow, in addition to a revolver, which was the constant companion of my slumbers.

The 1st of May dawned cloudless and bright. The rain of the previous night had cleared the atmosphere and refreshed the flowers and grass. Left to my own resources, the remembrance of a garden which had charmed me as we passed hurriedly through it two days before, enticed me back to Kazeroon. This garden was two or three acres in extent, and surrounded by walls high enough to keep out intruders and ensure privacy; within them were the coolest shade, the most brilliant colouring, the sweetest of perfumes, and the softest of nature's music. Tall graceful date palms waved their feathery branches aloft in the bluest of skies, gently fanning dark still groves of orange and lemon trees laden with golden fruit; below and amongst them were thickets of pomegranate-bushes, bright with their rich scarlet waxen flowers, and endless quantities of blooming roses and jasmine; the soft balmy air was luxuriously redolent with fragrant odours of orange-blossom and attar, and filled with the sweet warbling of nightingales and the soft cooing of turtle doves. In the centre, and approached by grassy avenues and long bowers of sweet lime-trees, stood a ruined kiosk and a broken fountain; there, in the checkered shade, my carpet was spread and my bed stretched: for, once within these fairy walls, why should I leave them? Was not this a spot where wintry cold, burning sun, dreary desert, the whole world outside, might be forgotten? Was there not here the beauty, the quiet, the contentment of Paradise? What was wanting? The sympathetic love of the fair Eve, whom most men search for, but few find: whom the most fortunate find in time, the most unfortunate, too late.

Dreaming of her, perhaps, but certainly dreaming,

A Garden at Kazeroon—Tribe of Nomads. 241

three days and nights sped quickly away. At early dawn I rode out sometimes to watch the natives scraping particles of oblivion from the poppies, or gathering bushels of rose-leaves from the rose-beds; at eventide I strolled forth to look towards the boundless west at the setting sun; but my garden ever enticed me back within its enchanted walls, until one night the last cold breeze of the season silenced the warblers, dispersed the perfume, and awoke me from my dreams. I ordered my horses and rode away towards Shiraz. But though the spell was thus broken, often and often I think of the garden of Kazeroon, as of one of the sweetest spots I have known.

Little of interest occurred on my march, which was broken by frequent halts wherever fancy dictated or game seemed abundant. On the Old Lady's Pass, I came up with some of the Shah's artillery, two six-pounders, which twelve horses and eighty men were slowly dragging up the hill by main force. Their wheels were the first I had seen in Persia, and the unusual sight caused all the beasts of my caravan to shy terribly. The harness for the horses was European and provided with blinkers, the use of which was evidently unknown to the drivers, for instead of being alongside the horses' eyes, they were either dangling about their mouths or caressing their ears.

Next day we joined a tribe of Nomads making for their summer pastures. The men looked hardy and wiry; the women, who eschew veils, had ugly weather-beaten features, showing signs of exposure and hard work. Before them, they drove endless flocks of sheep and goats, and long strings of cows, camels, horses, mules, and asses, on which were tied and strapped in promiscuous confusion lambs, kids, and children; black tents, pitchers and caldrons; cocks and hens; greyhounds, lamed on the march, clothes and carpets—a long procession, reminding one of Israel's exodus. In May these people tramp up to the Sirhad; in September or October they descend again to the Gherm-i-sir, occupying each year districts in both regions to which the use of centuries has given them prescriptive rights. I left them to re-enter the gates of Shiraz on the evening of the 7th of May.

On the hills to the north of the town are several objects of interest: the remains of a building, called Takht-i-Aboo Nesser, which, from the size of the stones employed in it, and the style of its sculptured portals, is evidently of the same date as the ruins of Persepolis; a series of Sassanian bas-reliefs, of inferior execution to those we have already seen, at a place called Naksh-i-Burmedillek; and the well of Ali— Chah-i-Murtesir Ali—a limpid spring in a cool grotto, hewn out of the rock some forty feet below the surface of the soil. Close to it a recluse inhabits a hovel under the shade of a solitary cypress, and draws water for the pilgrims who come to drink; and not far off are two other wells, of unknown origin, sunk through the rock, like the shafts of a mine, into the bowels of the mountain. I dropped pebbles down both; in one, three and a half, in the other six, seconds elapsed before I heard their splash. Visits to these places, and the beautiful gardens of Bagh-i-no (new garden), Takht-i-Kajar (throne of the Kajars), and Chehel Ten (forty Dervishes), occupied my mornings and evenings; in the daytime it was already too warm to stir much abroad. My chief resources were then books and the conversation of a Swedish doctor, the only European in the town, who complained bitterly of the difficulties he experienced in obtaining his fees even from the richest of his patients. On one occasion a considerable sum was due to him from a very wealthy man, whose wife he had attended through a long and dangerous illness; the bill was sent in over and over again, and payment was as often promised—and deferred. At last the doctor asked his client how he, a man of high standing in society, could so systematically break his word; the Persian noble replied, with a significative shrug of the shoulders, "I am not a European."

A week after my return to Shiraz, my companions arrived from Bushire minus a mule-load of traps which had been carried off by highway-men, and on the following morning we paid a visit to Sultan Ferhad Mirza, governor of the province and uncle to the King. Most Persian dignitaries have sonorous titles: the master of the court ceremonies is called "The Support of the Kingdom;" the minister of agriculture, "The Arms of the State;" and he of pensions, "The Confidence of the Empire." Sultan Ferhad's title is "Hissam-i-Sultaneh," the Sword of the State, an appellation which he is said to have justly earned by an unscrupulous use of this weapon in keeping the Shah's subjects in order. He received us with the stately courtesy and urbanity which distinguish, or can be assumed by, Persians of rank; and, though probably as sensitive as the rest of his countrymen to the fatigue of sitting on anything else than a carpet or cushion, did us the honour of ordering four chairs to be brought, and, seating himself on one of them, requested us to follow his example. The robbery was the first topic of conversation. The Prince said he well knew that the road to the south was infested with brigands; his predecessor had been too lenient with these people, and he himself had not yet had time to restore order, but, Inshallah, please God, he would soon do so. He exemplified his proposed treatment of the miscreants, if he caught them, by telling us that when on a previous occasion he had been named governor of this province, he had inaugurated his reign by causing twenty-four highwaymen to be executed at once on the maidan of the town. This act, he said, had inspired a very wholesome terror, and rendered government easy for a time; but the impression had worn off, and he added, with rather a ferocious chuckle, he must repeat it ere long. Altogether he seemed a bloodthirsty old gentleman, and talked of strangulation and mutilation with the utmost indifference, and as the only means of keeping his turbulent people quiet. Changing the subject to Europe, he asked many questions about inventions, especially about watches and chronometers, and then told us, with much animation, various anecdotes of his own country and its different dynasties. Aga Mahommed Khan, the first of the Kajars, was a great king, he said—a man of iron will and character, and a thorough soldier. One day, during a campaign against Russia, he found his nephew and successor preparing to lie down on a luxurious bed which his servants had prepared for him on a hill-side; enraged at such a want of warlike spirit in one of his own blood, Aga upbraided him to his heart's content, and then kicked bed and bedding down the hill. Kerim Khan, too, the founder of the Zend dynasty, came in for his meed of the Prince's praise: in Kerim's time there was justice in Persia, he remarked. One of his ministers having informed him that a poor man, in digging a well, had found a considerable sum of gold, insinuated that it must at once be taken from him. "No," said Kerim; "why should I deprive the poor fellow of that which God has given him. Let him keep it." That was a noble answer. Now, he added, treasure-trove was not only taken from the finder, but he was generally beaten and imprisoned for not giving up more than he had found.

The third round of tea, coffee, and pipes, the usual signal that a visit has lasted long enough, had already been served, but the Prince still retained us; and it was not till after he had shown us over a number of chambers, and a domed bath lined with slabs of a beautiful greenish species of alabaster, that he dismissed us, with the expression of a hope that we would come and see him again.

When criticising the régime under which they live, Orientals are generally more apt to allow their opinions to be inferred than to give them free expression. The anecdotes and conversation, at this and subsequent interviews, of the Sword of the State, all led to the inference that he considered that under the rule of his nephew Nasreddeen his countrymen had become both unjust and effeminate. That they had not become more honest was disagreeably evident to us; for we had hardly left the Governor's presence when another robbery, of which my friends were the victims, was reported. Their Peeshkedmet, who, as is usual in Persia, was entrusted with the purse and payment of all accounts, had that morning sent a Ferrash to fetch from his house a sum of about 25*l*. As the man did not return within a reasonable time, he himself went to his home, and learning there from his wife that the money had been given to the messenger, at once concluded that he had decamped with it. Information was given to the police, and diligent search was made during three days for the culprit. On the fourth he was discovered, in a nude state, within the precincts of a mosque; which, by the Governor's orders, were strictly guarded until hunger obliged him to surrender. He at once confessed the robbery, but stated that, in endeavouring to escape to a neighbouring village, he had been pillaged by Eeliauts, who had despoiled him of the money and his clothes, and left him in the naked condition in which he was found. Giving credence to this statement would have been tantamount to resigning all hope of recovering the money —the last thing the Peeshkedmet, or, indeed, any other Persian, could make up his mind to. So he set his brains and ingenuity to work to extract further confessions. Promises of pardon and threats of mutilation were tried in turn, until the prisoner, overmatched in the cunning game, was induced to avow that the Eeliauts had only taken half the money, and to indicate the spot where the rest of it was buried. Having once made this false move, it is needless to add that his opponent, by a judicious application of stick, soon made him produce the whole sum. As a punishment for his crime, the Governor sentenced him to be bastinadoed in the courtyard of our house and in our presence. I have already described the fellek and chub, and need only add that the spectacle of their application is one to be avoided.

The person next in importance to the Governor is the Eelkhaneh, or Lord of the Kashkai tribe of Eeliauts, which numbers above 25,000 black tents, and our second visit was to him. Though obliged by the government to live at Shiraz, as a hostage for the good behaviour of his clan, he is otherwise free to regulate his life according to his tastes. His dwelling, consisting of several buildings cased in handsome tilework, and a number of courts planted with chenars, cypresses and roses, is exceedingly pretty, and a proof that, though brought up in a tent, he knows how to make the best of his forced residence in a town. About a hundred retainers were idling about in the courts, smoking kalians and drinking sherbet. Their lord, a man of tall and imposing figure, with a look of keen intelligence in his eyes, wore a tall hat and robes embroidered and lined with the finest black lambs'-wool, the produce of his own flocks. He, too, had heard of the highway robbery, and at once betrayed his tribal extraction and opinions by attributing it, in the most positive manner, to the dependants of his mortal enemy, the chief of a powerful and rival tribe of this region, on whose head he heaped many curses and maledictions. Hatred of this individual seemed to be his *idée fixe*, and he talked of little else, until we happened to mention that we intended returning to Ispahan through the pasture-grounds of his own tribe. He was much pleased at this and promised us a gholam (mounted servant) of his household as escort, and a circular, which would insure us a hospitable reception from all his subjects.

Another important character at Shiraz was Mirza Mahommed Reza, whose acquaintance I made under circumstances which prove that a feeling of gratitude is not foreign to every Persian breast. Strolling one afternoon through the town, we met a portly Seyed, wearing a large green turban and a long beard carefully dyed red; contrary to the custom of his class, who generally make a point of showing their contempt of Christians by haughtiness and insolence, he greeted my friends with much cordiality and inquired who I was. Next morning a servant knocked at my door and, after declaring himself to be my sacrifice, presented me with a large tray of tea and preserved oranges, and the Seyed's compliments. Somewhat puzzled at this excessive politeness, I at once paid him a visit, and, on entering his room, was still more surprised when he opened the conversation by asking after the health of a near relative of my own. However, he soon explained all by telling me that thirty years previously he had resided for some time at Hyderabad, and had there made the acquaintance of the gentleman in question, and received some trivial service from him. Since then the world had gone well with him; he had made a large fortune in trade, and having returned to Shiraz, his native town, had had the pleasure of receiving my relative in his own house in 1848. I complimented the old gentleman on his good memory, and thanked him for his present, and we became great friends. His sojourn in India and his intercourse with Europeans had not increased his respect for his own religion and countrymen; in fact, he had become a free-thinker, and did not conceal from me that mollahs and priests were the bane of his life. On his return to Shiraz, he said, they had worried him to death, because he had a favourite dog and no wife; until at last, to escape their sermons and lead a quiet life, he had taken to himself a spouse and become the father of a fine blue-eyed boy. During the Moharrem, or month of mourning, they never allowed him to mourn in private, but overwhelmed him with invitations to weep and eat pilau in their society. At their instigation the Governor always requested him to supply suits of armour and clothes for the representations of the deaths of the sons of Ali, which are then given; in short, there was no end to the trouble he had with them. "This year, however," he said with a chuckle, "I have outwitted them. When the Governor sent for my contribution to the play, I replied that, being a descendant of the Prophet and having the blood of Ali in my veins, I already fully realized the loss I had sustained by the premature death of his sons, and was weighed down with grief and sorrow; but that there were many others who had not the same reasons for mourning, and that it was but just that they should be reminded of the solemnity of this season by being mulcted of what was necessary to represent the events which it commemorated. So I heard no more of the matter; but you see," he concluded, "I have no peace in my own country, and I therefore wish I was back in yours."

The climate of Shiraz during spring and autumn is delicious. May is, perhaps, the finest month; the whole plain is then fresh and green; the gardens are filled with roses and nightingales; cherries ripen, and Persians indulge in quantities of green almonds, of which, as well as of all unripe fruit, they are excessively fond. Its principal industrial products are glass bottles, rose-water, and damascened swords and daggers. The test usually demanded of a good blade and a skilled swordsman is the severance at one blow of an eider-down pillow suspended in the air. I have already spoken of its wine, which, with proper care, might be brought up to the standard of good Madeira, and need hardly mention its tembeckee (tobacco), since it is so fragrant and so highly appreciated that it has rendered famous the name of Shiraz wherever the kalian is smoked.

CHAPTER XIV.

RETURN NORTHWARDS — SECOND VISIT TO PERSEPOLIS — NAKSH-I-REJEEB — ISTAKR — OUJĀN — DISAGREEABLE RECEPTION IN AN EELIAUT ENCAMPMENT — A FLIGHT OF LOCUSTS — PISTOLS VERSUS DAGGERS — SUMMER QUARTERS — PERSIAN IDEAS OF EUROPE — MASSACRE OF JEWS — TROUT-FISHING AND SNIPE-SHOOTING.

THE Nomad instinct, which is said to be innate in us all, but is repressed in Europe by education and civilization, develops itself rapidly in a country like Persia, where there is no obstacle to its indulgence: impelled by it, and weary of the monotony of a residence in town—which, in the East, is, at best, camping without any of the incident or exciting variety of camp life—I determined to pass the interval of five or six days, which would elapse before my companion, the Doctor, would be ready to start with me for Tehran, on the plain of Merdasht, in preference to further inactivity at Shiraz. Accordingly, on the 24th of May, after duly celebrating her Majesty's birthday, by drinking her health in the topaz-coloured wine in which Hafiz found inspiration, I left the city of roses behind me, and retraced my steps to Zergoon. Diverging thence eastwards from the high-road to Ispahan, I rode in a few hours to the village which has given to the river Bendemir the name under which it is now known. Anciently it was called the Araxes, but, in the tenth century, an Emir, then governor of the province of Fars, dammed up its waters for purposes of irrigation, by throwing a "bund" or dyke across it, and since his time it has borne its present designation. The "bund," which is twenty-five feet high, has withstood the wear and tear of eight centuries, and still answers its purpose; but a bridge of thirteen arches, which surmounts it, will ere long be impassable. There is the same absence of bowers and nightingales on the river's banks at Bendemir as at the place where we passed it in marching southwards.

Crossing the plain, another day was passed in wandering amongst the ruins of Persepolis. Eeliauts had pitched their black tents just under the grand terrace; goats and kids were frisking about on the marble staircases, and sheep browzing in the shade of the great bulls. A troop of twenty of their owners were a source of considerable annoyance to me; they so dogged my steps, and kept such a constant watch on my movements, that I at first suspected them of some sinister intent. My suspicions were, however, speedily calmed by remembering the objects and motives which are attributed to the visits of Europeans to these ruins by all Persians. None of them can believe that they are prompted by curiosity or a desire to study the past. They listen with attention to one's expression of feelings of admiration for their antiquities, and apparently participate in them ; but a cunning twinkle of the eye betrays the secret thought of even the most educated amongst them. "Ah!" they seem to be saying to themselves, "you, too, have heard of the treasures buried in our country; you, too, have come to search for them. No one would be such a fool as to come such a long way with any other object." It is little use arguing against opinions so deeply rooted as this one, especially with people like my Eeliauts; so I was forced to submit to their importunity, and listen to a good deal of talk about Jemsheed, and the gold which is supposed to lie hidden beneath his throne.

About three miles north-east of the terrace, in a natural recess in the rocks called Naksh-i-Rejeeb, there are some more Sassanian bas-reliefs, but so much defaced that it is difficult to make out their subjects. Chardin, I think, relates that, during the reign of the successor of Abbas the Great, the prime minister of the day, annoyed at the interest taken by Europeans in the antiquities of this plain, employed sixty men for a considerable time in destroying them; and these relics, probably from their conspicuous position near the high-road, have, apparently, been the greatest sufferers.

Again crossing the plain in a westerly direction, I reached the foot of the hill of Istakr, which I have mentioned in a previous chapter as forming a prominent object in the view from the terrace of Persepolis. It has a conical base, sloping gradually up to a height of 1,200 feet, above which rises a zone of rock, half a mile in diameter, 500 feet high, and perpendicular as a wall. A guide from a neighbouring village led me up a zigzag path, and along some narrow ledges cut out of the face of the rock, and affording just sufficient space for the passage of a single person to the summit. The ruins which crown it date, I believe, from the tenth century, and consist principally of cisterns of hewn stone, the largest being fifty yards long by twenty broad. By its side stands the largest cedar (the only tree on the hill) I have ever seen: its trunk measures nearly six feet in diameter. Istakr was a stronghold of the Princes of Fars during the dark and middle ages, and must have been impregnable except by famine.

Having now seen all the points of interest in this, the most interesting district in Persia, I left it—perhaps for ever. Following the course of the Bendemir for twenty miles, and then turning north-east, I arrived at Mayeen, a village pleasantly situated on a green plain amidst fine walnut-trees; but, notwithstanding its apparently fertile neighbourhood, so miserably poor that bread was scarcely to be had, and many of its inhabitants were reduced to eating half-matured ears of barley. Here I was rejoined by my companion, the Doctor, and we set forth again on the 30th of May up a pretty valley, well watered and wooded with elm and ash —the last trees of spontaneous growth we were to see for a very long time. Gradually they decreased in size and number, as we ascended a steep, stony pass leading to the village of Imaum-Zadeh-Ismael (said to be inhabited exclusively by descendants of the Prophet), until we there again found ourselves amidst the russet-brown scenery which these pages have made familiar.

Surmounting the pass, a descent of ten miles (making the day's march about thirty miles in all) brought us to Rezabad, in the plains of Oujān; where, in default of better accommodation in the village, we camped and slept in a deserted tomb. Oujān is famous in Persian history as having been the favourite hunting-ground of Bahram Gour, and the place where he met with his untimely death. Surrounded by rugged, towering, gaunt mountains, the plain is covered from early spring till late autumn with the most luxurious herbage, and watered by a superabundance of streams which terminate, in its depressions, in fathomless black pools. It was in one of these that Bahram and his horse, carried away by the ardour of the chase, disappeared. Search was at once made, but their bodies were never found, and hence it is presumed that these pools have subterraneous exits. However that may be, they are dangerous-looking places; especially when, as is often the case, they are half hidden by reeds and rank grass. Game of varied sorts is still abundant—antelope, wild sheep and goats, partridges, wild-fowl, and the hobbarah, a small species of bustard: wild asses and bears are sometimes seen. But the neighbourhood is so unsafe, from its vicinity to the strongholds of the Baktiari, Mamaceni, and other marauding tribes, over which the Shah's authority can hardly be said to extend, that hunting excursions are always attended with considerable risk.

Our march on the 31st was to be a short one of sixteen miles, to the village of Assopas, at the opposite extremity of the plain. We started about 6 A.M. with our caravan, but finding the turf most inviting for a gallop, my friend and I, accompanied by a single servant, soon left it far behind us. The gholam promised us by the Eelkhaneh of Shiraz was in charge of it, and being thus relieved from all anxiety we continued to push on, until, after riding for four hours along the only track visible without seeing a single human being or habitation, we arrived at the foot of a steep pass, evidently leading out of the plain. Some Eeliaut herdsmen here told us that our destination was several miles off, and, though doubting the correctness of this information, we commenced the ascent, and at its top came in sight of another upland plain, beautifully green, level as a billiard-table, but entirely uninhabited as far as our view extended. It was clear we had missed our road, and ridden beyond our intended halting-place. Rather, however, than retrace our steps, we determined to march on, and perform two stages instead of one, trusting that our caravan-leader, not finding us at Assopas, would come on likewise. The descent to this second plain was rugged and fatiguing; but once on the grass, we cantered towards a projecting spur of the mountains which intercepted our view, in the hope that behind it we should see our manzil. From one spur we rode to another, and still no village was to be seen. At last, towards two o'clock, when both horse and man were well-nigh spent by heat and fasting, we reached a point whence the whole plain lay before us, and a large number of black tents was visible about three miles ahead of us.

My servant was at once sent on in front to announce us and request hospitality, whilst we followed at a more leisurely pace. Arrived in the encampment, a score of Eeliauts turned out to stare at us, and conspicuous amongst them was a young man of very handsome features, whose tall, well-knit figure was a perfect model of strength and activity. To him we explained our position and his lord's wishes as to our reception, requesting at the same time that a tent and breakfast should be prepared for us, and a horseman sent back to hasten on our baggage. Little credence seemed to be given to our statements, and no attention was paid to our requests; neither word, look, nor action gave any indication of the boasted hospitality of the dwellers in tents. We then tried stronger language. The model was informed that unless he at once gave us what we wanted, we should send a messenger back to Shiraz to report the conduct of the tribe to the Eelkhaneh. A consultation ensued, but only resulted in a sullen invitation to dismount and sit down in the shade of a carpet hung up outside one of the tents. This looked bad; for, according to the customs of Nomads, any one who has once crossed their thresholds and eaten of their bread, is safe as long as he is amongst them; and it was evident that, as these people omitted asking us to enter their dwellings, they intended to keep their hands free as regarded our future treatment. For us there was but one course to pursue. We hardly knew where we were, we were wearied and hungry; there was no village or house within sight; our horses were fatigued with an eight-hours' march; and any abatement in our demands or any apparent hesitation in our determination to enforce them, might have encouraged aggression. In the scanty shade of the carpet we therefore seated ourselves, with our rifles and revolvers ready to hand. An hour elapsed, during which arguments and threats were alike unavailing; the model and his comrades remained impassible and doggedly refused obedience to our orders. Covetous looks were cast on our saddles and arms, and indications of a desire to loot us were not wanting; but whether or not there was an intention to do so, it is impossible to say, for on its expiration we espied our gholam careering down towards us as fast as his horse could carry him. Galloping up to the crowd, and addressing himself to the model, he exhibited his written credentials from the Eelkhaneh, and summoned him on pain of all sorts of terrible penalties, to comply with their contents. But still the Eeliauts hesitated: and it was not until our caravan and servants hove in sight that they were convinced of the authenticity of the document, and of the necessity of according us the hospitality which our numbers now enabled us to exact. Then the model's tone changed: from haughty and sullen, it became obsequious and servile. He begged pardon ; he had misunderstood us : what were our orders ? He was our sacrifice, and only there to obey. The best tent was at once placed at our disposal ; a lamb was killed and spitted, and trays of bread, maust, honey, butter, and kebâbs were placed before us, whilst a deputation of the greybeards of the tribe requested permission to pay their respects.

Previous and subsequent experience has brought me to the conclusion that Persians, whether nomads or the contrary, must be treated with a high hand. The European traveller owes his safety to the fear which he inspires, and to nothing else : if he be not really able to enforce obedience, he must act as if he were. His prestige is luckily still so great that a display of firmness generally obviates the necessity of a recourse to extreme measures ; but he must always be prepared for them, and show that he is so. Then he will, as a rule, find little difficulty in procuring all that a traveller can justly demand, and have no reason to complain of his reception amongst them ; for, except when roused by religious fanaticism, they are naturally amiable, docile, and serviceable.

Things had now taken a favourable turn, the pangs of hunger were stilled, and our tempers were soothed by the return of a feeling of security and the kalian. My companion dozed off into a sound sleep, whilst I kept up a drowsy conversation with the greybeards ; who, seated in front of the open tent, examined guns, rifles and pistols with considerable minuteness, and a vast amount of astonishment depicted on their swarthy features.

All at once I was startled by a peculiar noise: at first it was like the sound of distant billows breaking on a rocky coast, but as each moment it came nearer and nearer, it resembled so much the roar of a rushing mighty wind, that I fully expected we should soon be enveloped in one of those devastating hurricanes which Eastern travellers have described as rising, by magic as it were, and sweeping everything before them. Still the sky was of the clearest blue, and my tent-hangings hardly moved in the almost imperceptible breeze. With serious faces my audience listened attentively for a minute or two, and then, as the roar increased, sprang to their feet, uttering the ill-omened cry, "Malek, malek," "The locusts, the locusts!" From behind the hills, about three miles off, a cloud appeared, casting a deep shadow over the plain and advancing fast towards us; in a few seconds it was upon us, and then, far as the eye could see, the atmosphere teemed with myriads of these fell destroyers: their serried ranks shut out the light of day and filled the Eeliauts' hearts with fear and disquietude. On they went in compact swarms, beating the air with millions of wings and apparently driven by some strong current; in half an hour they had vanished from view. All was still again; but hardly had my hosts had time to congratulate themselves on the departure of the scourge when the peculiar noise was again heard. The cloud reappeared, returning towards us; the sun was again obscured, and now the locusts descended on the plain. By sunset they had all alighted; the green turf was so thickly covered with them, that strolling about in the evening one could not avoid crushing them by half-dozens at each step, and a donkey's snort raised a cloud of them round his head; they penetrated into our tents, on to our beds and carpets: wherever we turned or looked there were locusts. Those I examined were of different colours, green, pink, yellow, and drab; many of them were above three inches long. Their voracity is well known, but it is not only on vegetation that they commit ravages; they try their jaws on almost anything, leather, canvas, cloth, &c.; and my friend the Doctor told me that a child was once brought to him at Baghdad with its eyelids and the skin of its nose completely eaten off by these gluttons.

As darkness came on, the flocks and herds were driven up to our encampment amidst much bleating and lowing; the women, of gipsy-like appearance and for the most part sparsely clothed in rags and tatters, busied themselves in milking their cows and goats; the men lighted their camp-fires and sat down around them to their frugal supper of curds: the full moon rose, in a violet sky, and hushed all, but the ever-watchful dogs, in the silence of sleep.

Next morning we could see that the locusts had done their work; they had eaten the grass bare in many places; heaps of them were lying about in all directions, killed by their own gluttony, or by the

Eeliauts. The latter had already decamped, and a smouldering log or two alone marked the place of their sojourn. We soon overtook them on their way to still higher pasture-grounds, and rode along with them in great amity for two days. Presents were exchanged between us; theirs consisting of dairy produce, dates, an antelope which they had caught alive in a swamp, and a greyhound; ours, of powder and money.

Our first day's march was for several miles along the plain, and then up a gradual ascent to another upland vale and to a curious caravansary called Kooshki-zerd, the Yellow Castle, probably from a yellow-tiled hunting-box which Bahram Gour is said to have had there. The second was over dwarfish hills, opening out now and then into grass-covered glens, backed by craggy mountains, to the alpine village of Dehgerdoo. The air is deliciously cool and invigorating on this high table-land, and hence the road which traverses it is, in summer, generally preferred by travellers to the ordinary post-road; in other respects, with the exception of the green plains already mentioned, there is little to recommend it. It is always more or less dangerous from the vicinity of the Baktiaries, accommodation is worse than in the lower land, and the solitude and silence seem more intense. We met neither caravan nor wayfarer of any description; for two days we saw neither animals nor birds, and locusts were apparently the only insects to be found there.

Dehgerdoo is such a miserably dirty place that we

camped outside its walls, on the banks of a stream, and only halted long enough to snatch a few hours' sleep under a willow-tree. Our next stage was to be long and fatiguing, and the muleteers, in order to escape the great heat of the mid-day hours, insisted on starting at two in the morning. Nothing, in my opinion, equals the discomfort of a night march with a caravan : obliged to move at a foot's pace for fear of outstripping the mules and losing the way, there is nothing to occupy the mind ; drowsiness comes on, and with it a constant and painful struggle to keep oneself awake ; if sleep gets the upper hand for a moment, one is disagreeably awakened the next by finding oneself on one's horse's neck, or within an ace of falling off altogether ; the hours of darkness, too, seem as if they would never end. We had a lovely moonlight night, but even the marvellous effects of light and shade, the clearness of the violet-coloured sky and the innumerable stars, ever visible in Persia's pure atmosphere, failed to interest us long, and to avoid breaking our bones we at last found it necessary to get off our horses and walk. When morning dawned, we found we had quitted the grassy upland and descended into a region of rocky glens and brown hills, which we only quitted to enter the valley of Yezdicaust, a sketch of which has been given in a former chapter. Here, after a tramp of eight hours, we rejoined the post-road to Ispahan. As the heat threatened to become each day more oppressive, and the weary slowness of the night's march had disgusted us not a little with caravan pace, we determined to leave our mules and baggage behind us, and perform the rest of the journey as quickly as possible on post-horses. Accordingly, before retiring to bed in the caravansary, a servant was despatched to the post-house to order our horses, and returned with an answer that they would be ready early in the afternoon.

At the appointed hour a groom went to fetch them, but brought back in their stead a message from the postmaster to the effect that he had received orders from Tehran to furnish no more horses to Feringhees. On the face of it this message was a lying invention, and also a gratuitous insult. The groom was therefore ordered to return and inform its author that if he persisted in his refusal to grant us the means of proceeding on our journey, we should be obliged to employ force. To this ultimatum came a reply containing more than one allusion to "Christian dogs," and couched in terms more insolent than the first message. There was, therefore, nothing to be done but to carry our threat into execution; and, as luck would have it, on leaving the caravansary with four servants for this purpose, a happy thought made me tell one of the party to bring with him my revolver, which, in the hurry of dressing, I had left under my pillow. We found the post-house door bolted and barred, and the postmaster and half-a dozen of his men seated on the roof smoking. Our request was once more repeated, and again refused; thereupon, an old telegraph pole which happened to be lying near was put into requisition as a ram, and the door speedily yielded before it. In the courtyard and stables there was but one horse, which, from its beauty and condition, was evidently no poster; we, however, at once ordered him to be led away to our quarters as a hostage, until the others should be forthcoming. Whilst engaged in superintending his departure, I heard the postmaster and his men descending the stairs from the roof, and had hardly time to turn and face them when three of them were upon us; so near indeed that their long knives gleamed in the air a few inches above our heads. Luckily my companion had been watching their movements and divined their intention; quick as thought he snatched my revolver—the only arm we had with us—from my servant's hand and pointed its five barrels full in the face of our nearest assailant. There was a moment of suspense; but only a moment: the revolver had won the day; the three knives were sheathed at once. Then ensued the usual scene. The most ample apologies were made; the most urgent supplications addressed to us not to report the matter further. This was not, however, a case in which we alone were concerned. These post-houses are maintained by the Persian Government for the use of travellers: each master receives from it annually a fixed sum for the keep of the requisite number of horses; and it is his duty to let them out at a fixed rate to all who demand them. The postmaster of Yezdicaust had not only attempted to evade this duty, but had likewise threatened to loot and tried to murder us, and if we had allowed this conduct to pass unpunished, it seemed probable that he would wreak his vengeance at having been foiled, on the next European who happened to pass this way. So, notwithstanding that he sent us our horses within half-an-hour of the above occurrence, we refused to accept any apology, and informed him that he would soon hear more of the matter. This he did, within a very few days; for on receipt of our letter stating what had happened, the Governor of the province, our friend the Hissam-i-Sultaneh, sent for the man to Shiraz, caused 500 sticks to be broken on his feet in the presence of the British agent, and dismissed him the service.

Meantime, we started on our ninety miles' ride to Ispahan, which town we reached next day, the 4th of June, without further mishap. Three days' repose was all we could allow ourselves, and on the 9th we were off again to Tehran. The road has already been described. The country looked browner, more arid and burnt, than when we previously traversed it, though every plain had its beautiful but delusive mirage lake; the heat and glare were excessive, the dust blinding, and the wind scorching. Through this we spurred and flogged for seventy-two hours, merely lying down on a carpet for half-an-hour's sleep at each post-house whilst fresh horses were being saddled. We were lucky in getting pretty good ones, and though we had several times to take them on for two successive stages, and often crawled in on them to our manzils at a snail's pace, we escaped the dilemma to which an English officer had been reduced some time previously when making a chapar journey to the South. He had ridden in advance of his servants and lost sight of them, when in the middle of a desert plain his horse broke down so completely that he was obliged to leave the poor beast to his fate; he was walking with saddle, bridle, and holsters piled on his head towards the next post-house, when he was met by a Persian nobleman, who, puzzled no doubt at seeing a solitary European in such a plight and place, asked him what he was doing. "I am riding post to Shiraz," replied the officer.

The heat was already so great at Tehran that the Shah and his Court, and all those who could follow their example, had left the town for their summer quarters on the slopes of the Elburz; whilst those who remained were passing their days in zyr-i-zemeens (underground chambers), and their nights on the housetops. The English Legation was established at Gulhek, a village situated about six miles off on rising ground to the north of the city, which was given some years ago in fief to the British Government by the Shah. Close to it a garden, several acres in extent, and inclosed by a substantial wall, contained the dwellings of her Majesty's Minister and his secretaries. The Minister's house was two-storied, but afforded so little accommodation that it was supplemented by a large marquee, which served as breakfast and dining-room; bell tents were pitched around amongst the trees for the servants and kitchen, and the horses were stabled in temporary huts roofed with branches. For the junior members of the Legation there were smaller houses of two or three rooms each, scattered about in different parts of the garden, and likewise supplemented with bell tents and huts, so that their occupants had their servants and horses within call. An abundant stream of water irrigated the garden and fed a couple of tanks large enough for a swim in the morning and at sunset,—the only exercise it was possible to take between the 15th of June and 20th of August, when the thermometer stood at 95° in the daytime and 86° at night. In such a temperature I found it impossible to sleep except in the open air,—a proceeding which is unattended by any risk to one's health, as no dew falls, and the atmosphere is so dry that a steel blade may be exposed for months without contracting a particle of rust.

The villagers of Gulhek enjoy several privileges in consequence of their village having become British property. They are exempt from furnishing recruits or having troops quartered on them; their tribute, due to the Legation, is always remitted; and, except in case of revolt, criminal and civil jurisdiction is exercised within their walls by a kedkhoda nominated by the British Minister. I never, however, perceived that they were particularly grateful for these boons, or that they were better disposed towards us than their neighbours. More than once they diverted our stream to their own fields; and I daresay would have had no scruples in appropriating other property, had not all our garden gates been watched day and night by sentinels who allowed no one to come in or go out without the password. The Russian, French, and Turkish Legations were located in villages, held on the same terms, at no great distance; and the society of their members, with that of the English telegraph officers, was our only social resource, unless the visits of the dellal be considered of that nature. The dellal is a pedlar of antiquities and retailer of bazaar news. His wares consist of carpets, arms, calamdōns (papier-mâché pen-trays), Kerman shawls, silk abbas, engraved copper vases, china; in short, all sorts of bric-à-brac. Of all Persians he is the blandest and the least hampered with conscientious scruples or honest principles. For all his articles he has always numberless purchasers, but has refused their offers and kept his goods especially for the client in whose presence he happens to be. He is as adroit in passing new things off for old as his compeers in Europe, and as little credit can be attached to his words as to theirs; but he is generally amusing, and a welcome, though sometimes an expensive, guest.

On the 20th of June, the Shah's birthday, we all went to congratulate his Majesty, who was living a few miles off, at his summer palace of Neaveran. He had just then heard rumours of a probable outbreak of hostilities in Germany,—the subdivisions of which were united and amalgamated long before the time of Bismarck, in the Persian language, under the name of Lampza,—and had apparently much difficulty in understanding the co-existence in one country of two such potentates as the Emperor of Austria and King of Prussia; for, in referring to these sovereigns, he said that if there were two Shahs in Iran, it was certain that they must fight until one had destroyed the other. He further expressed surprise that England was not going to take part in the impending war, remarking that formerly she had always been the foremost in every fight. Was she growing old?

Persians, as has already been stated, have very vague ideas as to the geography of Europe and the relative strength of European powers. Russia is generally considered the most powerful of them, and has, by her recent conquests in Central Asia, somewhat dimmed the prestige which England enjoys from her possession of India. Turkey, from its vicinity, is known to be formidable; but the other nations of the West are supposed to be little more than petty principalities, whose princes are ever warring on each other, and whose overcrowded inhabitants are ever kept working like slaves, in manufactories. As to their own country, they think there is none other like it. Its king is the king of kings, its mountains are the highest, its plains the vastest, its climate the best in the world; its horses are the fleetest, its women the most beautiful, and its fruit the most mellow: there is no place like Iran.

The prevalence of such ideas is not surprising when the geographical and intellectual isolation of Persia is considered. The number of Europeans who visit it is excessively small, and their intercourse with the natives of the most limited nature. Few of its inhabitants have ever been west of Constantinople and Nishni-Novgorod, or east of Bombay; and the accounts which these few bring back with them of what they have seen are always toned down so as to flatter the national vanity. Books relating to foreign countries hardly exist; and caravans and the monthly couriers of the French and English legations are the only means of communicating with them. The Shah is, probably, the only person in his kingdom who sees foreign journals, and even his knowledge of them is confined to illustrated papers. Thus there is, generally speaking, amongst all classes profound ignorance of, and complete indifference to, all that goes on outside their immediate circle; probably, a Cornish miner or a Cumberland ploughman knows as much of Central Asia as an enlightened Persian does of anything beyond the frontiers of his own country.

Some years previous to my visit, the Shah ordered a weekly journal to be lithographed and published in the capital, and commanded all his officers, civil and military, to subscribe to and read it. For some months its columns were filled with descriptions of European countries, their inventions, trades, and arts; but, just as children get tired of good books, both editors and readers had soon more than enough of this information, and at the time of which I am speaking the *Tehran Gazette* contained nothing but a short Court circular, long disquisitions on the art of making gold, and the probability of the discovery of the philosopher's stone, almost the only subjects in which Persians take an interest.

As letters and papers only reached us once a month, and the same post which brought us the news of the declaration of war contained the intelligence that the Prussians were before the lines of Vienna, it was difficult even for us to follow very closely the changes which were being brought about, two thousand miles off, by the events of 1866. Our attention, too, was soon diverted from them, for the moment at least, by the accounts of a horrible massacre of Jews which took place about this time near Barfouroush, a town in the province of Mazanderan, not far from the Caspian Sea.

The Children of Israel are the world's scapegoats. Christians and Mahometans unite in looking upon them as legitimate objects on which to vent their spleen, and in considering, in some countries at least, their persecution as a laudable proceeding, a means of propitiating God and averting calamity. Being once on a visit to Tetuan, I was startled one evening by hearing an immense hubbub in the generally quiet streets, and, issuing forth to inquire its cause, found the entire Jewish population of the town, men, women, and children, some 10,000 souls in all, prostrate on their knees, addressing loud prayers and supplications to heaven. The spring had been very dry, fears were entertained that the crops would suffer from the drought, the Moors had prayed in vain for rain, and, as a last resource, the governor had ordered the Jews to intercede with the Deity. Next morning there was a shower, and I heard a Jew and a Moor wrangling in a bazaar as to the efficacy of their respective prayers. The Jew pointed with an air of triumph to the falling drops as proofs of the influence of his people with their beneficent God. The Moor shrugged his shoulders, and contemptuously remarked that Jewish prayers were so distasteful to Allah's ears, that he had sent rain in order to hear no more of them.

At Barfouroush, another expedient is used when the elements are unfavourable. The disinterment and dispersion to the winds of a Jew's dust is there found to be efficacious in securing a supply of rain; and it is possible that, the usual remedy for scarcity having been tried without producing the desired results, the disappointed Barfouroushees may have thought that violent measures might succeed where mild ones had failed. However this may be—for the immediate cause of the massacre was never elicited—they rose one night, attacked and set fire to the Jewish quarters of the town, massacred eighteen men and six women (two of the former were besmeared with petroleum and burnt alive), and drove the survivors almost naked into the woods.

The European missions have always used their influence to prevent occurrences of this nature, and to obtain the punishment of their authors, and reparation for the sufferers; but on this occasion the English mission alone made formal representations. A letter was written by the British Minister, stating the painful impression which would be produced in England by the news of this massacre, and expressing the hope that his Majesty would make such an example of its perpetrators as would deter others from following in their steps. With this letter I was despatched to the royal camp, which, after a day and a half's ride, I found established in a secluded and well-watered valley, called Sheristanek, on the north side of the Elburz mountains.

The Shah usually passes five or six months of the year under canvas. Like all Persians, he dislikes the restraints of town life, and, as soon as summer commences, departs to the hills, where he can enjoy freedom and indulge his passion for hunting and shooting. His camp is no temporary bivouac, but a summer residence, as comfortable and luxurious as any of his palaces. He is generally accompanied by forty ladies of the harem, and his own and their marquees, which are scarlet, form the centre of the encampment. At a respectful distance are grouped the white tents of ministers, courtiers, and guards; the abode of the chief executioner, distinguished by the display before it of several felleks, and a plentiful supply of sticks, being conspicuous amongst them; and around these, soldiers and servants, to the number of three or four thousand, bivouac, and horses, mules, &c. are tethered. After passing the outposts, I threaded my way to the tent of the Shah's aide-de-camp, delivered my letter, and then found cordial hospitality with his Majesty's French physician. Dinner, consisting of several dishes of the snowiest and most delicious rice I have ever seen, of ragoûts of lamb and chicken strongly flavoured with saffron, of sauces sweet and sour, and dried fruits, was served from the royal kitchen. In the evening the aide-de-camp returned my visit, and, in handing me his sovereign's answer, begged my acceptance of a wild sheep and a wild goat, which his Majesty had that day shot. Next morning, as I rode away, I was stopped by a sentinel on guard near the scarlet tents, and informed that, in accordance with the etiquette of the camp, I must dismount and walk past the sacred precincts of the harem. The ladies were, apparently, not yet up, for, though I purposely dallied as much as possible, I saw not even a veil.

The Shah's answer was all that the most ardent humanitarian could have desired. His feelings, he wrote, had been much shocked at the barbarous conduct of the Barfouroushees; he was determined that similar atrocities should no longer disgrace his kingdom, and he announced that a Commissioner should at once be sent down to the place with full powers to punish the offenders and compensate the surviving victims. His Majesty evidently meant to be as good as his word, and the immediate despatch of a functionary of high rank to Barfouroush encouraged us to hope that justice would be done.

On approaching the scene of the massacre, the commissioner was informed by the chief mollah of the place, that the populace was so exasperated that his entry into the town might be followed by the most disagreeable consequences; he therefore remained encamped outside its walls, and demanded further instructions from the government. The wily mollah, having thus gained time for negotiation, set to work to shake the Shah's determination, and found most willing allies amongst his brethren in the capital. The mushtehed, or chief priest of Tehran, admonished the King for attempting to punish good Mussulmans merely because a few dogs of Jews happened to have been killed, and insinuated that Islamism was in danger when foreigners and Christians dared to urge his Majesty to take rigorous measures against his own co-religionists, the most faithful of his subjects. The fanaticism of the populace was, at the same time, aroused, and a crusade against Feringhees was openly hinted at in the bazaars. At first we paid little attention to all this; but after a time our reports of the state of popular feeling towards us became so alarming, and rumours of an intended attack on the Mission so rife, that they could no longer be disregarded; a member of the Legation was therefore sent to the Minister for Foreign Affairs to obtain information as to their authenticity. His excellency replied that these rumours had not reached his ears; he would make inquiries about them, and, should there be any foundation for them, he would at once bring them to the knowledge of the

Shah. He knew, he said, from intercepted letters, that the mollahs were highly indignant at his Majesty's expressed intention of punishing the Barfouroushees, and he himself had been threatened with excommunication for having seconded that intention. The Shah was very uneasy; the situation was very serious; dissimulation was necessary; the mollahs must be appeased for the moment by dropping this question of the Jews until an opportunity occurred for diminishing or annihilating their influence with the people.

Put into plain English his reply amounted to this: The priests' influence is paramount: we are powerless against it; if you persist in interposing in favour of the Jews, we wash our hands of the consequences; if you let the matter drop we can calm the storm that is brewing. That a storm was brewing was evident, not only from the Minister's words, but also from reliable reports which we received from the Affghan residents of Tehran; who, though living under the protection of Persia, cordially hate the Persians, and, being Sunnies, would sooner fight for Christians than side with Shiahs against them. Several of them are *protégés* of the British Mission, and, believing there was some risk of an attack upon us, they offered to furnish a guard of 200 men for our defence. Their offer was of course declined; but the fact of its being made, proved that our interference in favour of the Jews had brought us into a difficulty which might become a danger; and which, since neither we nor the Shah could crush the mollahs, could only be turned by conciliating them.

The first moonshee of the Legation, accordingly, had an interview with their chief men, who stated frankly that they and all good Mussulmans were incensed against us, because it was understood that we were hostile to Persia and Islamism, and that we insisted on the exile of the chief priest of Barfouroush, a very holy man and a pillar of their religion. The moonshee had little difficulty in refuting the two first accusations, by showing that it was the interest manifested by England in the maintenance of Persia which prevented it being dismembered by Russians, Turks, and Affghans; and by pointing to India, where we had millions of Mahometan subjects who had never yet experienced persecution under our rule. As to the third count, he said that it was untrue; and that if we had given advice in the matter we were not actuated in doing so by any hostile feelings for their religion, but simply by a desire for the welfare of our ally the Shah. Upon this the mollahs put their heads together, and finally a tacit understanding was come to, to the effect that they would pacify the people of the bazaars, and that we would leave the Jews and their persecutors to the fate which the Shah's sense of justice might decide.

Our action in the affair was thus terminated; but the excitement and commotion it had caused was so serious that the King summoned a grand medjlis, or council of all the high functionaries of Church and

State, and some representatives of the mercantile and industrial classes, for the purpose of taking the position of the country into consideration. The clerical party at first advocated the expulsion of all Europeans, but finally contented themselves with demanding the dismissal of five French army instructors; a demand with which the Shah at once complied. The public irritation being thus calmed, in a few days things began to resume their ordinary course, and the council turned its attention to other matters. Some time afterwards I asked a Persian what it was doing, and was told that the result of one week's deliberation was that shoes were to be divided into two classes, and that the maximum prices of the two classes had been fixed at forty and twenty francs respectively. Beyond this important enactment the public heard no more of its proceedings, and soon afterwards it was dissolved.

As to the massacre, the sequel of the story may be told in a few words. For form's sake, a few of the Barfouroushees—those of them probably who could not prove their innocence by bribing the commissioner —were arrested and brought in chains to Tehran, whence they were speedily allowed to escape. A considerable indemnity was promised to the surviving Jews for the loss of their houses and property; but its payment was postponed from week to week, and with each postponement it decreased in amount, until at last it was reduced to a wretched pittance. Thereupon a deputation of half-starved old men came across the mountains, and, after long waiting, found an opportunity for presenting themselves as suppliants to the Shah as he was returning one day from hunting. "Who are these people?" he asked, when he saw them bowing in the dust by the roadside. "The Jews of Barfouroush," was the reply, and the King passed on, saying, "I have settled their affairs. What more can they want?" No sooner was his back turned than the royal ferrashes fell upon the suppliants and beat them within an inch of their lives. Some of them then sought asylum in the Mission stables, and we learnt from them that the settlement referred to by the King was a grant of 7,000*l*., to which sum the original offer of 16,000*l*. had been reduced as soon as the government were relieved from the fear of further interference on our part. The King had ordered the 7,000*l*. to be paid in specie, and no doubt thought his orders had been executed. His ministers, however, could not make up their minds to what they considered a waste of good coin, and made the following arrangements with regard to it. First of all they decided that, in consideration of the protection afforded them, the Jews should make the King, *i.e.* his ministers, a present of 1,600*l*. They then proposed to relieve them of debts due to Mussulmans (most probably fictitious) to the extent of 1,800*l*., and to restore clothes and property recovered by the Commissioner, that were really worth about 400*l*., but were valued by the Persians at just double that amount. And, finally, they would give the remnant of the King's grant, *i.e.* 3,800*l*. in hard cash. In vain the Jews murmured against these hard conditions, and made pitiable representations of the sufferings of their friends and families, who, to the number of 450, were wandering houseless and starving in the woods of Mazanderan. They had played their last card by supplicating the Shah in person, and had lost: so they took their money and returned whence they came. The ministers likewise took theirs (every one said), and, in view of this last act of the tragedy of Barfouroush, have no reason to deprecate a monthly recurrence of a massacre of Jews.

Little else of interest occurred during the summer and autumn of 1866. The Debeer-ool-Moolk, Councillor of the State, was dismissed from the post of governor of Tehran for peculation, and was succeeded by the Zaihir-ed-Dowleh—the Kingdom's Backbone. Our friend "the Sword of the State" fulfilled his promise, and caused eight brigands to be executed at once on the Maidan of Shiraz, and the Baktiaries became so bold that they extended their marauding incursions to the gates of Ispahan, and stripped the banks of the Zeinderood of their usual robe of bleaching calico.

There was happily less insecurity around the capital, and I was unmolested in two or three excursions which I made across the Elburz for fishing. One of these was to a remote valley, some forty-five miles from Tehran, at the foot of Mount Demavend. There amidst the grandest of mountain scenery I camped for three days in perfect solitude, and fished morning and evening in the river Lar. Like most of the streams which fall into the Caspian, it is full of trout, which had probably never before seen artificial flies and were most desirous of becoming acquainted with their flavour, for they rose by twos and threes to every throw of my line, and before leaving I had 450 in my creels: the best of them varied from one pound to one pound and a half in weight. In the month of September we returned to town, and I made a trip to the Caspian, which it is unnecessary to describe, as we shall before long proceed to Europe by that route. In November we had very fair snipe-shooting, some twenty miles from the town, in the marshes in which the river Kerrij terminates its course, and on one occasion, when there was a good flight, got twenty-five brace to two guns before a late breakfast at noon.

In December winter set in, and towards the end of the year skating again became our pastime; it attracted crowds of native spectators, who were under the impression that we all suffered from some excessively hot disease, and were recommended this exercise as a cooling medicine. Commiseration for our supposed maladies did not, however, prevent the owners of ice-ponds from attempting to make a good thing out of the remedy, for they charged a high price for their use, and when one day a couple of favourite puppies followed us on to them, declared the ice to be nejjys—defiled, and consequently unfit for the use of Mussulmans, and demanded compensation for its full value.

CHAPTER XV.

A Persian Marriage—Khorassan—Kermanshah—Tag-i-Bostan—The Loves of Ferhad and Shireen—Bisitoon—Dancing-Girls—Hamadan—Tombs of Esther and Mordecai—Climate—Sunnies and Shiahs—Passion-Plays.

" To the High and Lofty One, whose companions are greatness and glory, to my kind and beneficent friend :

" Whereas, by the favour of God, and under the shadow of the graciousness of his Royal and Holy Majesty the King of Kings (may his Kingdom and Sovereignty be perpetual), arrangements have been made for the marriage festival and ceremony of my son Mirza Moostafà Khan, I, in accordance with the precepts of amity and friendship, beg my kind and beneficent friend, Mr. Mounsey, to take the trouble of coming to my town residence on Monday night, one hour and a half after sunset, and partaking of sweetmeats and dinner, and making me joyful by the sight of his countenance and the benefit of his conversation."

Due allowance being made for the extreme difficulty of rendering into correct English the superabundance of flowery epithets and expressions of the Persian language, the above is a faithful translation of an invitation which I received early in the month of January, 1867, from the Muyer-el-Moolk, or Minister of Finance, on the occasion of his son's marriage with one of the Shah's daughters. The functionary in question owed this apparent distinction to the riches which his tenure of the most lucrative office under the Persian crown, and his prudent observance of the practices traditional in it, had enabled him to accumulate. The greater part of the revenue,* which amounts to about two millions sterling, passes through the hands of the Minister of Finance ; not like water through a sieve, but leaving a percentage, varying according to circumstances, behind it. He is charged with the payment of the chief items of national expenditure,† and, having always a considerable sum

---

* The revenue is raised from a tax, varying from twenty to thirty per cent. on all cultivated lands, except those belonging to the church ; from imposts on gardens, vineyards, mills, watercourses, wells, shops, beasts of burthen, cattle, sheep, and goats; and from duties on exports and imports. The former, chiefly silks and carpets, were valued in 1866, at 1,600,000*l*., and the latter, consisting of cotton and woollen goods and hardware, at 2,400,000*l*.

† The expenditure is thus distributed :—Army, 720,000*l*. ; Civil Service, 300,000*l*. ; Church, 100,000*l*. ; Extraordinary, 200,000*l*. ; Total, 1,320,000*l*. Persia has no public debt. The surplus of the revenue is paid into the King's privy purse for the expenses of his court, harem, &c. ; and the residue, after this payment, into his private treasury, which is said to contain above a million and a half sterling, besides jewels and plate to the value of two millions. Amongst the jewels the finest are the Darya-noor, weighing 178 carats, and valued at 200,000*l*., and the English diamond, which weighs 73 carats, and was presented by George IV. to Futteh Ali Shah.

of ready money at his disposal for this purpose, he can turn a pretty penny by lending at high interest. His patronage also—which he, of course, never dispenses gratuitously—brings him in a handsome income.

These opportunities had not been neglected by the Muyer. He had used them prudently and very advantageously for a number of years, but latterly his great wealth had somewhat turned his head and made him forget that a Persian subject must conceal both his prosperity and power if he wishes to retain them. During the previous year he had built himself a country palace not far from Tehran, the beauty and luxury of which became so much the talk of the court and town, that the Shah thought it advisable to put a stop to what he considered a piece of improper ostentation. With this view he asked his minister for whom he had built his beautiful palace. The Muyer, who well knew the purport of this question, and had made up his mind to execute himself gracefully, at once replied that it was for his Majesty if he would deign to accept it. About this there was no difficulty, and it accordingly became royal property. He was still, however, a very rich man; too rich for the royal mind to be quite easy about him: he must be bled a little more, but in a gracious manner. The King had a daughter to marry, and the Muyer's son was the best parti in the kingdom. The match suited the King, because by it he reduced his subject's wealth to proper proportions, and secured a portion, at least, of it to his own flesh and blood. It likewise suited the Muyer, who was getting old, and probably had reason to think that his tenure of office would not be much prolonged; for though he knew it would cost him an enormous sum of money, and that he must give a very large dowry to his daughter-in-law, he hoped that on her account he would afterwards be left in the undisturbed enjoyment of the rest of his fortune, and this he no doubt argued was well worth the price he had to pay for it.

Accordingly the marriage was arranged and the diplomatic body was invited to some of the festivities ; which, in conformity with the custom of the country, lasted seven days. On the first of them the ceremony took place : it was short and simple. The bride and bridegroom, who then saw each other for the first time, appeared before a mollah with two witnesses and declared their desire to enter into the bonds of matrimony. A short exhortation to lead a good life was addressed to them, the contract was signed, and the couple departed; but not together, for though virtually man and wife, etiquette separated them during the remaining six days' feasting, which was carried on on a grand scale, in the Muyer's house, where doors were kept open day and night to all comers, and eating and drinking went on continuously. It was the finest palace in the town, surrounded by large courts and gardens, which on the night of our visit we found brilliantly illuminated with Bengal lanterns and filled with guests. Traversing these, we mounted a handsome staircase, and were welcomed at its top by our host, who had put on his bravest apparel and successfully concealed the signs of his advanced age by an extra application of indigo dye to his beard. He wore a robe of the richest cashmere, the Shah's portrait set in diamonds on his breast, and a belt studded with brilliants and rubies and clasped with a buckle formed of one big emerald. After receiving our congratulations, he conducted us through several handsome rooms, some of which were ablaze with lights reflected from numberless squares of mirror glass encrusted in their walls, whilst in others there reigned merely a rosy semi-obscurity. We then entered a large saloon ornamented from top to bottom with the most elaborate stucco modellings, in high relief, of trees, flowers, fruits and birds : colour alone was wanting to make it appear like a bower. Its windows looked on to a garden, where were collected all the mummers, rope-dancers, athletes, musicians, and singers of the town ; and for an hour or more we had to look at and listen to their performances, eat sweetmeats, and smoke gold and jewel-headed pipes.

At last dinner was announced, a meal half European half Persian. The West was represented by chairs and a table crowded with a motley array of crystal, bronze, and porcelain vases filled with fruits and flowers; by a complete service of plate, glass, and earthenware, and a menu containing twenty-five dishes : the East, by large bowls of sherbet and mountains of rice, by a constant din of tomtoms and guitars, by the wild discordant ditties of a troop of singers squatted on the carpets, and by dancing-boys in female costume, who kept turning continually round the table, and accompanying their measured movements with castanets. Amongst the guests were several of the greatest men in Persia. They, too, had donned their richest robes and finest jewels and brought their prettiest pages with them; handsome youths many of them, beautifully dressed, and evidently treated more as favourites than menials by their masters, for their only duties were serving coffee, sherbet, and pipes. The bridegroom was not present at dinner, but when his health was proposed the Muyer sent to request his attendance. He entered the room escorted by a train of servants bearing lighted candelabra, made a low bow, and then stood still for a while with downcast looks, without uttering a word, like a man afflicted with all the woes of humanity, or about to mount the scaffold; having thus shown his good breeding, according to Eastern notions, he departed as he had come. After dinner—which lasted many hours, and would have been insupportably tedious to us had we not, by the advice of our host, caused our servants to bring a supply of wine from our own cellars, and was dreadfully fatiguing to the Persians, who hate sitting on chairs—there was a grand display of fireworks, in the manufacture of which the natives are great adepts; we were then ushered into a dimly lighted hall, thickly carpeted and cushioned, where more music and fresh bevies of boy-dancers helped to while away the hours until midnight.

A few nights later we witnessed the last ceremony

of a Persian marriage,—the bringing home of the bride. As she was a royal princess, the troops were on duty, each man with a burning candle in the place of his bayonet, to light the procession on its way from the Palace to the bridegroom's home. Torchmen led the way and were followed by several military bands, all playing different discords at the same time. Then, surrounded by courtiers, ferrashes and troops, came an elephant in red trappings bearing a turret on his back, in which were the Muyer, one of his wives, and the bride enveloped in a veil of silver tissue spangled with jewels: a ladder being carried close behind them in case of accidents. This was succeeded by a dozen takhterawans—covered litters borne on poles by two mules, containing the bride's women and trousseau, and by more troops and servants.

This marriage is said to have cost the Muyer 160,000*l*., viz. 80,000*l*. for the bride's dowry and the seven days' feasting, 60,000*l*. as a present to the King, and 20,000*l*. to the Queen-mother. But then in a country where no man can call his house his own, half your own loaf is better than no bread. A short time afterwards, the Shah bestowed the hand of his sister on the son of the Minister for Foreign Affairs, and we had more *fêtes*, but on a much smaller scale; for, unlike his colleague of the Exchequer, the Persian Foreign Secretary has few opportunities of putting money in his pocket.

Spring came on early, and about the 15th of March the natives began their usual preparations for their great national festival of New Year's Day. Each night at sunset much powder was blown away in saluting the coming new year, and during the day many rockets were despatched aloft, apparently for the gratification afforded by the noise of their reports. The astrologers, who had been busy with their calculations for some time, announced that the sun would enter Aries at half-past 4 A.M. on the 21st of the month, and it was fully expected that in accordance with all precedent, the Shah would, like a good orthodox Shah-in-Shah, at that moment admit his Ministers and the functionaries of his Court to the usual private salaam. The earliness of the hour, however, being inconvenient, his Majesty sent for the wise men, and assured them they were out in their reckoning, and that it was quite impossible that the year could commence before he had had his customary amount of sleep. Whether they were originally wrong in their calculations, or adapted them, subsequently to this interview, to the wishes of their master, does not appear; but it was not until half-past seven o'clock that the year 1283 of the Hejira began.

His Majesty received us with the usual ceremony and announced his approaching departure from the capital on a visit to the province of Khorassan. His motives for this visit were twofold, spiritual and temporal: firstly, to overawe the Turcoman tribes on the northern frontiers of the kingdom, who had lately been making incursions and carrying off a good many of his subjects into slavery; and secondly, to perform a pilgrimage to the Shrine of Meshed, the most holy place in Persia. Great preparations were requisite for this journey, for Meshed is 500 miles from Tehran, and a large force is necessary to prevent the possibility of an attack from the marauders who constantly infest the road. Some weeks were therefore employed in collecting troops and provisions in a temporary camp near the town. In April all was ready, and his Majesty started with 16,000 soldiers and camp-followers and several cannon. A friend of mine, who accompanied him, wrote me the following lines from Meshed :—

" A more uninteresting place than this to any one but a Mahometan pilgrim you can scarcely conceive, and indeed the same thing may be said of the whole march from Tehran, with the exception of the turquoise mines and the district of Nishapore, which is extremely rich and fertile. These two places are the only points worth notice on the road. The rest is a howling wilderness, with here and there a miserable village and a paltry stream of water just sufficient to irrigate a few fields. Damghan, Semnan, and Bostam are towns more than half ruined. Shahrood is a little better, having some trade and showing some signs of life. Sebzewar is only partially ruined. Outside Meshed, the country is rather worse than the neighbourhood of other Persian towns—quite a desert apparently. Within the walls, which are twelve miles in circuit, a large extent is taken up with fields and well tenanted cemeteries. The Shrine and Mosque are very handsome. We saw no wild asses on the road, but the Shah had one brought to him, and we got a portion of it, which we cooked in various ways and ate, without however relishing our dinner; to my taste it was something between bad pork and venison, rather tough and coarse, and decidedly not to be preferred to mutton or beef. It is quite possible that before this journey is over, I may have brought myself to look upon Gulhek as a sort of earthly paradise."

Whilst my friend, from whom I subsequently received this information—all I can give about the province of Khorassan—was journeying eastwards, I myself started off in a south-westerly direction, and after posting for 300 miles in three-and-a-half days, reached Kermanshah on the 21st of April. Thence it was my intention to proceed to Baghdad. Several reasons, however, induced me to change my plans. The time at my disposal was so short that I could have paid merely a flying visit to the city of the Caliphs; the distance thither was above 200 miles, the hot weather was coming on, and the Engineer officer who superintends the telegraphs in this quarter of the kingdom was about to march back to Tehran. So I determined to retrace my steps, and visit, at leisure and in the society of an agreeable companion, the numerous objects of interest which I had galloped past during the preceding days.

Kermanshah * is situated at the south-western

---

* In the neighbourhood of Kermanshah are made the carpets so justly admired in Europe for their brilliant and durable colours as well as for their elaborate designs. In addition to these qualities, they have another and useful one—each side is presentable.

extremity of a noble plain, well watered by three considerable streams, which on their junction not far southwards take the name of Karasoo, and discharge their waters into the Tigris near Bassora. It contains from 20,000 to 25,000 inhabitants, but no buildings or mosques worthy of note. A day within its mud walls sufficed for repose, and, our caravan being already organized, we quitted it, twenty-four hours after my arrival, on our return journey.

Four miles to the north of the town is a romantic spot, called Tag-i-Bostan, renowned throughout this portion of Persia for the limpidity of its springs, and some very fine sculptures, which commemorate the loves of Khosroo Purviz, Shireen, and Ferhad. At the base of a mountain of sombre rock rising perpendicularly from the plain, a large volume of the purest water comes gurgling up to daylight in the lower chambers of a summer-house lately constructed by the governor of the province, and after feeding a large reservoir, escapes in graceful falls to the plain, spreading verdure on all sides. All around are weeping willows, drooping their feathery branches into the cool pellucid stream, to meet the kiss of golden-centred lilies, or to caress the blushing rose and retiring iris; and close by are park-like groups of trees, rising here and there on the greenest turf. The spring is still called Shireen, the Persian word for sweet, and the legend of the beauty who is thus immortalized in its waters is still the common talk of the neighbourhood.

In the beginning of the seventh century, Hormuz king of Persia was dethroned by one of his generals, and his son Khosroo fled for protection to the Court of the Roman Emperor Maurice. There he fell violently in love with Shireen, whom tradition makes out to have been the Emperor's daughter. He married her, and by the assistance of his father-in-law soon recovered his kingdom, and returned with his lovely bride to his own capital. He loved his wife to idolatry, and being desirous of perpetuating her beauty, sought an artist able to carve her likeness in stone. Ferhad, the most celebrated sculptor, and, at the same time, the handsomest youth of his age, presented himself as a candidate for the work, and at first sight became madly enamoured of Shireen; who, it appears, was not untouched by the passion she had excited. His love waxed stronger and stronger as he studied more closely the fair features and limbs of his model, and at last became so franticly wild that he demanded the possession of the Queen as the price of the completion of his work. Khosroo, who was fascinated by the wonderful skill of the artist, gave a rash intimation of consent. The statue was finished, but other works were provided for Ferhad: palaces were to be built, reservoirs constructed, mountains of rock pierced for the passage of rivers, and fountains made to play for the pleasure of Shireen. Nothing daunted the sculptor, his love gave strength to his arm and accuracy to his chisel; he performed prodigies, and at length arrived at the last of the tasks assigned to him. With horror the king saw the moment approach when he must pay the debt of his rashness and surrender his idol to another. He determined to rid himself of his creditor, and whilst Ferhad was at work high up on the rocks, sent an old woman to tell him that his toil was now useless, for Shireen was dead. In an agony of despair the sculptor seized the unlucky messenger, and throwing himself with her from the top of the peak, was dashed to pieces. When the fate of her lover was told to her, Shireen "drooped her head and withered like the rose deserted by the nightingale." Khosroo, disconsolate and broken by remorse, caused the lovers to be interred in one grave, with the old woman's corpse between them; and the villagers say that at Kasr Shireen (a hamlet on the road to Baghdad) two rose-trees and a thistle mark the spot where the luckless couple and their betrayer lie buried. Such is the legend; but history tells us that Shireen was the most faithful and loving of wives, and that, when Khosroo was murdered by his son, she stabbed herself on her husband's body to escape the incestuous embraces of the murderer.

The principal sculpture is protected by an arch, several feet in depth, hewn out of the rock, and is divided into two compartments. In the upper one, Khosroo appears on foot between Shireen and Maurice; in the lower, he is alone on horseback, habited in chain armour, and poising a spear. The figures are in the same style as those at Shapoor, but in higher relief. On each side of the arch there are some remarkable bas-reliefs, representing hunting-parties. The scene of one of them is laid in a swamp, where troops of wild-boars are being slaughtered by men armed with bows and arrows, and either mounted on elephants or seated in boats, whilst ladies play an accompaniment on harps. The subject of another is a stag-hunt. Near it lies a torso, so mutilated as hardly to be recognizable; perhaps the remains of Ferhad's statue of Shireen.

After breakfasting near her cool fountain, we rode on again along the base of the mountains which bound the vale of Kermanshah to the north, and towards evening arrived at Bisitoon, alias Behistun, alias Bagistan, where they terminate in an abrupt bold mass of rock 2,000 feet high. On its perpendicular face are the famous sculptures which so long engaged the attention and puzzled the brains of savans, and were never satisfactorily explained until Sir H. Rawlinson copied and deciphered the cuneiform inscriptions upon them. Persepolitan in style and execution, they represent a king holding up his right hand with an authoritative air, and treading on a prostrate body; with his feroher, or guardian angel, above him, two armed attendants behind him, and nine captives, with their hands bound behind their backs and a rope round their necks, before him. They are so high up that it was only by the aid of a field-glass that I could make them out; hence it is, no doubt, that travellers have given such different accounts of them. Some have taken the figures for the twelve apostles, and the feroher for the cross; others have maintained that the scene depicted is the carrying away into captivity of the ten tribes by Salmanezer. The readers of cuneiform have now decided that the subject is the apotheosis of Darius, and that the sculptures date from B.C. 515.

Below them a large portion of the rock has been cut down to a flat surface, and along its base there is a narrow gallery, about 150 feet in length and provided with a low parapet, hewn out of the mountain. In front of this are the remains of a terrace wall, composed of enormous blocks of stone, some wrought, others rough. The origin and purpose of these works are unknown, but Diodorus Siculus and tradition ascribe them, the one to Semiramis—who, he says, halted here on her way to Ecbatana, and performed the gymnastic feat of ascending to the top of the mountain by means of a staircase formed out of the packs and fardels of the beasts of her caravan; and the other, to Khosroo, who is stated to have here caused a palace to be built for Shireen by Ferhad.

The village of Bisitoon, which lies immediately under the rock, is a very miserable one, but having a tent with us we had fortunately no necessity to enter it. Next day we marched sixteen miles through a green and fertile country to Sahna, a hamlet inhabited principally by members of the Susmani tribe, which is said to practise communism in all things, and is therefore kept at a respectable distance from the good Mussulmans of the interior. The women of the tribe, who have no prejudices about veils, or indeed about anything else, are accounted the best dancers in Persia; so, having a long afternoon before us, we requested the attendance of some of them in a shady garden near our tent. Two damsels, accompanied by an aged male relative who acted the parts of chaperon and tappeur, accepted our invitation. They had bronzed gipsy-like features, fine black eyes, and good figures, which the peculiarities of their costume allowed to be seen a little more perhaps than is compatible with our conventional ideas of fitness; it consisted of bright scarlet kerchiefs twisted into their streaming black locks, a short shift—so short that their elaborately tatooed waists were at each movement exposed to view—and parti-coloured skirts descending from the loins to the knees. Necks, arms, legs, and feet were bare, and adorned with armlets, bracelets, and strings of coins. Their dancing was like that of the Almæ and Bayadères, a succession of plastic movements, proceeding principally from the hip, and in which all the members of the body participated in producing an alluring effect. After performing for an hour or so, they drank tea and smoked kalians with us, and departed well satisfied with a present of a few francs.

Our next stage was twenty-four miles, through narrow grassy valleys shut in by rugged hills, to the village of Kangawar, which is stated to be the site of Elymäis; the arguments in favour of this statement being the shafts of several enormous marble columns, ten feet in diameter, which rise from a basement of large squared stones and are built into one of its mud hovels. They are supposed to be the remains of a temple, dedicated, in the days when Zoroaster's religion was corrupted by the Magi, to Astarte, the Queen of Heaven, and which was plundered about two centuries before our era by Antiochus Epiphanius : about whom I confess to knowing nothing further. The two following days were devoted to shooting on a swampy plain, which extends from Kangawar to Sahadabad (a distance of twenty-four miles) and is a favourite haunt of wild-fowl. Our sport was very fair, and we were lucky in finding and bagging a considerable number of solitary snipe, which formed a most delicious addition to our camp fare. At Sahadabad we quitted the verdant province of Kermanshah, and after a steep ascent of four miles, had a long march of twenty more along the brown slopes of the Elvend chain to Zageh ; here the village squire, a tribal chieftain, invited us to a drinking-bout, at which he got so tipsy that he was carried off to bed by his servants at four o'clock in the afternoon. A ride of ten miles next morning brought us to Hamadan, where we found our tent pitched in a charming garden on the edge of a reservoir of the purest water : the greatest luxury, because so rare, in Persia.

It is now agreed on all hands that Hamadan stands on the site of Ecbatana, the capital of the great Median empire founded by Dejoces—Arphaxad of the Bible—B.C. 709. "Dejoces," wrote Herodotus, "the founder of Median independence, compelled the

Medes to build themselves one single town, and to attend to adorning it without taking much account of the others. The Medes obeyed, and he created a large strong place, the same which is now called Ecbatana, fortified with concentric walls, so arranged that each circular wall was higher than the preceding one by the battlements only; the site, which was on a hill, contributed in some measure to this plan, but it was principally so constructed by design: the whole number of circles was seven, and within the innermost stood the palace and treasury. The largest of these walls is nearly equal in extent to the ramparts of Athens; the battlements of the first circle are white; those of the second are black; those of the third, purple; those of the fourth, blue; those of the fifth, buff: thus the battlements of five circles are coloured with paint; but the two inmost have their battlements covered, the one with silver, the other with gold."

Supposing its palaces and buildings to have been on the same scale of magnificence as its walls, Ecbatana was probably then the grandest city in the world. Its terraced parks and groves are said to have been so beautiful that it was from them that the wife of Nebuchadnezzar drew the model of her famous hanging gardens at Babylon. Cyrus the Great made it his summer residence, and dated from it his order for the rebuilding of Jerusalem; and, after the destruction of the Kaianian dynasty, Alexander banqueted and revelled in the golden palace of the Medes, and caused the plays of Eschylus to be acted in its courts. Until the third century of our era it retained much of its magnificence; then Tiridates, king of Armenia, stript it of its splendour to ornament his own capital. Mahomet's fanatical troops overthrew much that he had left standing, and the Tartar hordes of Tamarlane sacked, pillaged, and ruined the rest. Aga Mahomed Khan, the first of the Kajars, completed its degradation by ordering every remnant of the past to be destroyed, even to the iron gates which still hung from its crumbling walls. Here and there the remains of solid stone foundations cropping up above the surface of the soil, or a block of marble projecting from a mud-built hovel, may still be seen; but this is all there is to remind one of its former greatness.

The modern Hamadan is only distinguished from other Persian cities by the natural advantages of its situation on the slope of Mount Elvend, whence copious streams of water descend to traverse its streets and alleys, and irrigate its numerous gardens and fertile plain. Were it not for these, the town would probably long ago have become a shapeless mass of ruins. As it is, it leads a languishing sort of existence and shows many marks of continuous decay, such as deserted dwellings and crumbling walls. The inhabitants, about 30,000 in number, gain their livelihood chiefly by the manufacture of leather, for the tanning of which great facilities are afforded by the never-failing supply of water. They have many superstitions about Elvend, the classical Orontes, which towers above the town to a height of 10,000 feet, and say that certain herbs and grasses which grow upon its sides—but which have apparently not yet been found, or, if found, have been improperly applied—have the property of curing all diseases, and of transmuting the baser metals into gold : they also believe the philosopher's stone lies hidden in its entrails. The origin of this latter belief is explained by the existence near the top of the mountain of some arrow-headed inscriptions, to which the natives have given the name of " Gunj Nahmeh "— " History of the Treasure," and which they say, when read with the proper key, will indicate the exact position of the stone—and the means of getting at it. I am not aware that these inscriptions have been deciphered by our cuneiform professors, nor had I time to ascend the mountain and visit them.

The only objects of interest in the town are the tombs of Queen Esther and Mordecai. The original structure, which covered their remains, is said to have been destroyed by Tamarlane ; the present one was erected soon afterwards at the expense of the Jewish inhabitants of the place. It is a square building of brick, surmounted by a dome, sadly in want of repair, and much resembling a Persian mosque. The door, which is a single slab of stone, opening from one side on its own pivots, is so small that we could only enter it in a stooping posture. Inside is a vestibule in which are the graves of several Rabbis, and from it, a still smaller door, through which it was necessary to creep on hands and knees, admitted us to the tombs—

two sarcophagi of dark wood, lying immediately under the centre of the dome, and ornamented with rich carving and Hebrew inscriptions. The walls around are likewise covered with writing, and let into one of them, is a block of white marble, which is said to have formed a part of the original sepulchre of Mordecai. Engraved upon it, in Hebrew character, is this inscription :—

"Mordecai, beloved and honoured by a King, was great and good ; his garments were as those of a Sovereign. Ahasuerus covered him with this rich dress, and also placed a golden chain around his neck. The city of Susa rejoiced at his honours, and his high fortune became the glory of the Jews."

The inscription on the tomb of Esther has been translated as follows :—

"I praise thee, O God, that thou hast created me! I know that my sins merit punishment, yet I hope for mercy at thy hands, for whenever I call upon thee, thou art with me : thy holy presence secures me from evil.

"My heart is at ease and my fear of thee increases. My life became, through thy goodness, at the last full of peace.

"O God! do not shut my soul out from thy divine presence! Those whom thou lovest never feel the torments of hell. Lead me, O merciful Father, to the life of life ; that I may be filled with the heavenly fruits of Paradise! Esther."

On the sarcophagus of Mordecai are the following sentences :—

"It is said by David, Preserve me, O God! I am now in thy presence. I have cried at the gate of heaven, that thou art my God ; and what goodness I have received came from thee, O Lord!

"Those, whose bodies are now beneath in this earth, when animated by thy mercy, were great ; and whatever happiness was bestowed upon them in this world, came from thee, O God!

"Their griefs and sufferings were many, at the first, but they become happy, because they always called upon thy holy name in their miseries. Thou liftedst me up, and I became powerful. Thine enemies sought to destroy me in the early times of my life; but the shadow of thy hand was upon me and covered me, as a tent, from their wicked purposes! Mordecai."

The Rabbi who showed us the tombs informed us that they were dated 1718 years after Alexander, which would be equivalent to A. D. 1387, and that his co-religionists regard them with great reverence, and make frequent pilgrimages to them from all parts of the country. His name was Lalazar or the Tulip Bed, and he wore a large blue turban and a rich silk abba of a brickdust colour, which showed his features and figure, the handsomest I have almost ever seen, to great advantage. From the ostentation thus manifested in his dress and other facts related to us, it appears that the Jews are less molested in Hamadan than in other Persian towns.

The book of Esther is so graphically written and the manners and customs of Persians have undergone so little change since her times, that on re-perusing it in my tent, I could, without at all straining my imagination, easily conceive all the incidents of the story occurring at the present day. A modern Vashti might at any moment be disgraced and succeeded by a new favourite whose influence might become supreme with her lord. A modern Haman might, in like manner, arise to dispute her power over his sovereign's mind : he might, even at this day, obtain a decree for the banishment at least of all Jews from the kingdom.

Now, as in the times of Esther, the favourite wife would "stand in the inner court of the king's house, over against the king's house," at the risk of her life : now, as then, she might procure the reversal of the decree, and "letters sealed with the king's ring would be sent by posts on horseback and riders on mules, camels, and young dromedaries," to " the lieutenants and deputies and rulers of the provinces," countermanding the king's orders. Finally, now as then, her relations would at the king's command be "arrayed in royal apparel of blue and white, and with a garment of fine linen and purple," and the minister, her rival, might be hanged on a " gallows fifteen cubits high."

There is one other interesting tomb at Hamadan, that of the philosopher Avicenna. On his stone sarcophagus, which is protected by a small mud building and is situated in the Mussulman cemetery, his Persian name, Aboo Sennah, is inscribed.

Having thus seen all the lions of the place, we had but one more visit to make, to the Isz-ed-Dowleh— Glory of the State, a half-brother of the Shah and governor of the province, who had expressed a wish to see us. Sunrise was his highness's reception hour, and on our proceeding to the palace, we found the corpses of three villagers lying immediately before the gate. They had been killed in a brawl on the previous day, and been brought into the town by their relatives for exposure to the governor's eyes, until the murderers should be punished or an award of blood-money granted; a method of obtaining justice of common occurrence in Mahometan countries, where to refuse or delay interment is considered the extreme of inhumanity. The prince, who is very like the Shah, was suffering from an attack of ague, and had put on over his handsome Persian dress a thick military greatcoat of European cut, which gave him a most eccentric appearance. His manners were most polished and agreeable, and he seemed better educated than most men of his rank, for he was able to speak a few words of French and showed a considerable knowledge of geography.

Between Hamadan and Tehran there are seven stages, viz. Melagird, Zerreh, Noveran, Kushkek, Khaneabad, and Kolmeh. The distance is 190 miles, and the country through which the road runs is a succession of plains and passes, generally barren and arid, and sparsely inhabited. There being nothing to see, we performed the journey as quickly as possible on post-horses, and re-entered Tehran on the 1st of May in a tremendous thunderstorm, which washed down several houses in the town and neighbourhood.

A week later, when strolling one cloudy afternoon in the Mission garden, I saw the whole population of the neighbourhood on the housetops and ramparts, casting anxious looks towards the mountains. Following their example and mounting to my upper chamber, I soon perceived the cause of their anxiety. A waterspout had burst about three miles to the north, and a huge torrent was rolling down the hill slopes towards the town. It came on at a great pace, washing down the mud walls of the gardens and the houses of sun-dried brick in the suburbs as if they had been built of cardboard, and sweeping everything before it. The town ditch was soon filled, and the water not finding sufficient exit to the plain, began to flood its low-lying quarters. In a few minutes more than 120 houses had melted away, as it were, and been converted into a lake of liquid mud, in which floated beams, rafters, and furniture. The flood luckily subsided before further damage was done, but had it been fed by a second water-spout the whole of the capital would inevitably have been destroyed, since no modern Persian buildings can resist the action of water. So frail are they that twenty-four hours' rain is a cause of much apprehension to householders, and always necessitates a good deal of patching to walls and roofs, if not their total reconstruction. Happily moist days are very rare, and I find from a register which I kept (hydrometers don't exist at Tehran), that during the first six months of 1867 there were only forty-nine days on which snow or rain fell, and that on thirty-four of these we had merely slight showers or a few drops. There were thus only fifteen days on which any considerable amount of moisture reached the earth. The second half of the year is generally dryer than the first: in August and July rain never falls. Towards the autumnal equinox there are some stormy wet days. During October and November the sky is generally cloudless, and it is only late in December that snow begins to fall.

The sensation caused in the town by the above

catastrophe, in which several persons lost their lives, had hardly subsided when the Moharrem or month of annual mourning for the death of the sons of Ali came round, and preparations were commenced for the Passion Plays with which that event is commemorated all over Persia. Before proceeding to give a sketch of those I saw, I must say a few words relative to their subject and to the two rival sects of Mahometans.

The Persians, as is well known, were not voluntary converts to the religion of Mahomet. When the last of their monarchs of the Sassanian dynasty, Yezdigird, was defeated and killed by the Saracens, they accepted it as a consequence of the loss of their independence. The victors offered them their choice between the book, the sword, and the tribute. They took the book ; but they took it with much reluctance, and it appears doubtful whether their descendants under the successive rule of the Caliphs, the Seljuks, and the Moguls ever became conscientious adherents of the new Faith. It probably always reminded them of their subjugation by alien races, and thus brought them to think that dissent from the religious opinions of the Turks, Arabs, Tartars, and Affghans, who surrounded them, would be the only means of throwing off a foreign yoke and reconstituting themselves as an independent nationality. That some such feeling existed may be presumed from the fact, that when in the fourteenth century Sultan Mahomed Khodabund, King of Persia, publicly declared himself of the sect of Ali, his example was at once followed by the whole nation. On still stronger grounds may it be presumed that the Sultan's declaration was made rather for political purposes than from religious conviction. Since his time all Persians have remained adherents of that sect and have been called Shiahs, in contradistinction to all other Mahometans, who go by the name of Sunnies; an appellation derived from the word Soona—law. The chief point of controversy between the two sects relates to the succession to the Caliphate. The Sunnies hold that Aboubekre, Omar, and Othman were lawful successors of Mahomet, and that their interpretation of the Koran is the only legitimate one. The Shiahs on the contrary consider these three Caliphs as usurpers, and their writings as heretical, and affirm that Ali was the second Caliph, and that his commentaries are alone correct.

The facts upon which this controversy bears are as follows. Mahomet had no sons, and gave his only daughter Fatima in marriage to his cousin Ali. When he died, a dispute arose between Ali and Aboubekre, Mahomet's father-in-law, as to which of them was the rightful successor. Aboubekre won the day, and was in turn succeeded, in spite of the protests and opposition of Ali, by Omar and Othman. On the death of the latter, the party of Ali were at last able to raise their candidate to the Caliphate; but after a short reign he was assassinated in the mosque of Cufa, and his son Hossein laid claim to his succession. Accompanied by his wife, a daughter of Yezdigird, and his children, he set out for Cufa, in the hope of there finding support; but was overtaken in the desert plain of Kerbela, not far from the Tigris, by the troops of Yezyd, who was already installed as Caliph. Hossein's little band, surrounded and cut off from the river by superior forces, suffered torments from heat and thirst. One after the other his followers were massacred as they attempted to pierce the circle of their enemies and procure water for the women and children; and, finally, he and his male children were killed, whilst slavery became the lot of his female relations.

On this story, many of the details of which are exceedingly touching and dramatic, are based the Passion Plays,* which are the most perfect expression of the feeling with which Ali and Hossein are regarded by all Persians. For them Ali is not only the prophet, but also the vicar of God: Hossein is not only a saintly martyr, but also the door of Paradise, and through his wife, the representative of one of their native dynasties. The descendants of their murderers, the Sunnies, are therefore hated by them with a hatred, the intensity of which is only equalled by that of the reverence and adoration paid to Ali and Hossein.

The plays, or tāzyehs as they are called, are held in tekkyehs, large canvas tents erected for the purpose in the public squares, and have become so much part and parcel of the Shiah religion that it is considered a meritorious action to contribute furniture

---

* For a complete and most interesting account of these Passion Plays, vide *Les Religions et les Philosophies dans l'Asie Centrale*, by M. de Gobineau.

for their decoration and costumes for the actors : indeed a refusal to do so exposes its author to vituperation and persecution. The Shah and most of his grandees have their own private tekkyehs, which are fitted up with considerable splendour; but, though application is frequently made to Europeans for the articles which are required for the dresses of the foreign ambassadors, who play an important part in them by interceding with Yezyd for the lives of Hossein's family, Christians are now as absolutely excluded from these performances, as they are from all the mosques and the baths used by Mussulmans. I was, therefore, obliged to content myself with witnessing two of the ten acts into which the drama is divided—one for each of the ten days of mourning—in an inferior or bourgeois tekkyeh, the proprietor of which happened to be a personal friend of mine, and a man of sufficient influence and standing to disregard, for once in a way, the popular prejudice against the admission of foreigners to these mysteries. His tekkyeh was arranged somewhat after the manner of a theatre, and tastefully ornamented with carpets, shawl hangings, vases of flowers, mirrors and candelabra. On each side of the stage were two or three boxes for the owner and his intimate friends; but the mass of the audience, in which the fair sex (veiled, of course,) predominated, was seated on the ground in the pit, where tea, coffee, sherbet, and pipes were handed round during the *entr'actes*.

By way of prelude to the piece, a band of music traversed the stage, playing a most dismal air. Yezyd, made to look as fierce and inhuman as possible, then entered, attired in red cloth-of-gold and wearing a huge Arab turban, and placed himself on his throne, an iron bedstead covered with cushions. He appeared to be suffering much mental and bodily pain, the cause of which he attributed, in a long oration and with many curses, to his enemy and rival, Hossein; he rolled himself about on his throne in contortions, in vain seeking relief from the contents of several medicine-bottles which stood on a table beside him. A fatal termination to his illness seemed imminent, when a warrior in chain-armour arrived with the head of Hossein in a dish,—a sight so grateful to Yezyd, that he threw his medicines away and at once recovered his health. Then, mounted on camels, and dressed in black, the members of Hossein's family were brought before him by his general, Shamar, who detailed at length the circumstances of their capture. They had each of them a supply of straw and ashes, which they scattered profusely on their heads as they told their pitiful tale and entreated clemency from their conqueror. Yezyd remained unmoved by their entreaties, maltreated the women, and was on the point of ordering the men to execution when the three foreign ambassadors were introduced. They entered in great state, dressed as far as possible in the costume of European diplomates, and preceded by led horses, richly caparisoned.

Unluckily, it had been impossible to find cocked hats for the whole party, and the senior and spokesman of the three was obliged to content himself with what is commonly called a chimney-pot. In this ludicrous head-piece he made a long intercessionary speech to Yezyd, urging him to have mercy on the captives; he fondled the children of Hossein, and, when at the Caliph's command the executioner was about to cut their throats, rushed across the stage and wrested the sword from his hands. But even this active intercession was unavailing: the ambassador was obliged to surrender the weapon, and the captives were led away and supposed to be put to death. Thereupon the foreigners, to my disgust, turned Mahometans; and, to my delight, were rewarded by Yezyd for their apostasy by being ordered off to be hung.

Such was the first act. Each of the performers in it had his part written on a bit of paper in his hand, so as to be able to refresh his memory whenever it failed him, and was conducted to his proper place and put in position by the prompter; who never quitted the stage, and gave us frequent explanations of what appeared to him ambiguous in the acting or declamation. From the beginning to the end of the piece the audience kept up a continuous wailing and weeping, which became louder and more vehement at the touching moments. The intercession of the foreigners, for instance, was received with a great burst of lamentations, and at one moment I thought that my host, who sat beside me, would choke himself with sobbing.

The scene of the second act which I saw was laid in the desert of Kerbela. Hossein had already been killed, and a man in armour was seen bearing his head fixed to the end of a lance, through his encampment, which was represented by some bits of canvas stretched on poles. Near these, three boys, the martyr's sons, were laid out in grave-clothes. A ferrash approached them, and proceeded with great *sang-froid*, but amidst loud cries of "Wai, wai!" (woe, woe!), and violent expressions of grief on the part of the audience, to stick pegs, in the form of arrows, into the pretended corpses, and to sprinkle them with pomegranate juice, so as to produce the effect of blood. A lion was then led in, and made to lie down peaceably by the side of the murdered boys, in order to show that even wild beasts have better hearts than Sunnies, and can commiserate the fate of the descendants of Ali. The act terminated by the arrival of a band of ruffians who simulated the looting of the camp by carrying off a few pots and pans, and its burning, by setting fire to a heap of straw, placed on the stage for the purpose. The bearer of Hossein's head and the Ferrash recounted in turn the whole of the tragic story in an exulting tone, and at one time seemed in imminent danger of being set upon and throttled by the spectators. The performance of the lion was saluted with much moaning, and towards the end of the representation the whole audience went into convulsions of the most passionate grief: a perfect phrenzy, in fact; for the women tore their veils and hair, and the men rent their garments, and beat their bared breasts until the blood flowed.

CHAPTER XVI.

Tehran to Resht—Enzelli—Ashorada—Turcomans—Baku, Astrakhan, and the Volga.

The 3rd of July was the day fixed for my departure for Europe. The previous night an English officer was attacked, on the road I was about to take, by the advance guard of a regiment on its march home to Azerbaijan to be disbanded. He was cantering along by moonlight when he saw his postboy, who was leading, struck with a long knife by one of the soldiers; the boy flung his arms in the air, shrieked, and fell from his horse. The Englishman and his servant had time to swerve from the path and escape a similar fate; but after the lapse of half an hour, sufficient as they thought for the soldiers to move on, they attempted to return to the spot and pick up the boy. More soldiers, however, frustrated this charitable intention by charging them with their bayonets, and they therefore rode away to the next post-house to give notice of the murder. There no one believed their story; in fact I subsequently found, that a small sum of money which the Englishman left for the boy's parents was looked upon as blood-money, and considered as a confirmation of what was universally believed along the road, viz. that he himself was the murderer.

The possibility of my falling in with the regiment and having a similar rencontre with it was not an agreeable prospect; but as all my preparations were already made, and I was anxious to be off as soon as possible, I bade adieu to my friends and left the capital at the appointed hour. As I mounted my horse at dawn the thermometer marked 95°: what the heat was at noon I have no idea, but the sun's rays raised blisters on my skin, and the air was like the breath of a furnace. My road, for 100 miles, was the same I had traversed on first coming to Tehran. Then the whole country was covered with ice and snow; now it was parched, scorched, and burnt. The dust and the arid heat of the atmosphere generated a thirst which there was no means of slaking except at the post stations, at each of which I swallowed a kettle of tea like a glass of water: it was therefore with no little pleasure that, at sunset, I entered Kasvin, having fortunately seen no traces of my friend's assailants of the preceding night.

The first stage from that town towards the Caspian is long (seven hours) and fatiguing, one half of it being over a barren plain, and the other up a formidable ascent to a wretched village called Kharzan, on the top of the Elburz chain; which is here 9,000 feet high, and forms the boundary between the provinces of Irak and Ghilan. The view from this point extends, wherever the eye can reach, over a conglomeration of the wildest and most desert mountains it is possible to imagine. Neither tree nor herb of any description seems to grow on them, and their monotonous brown colouring is only relieved at rare intervals by reddish seams and patches of snow. A steep descent on the northern side of the pass brought us to the Shahrood (King River), which has some signs of sparse vegetation on its banks. Following its course through a lonely valley for four hours, we reached Mangil, where I hoped to have some sleep; with this view, I laid a thick train of Persian insect powder around my bed, which was prepared on the clay floor of the post-house, hoping thus to keep out the vermin, for which and for its windiness this place is notorious. But either the powder was spurious or the insects of Mangil are insensible to its effects, for they broke through my lines of circumvallation on all sides, entered my fortress, and drove out the garrison. After tossing about for an hour or so, I was so completely covered and so terribly bitten by these loathsome swarms, that I ordered my horses and rode away at midnight.

There was luckily a moon, and we could thus see our way across a long dilapidated bridge which spans the Seffeed Rood, or White River, the largest I know in Persia, about a mile below Mangil, and thence over a stony road carried along the edge of its precipitous banks. The scenery began to change soon after passing the bridge, and my eyes greeted with pleasure the sight of natural wild trees, which I had not seen since leaving the oak forest near Kazeroon fourteen months previously. The first we approached were junipers of great size, growing thickly on the hill-sides; lower down we traversed plantations of olive-trees in the valleys, and on reaching Rustamabad (four hours from Mangil) at dawn, found the appearance of the whole country so changed that I could hardly believe myself still in Persia, and could have imagined I had been transported during the night to a Swiss valley. Green sward, on which grazed herds of fine cattle, covered the low ground, and around it rose hills and mountains clothed to their summits with magnificent forests of oak, ash, elm, fir, &c., in fact all our European trees.

Farther on vegetation became still more luxuriant, and the path descended through shady green lanes where brooks and dark blue pools abound, to Kudum on the flat region bordering the Caspian. Hence there is a macadamized road (the only one in Persia except a small bit six miles in length from Tehran to one of the Shah's country palaces), running through virgin forests, where wild grapes were already ripening on the topmost branches of the trees; and underneath them were dense thickets of wild fig-trees, pomegranate bushes, hops, auricarias, and a species of acacia, called by the natives Derakht-i-Abrishum, the silk-tree, from its beautiful flower, a deep pink bell, out of which grows a bunch of pendent tongues like the ends of a skein of silk. Here and there were rice fields and mulberry plantations, and huts raised on log stages above miasmatic swamps, whose tenants bore evident traces of fever and ague in their haggard features. Through this sort of scenery we cantered for six hours, reaching Resht in the afternoon of the third day's ride from Tehran, the total distance being about 220 miles. During this ride I only met one traveller, a Gholam of the Shah, who had been sent down from the capital to collect arrears of revenue, and at whose approach the villagers were decamping and concealing themselves in the jungle.

Resht, the capital of Ghilan, is situated some twenty miles from the sea, and contains about 25,000 inhabitants, occupied chiefly in the cultivation of the silk-worm. It covers a large extent of ground, as each house is surrounded by a garden, and within its circuit there are several large open spaces like our village greens. The houses, bazaars, and mosques are built of red kiln-burnt bricks, and have pointed roofs, projecting eaves and gable ends; as is universally the case in Ghilan, Mazanderan, and Astrabad, the three Caspian provinces of Persia. Altogether the aspect of the town is pretty on a fine day—a rare occurrence, I was told; for the amount of rain which falls on this northern side of the Elburz chain is as excessive as is the aridity to the south of it. The climate would seem to be very similar to that of the lower parts of Bengal, and a further point of resemblance between the two localities may be found in the existence, in the jungle, of tigers, wild-boar, pheasants, leeches, snakes, &c.

A good deal of silk is exported from Ghilan (in

1866 the total amount produced in the province was valued at 1,000,000*l.*), and an English Commercial House, that of Ralli and Sons, has a comptoir at Resht; to which is attached the most comfortable dwelling in the whole of Persia, built on the plan of an English country-house and fitted up with every European comfort. Its owners received me most hospitably, and in their society and that of the English and Russian consuls, the only other Europeans in the place, I passed three very agreeable days. Whilst there, an eclipse of the moon occurred, and the whole population, men, women, and children, turned out into the street with all their pots, pans, and irons, everything in short which would make a noise and frighten away the monster which was supposed to be eating up the poor moon: perhaps they too think it is made of green cheese.

The port of Enzelli, at which I was to embark, is a day's journey distant from Resht; a journey not exempt from a certain amount of risk. The first part of it is performed on horseback through the densest of jungles, where the soil is of the same consistency as that of an Irish bog, and where the Persians purposely abstain from making a road, on the supposition that, if they did so, the Russians would next day march into and take possession of the province. The consequence is that the traveller must wade his horse almost the whole distance through liquid mud, and is in constant danger of being engulfed in ooze and slush. The ponies used on this stage are very sagacious, and generally avoid the worst holes, but some of these are so deep that a man on foot is sent in first to sound them. Having, by good luck, safely traversed this Slough of Despond, I reached an assemblage of reed huts, called Pyr-i-bazaar, on the banks of a sluggish stream, and entered a cranky flat-bottomed boat, of rough planks and wicker-work, with wooden spades for oars. Twelve Persians set themselves to row with these implements, and encouraging each other by constant appeals to Ali and imprecations on the head of Omar, pulled slowly down the narrow channel; which is in some places so overhung with trees and blocked with rank brushwood and reeds that we could hardly pass, and in others so shallow that the crew were obliged to haul us through the mud. At last, in about two hours we got out into a lagoon some eighteen miles long and ten broad, swarming with aquatic birds, pelicans, storks, herons, and wild-fowl. Crossing, by the aid of a tattered sail, to its northern side, we reached a narrow channel, cutting at right angles the tongue of land which separates the lagoon from the Caspian Sea, and connecting their waters together.

On the western bank of this channel stands Enzelli, a village of some 200 or 300 inhabitants, who dwell in reed huts surrounded by orange-groves, and are very proud of their lighthouse and three small forts. The former is built on the model of all lighthouses, and would resemble them in all respects, if it was oftener lighted; the latter are only in name what they pretend to be, as the guns mounted on them cannot be fired without the risk of killing more friends than foes. As to the port, it is simply what nature has made it, and nothing more appears requisite for the infinitesimal amount of commercial business transacted at it. Half-a-dozen rotten old vessels, which, to judge from their build, date from the time of the Spanish Armada, were lying moored close in shore. What they were doing there it is impossible to say: they were neither taking in nor discharging cargo; there was no freight visible for them, and none seemed to be expected; warehouses there were none, and the only edifice, above the rank of a hut, was the custom-house.

Persians, even of the seaboard, regard nautical pursuits with the utmost fear and abhorrence; the imports and exports of the place are, therefore, carried by the Russian steamers which call here once a fortnight, weather permitting; but are prohibited from entering the lagoon, and consequently obliged to lie-to a mile and a half from the coast—a most inconvenient arrangement, as communication with the shore is often impossible, and at all times attended with risk. Such being the case, it is matter for surprise that Russia, which long ago forced Persia to renounce her right to maintain armed vessels on the sea, should have so long submitted to a prohibition which exposes her merchantmen to considerable danger; there being along the whole of its southern shore and outside the bar of Enzelli, no harbour, worthy of the name, for which they can make in stress of weather.

My steamer was not due until the morning after my arrival, and there being nothing beyond what I have mentioned to see in the village, I took a stroll on the flat sea-sands and had a salt-water bathe. On my return, my attention was attracted by a large iron boiler and a quantity of machinery lying neglected on the beach. Their story is illustrative of "cosas de Persia." Two years previously, the Shah, by the advice of course of some one who had a private interest in the matter, had determined to re-coin the currency* of his realms on a European basis, and instructed his Minister in Paris to purchase the necessary machinery and engage some Frenchmen to superintend the new mint. The men arrived at Tehran, and the machinery entered the Caspian. There the steamer on which it was freighted burnt out her wood, and the cases in which it was packed were used to supply the deficiency and enable her to reach Enzelli; where boilers, wheels, and all the delicate apparatus for coining were landed pell-mell on the sand. Meantime, a building had been erected at Tehran for their reception, and as soon as it approached completion they were ordered up to the capital. Then, and not till then, was it discovered that it was absolutely impossible, even with the assist-

---

* The coins current in Persia are, 1, Tomans (gold) = 10 francs; 2, Kerans (silver) = 1 franc; 3, Shahis (copper) = 1 centime. They are all unmilled, and by being constantly submitted to the process of sweating, soon lose their proper weight. Sovereigns and napoleons are the most useful foreign coins.

ance of the Shah's elephant, to transport them any further. So there they lie, and there they will continue to lie till they are buried in the drifting sand. Some centuries hence they may perhaps be dug up and returned to Europe to figure in a Hyrcanian museum!

On the morning of the 11th of July the steamer hove in sight; my rickety boat was manned, and we got through the surf, which was running rather high, with nothing worse than a wetting. She was a Clyde-built vessel of 600 tons, which had steamed to Petersburg, had there been taken to pieces, and thus transported by canals and down the Volga to the Caspian, where she was put together again. Her captain was a Swede, who, luckily for me, spoke German, and we two had the ship to ourselves. At 2 P.M. we started eastwards, and after calling at Meshed-i-syr, an insignificant Persian village, came to anchor on the afternoon of the 12th, off Ashorada; which has already been incidentally mentioned as being a Russian naval station. It is a low unhealthy island, in the south-eastern corner of the Caspian, about four miles from the mainland. Its soil is barely three feet above the sea-level, and it measures only a mile in length, and 300 yards in breadth, one half of it being sand and the other marsh. Besides being a hotbed for fever, the latter is the favourite breeding-ground of mosquitoes, which are there generated in sufficient numbers to exasperate the tempers of the whole of mankind. Happily they remain where they are, and content themselves with worrying the 300 sailors and their families who form the garrison of the island; and who, together with a flotilla of two steam schooners, two sailing yachts, and two steam launches, represent the naval power of Russia in this remote quarter. The commandant of the station, Captain Prince O——, for whom I had letters of recommendation, received me most hospitably; but informed me, to my regret, that it would be impossible for me to carry out my intention of paying a visit to Astrabad, a Persian town about forty miles inland and eastwards from the island.

The Turcomans, who roam over the vast steppes which stretch almost uninterruptedly from the eastern shore of the Caspian to the khanats of Khiva and Bokhara, are ever warring with the inhabitants of the north-eastern province of Persia; and one of their most powerful tribes, the Yemoots, who have their pasture-grounds on the banks of the Attrek, had lately made a formidable incursion into the country of their hereditary enemy. Headed by an Affghan adventurer, who had persuaded them that he was a prophet and that God had rendered him invulnerable, they had assembled in great force, and surprised and surrounded the Governor of Astrabad as he was returning to that town from a visit to an outlying fort. The Persian, though vastly outnumbered, rather than surrender himself and his men to slavery for life, had cut his way through his foes, and had killed the would-be invulnerable prophet in a hand-to-hand encounter. The Yemoots had thereupon dispersed, but were still in the neighbourhood, and rendered all communication between the town and the sea exceedingly dangerous. Under these circumstances, to persist in my intention would have been like putting my head into the lion's mouth, and I therefore desisted from it. Even in quiet times, this journey to Astrabad ought never to be undertaken without a strong escort, for the Turcomans are as irrepressible as the Uhlan : on their swift, powerful horses they are here, there, and everywhere. Nor is it only on land that they are so formidable : they make frequent descents, in their long log canoes, on the coasts of Mazanderan; and are so much dreaded that the peasants till their rice-fields and gather their mulberry-leaves with fire-arms slung on their shoulders.

To compensate me for my disappointment, the commandant steamed me about the vicinity in one of his launches. One day we landed at a place called Gez, where there is a very primitive *depôt* for Russian merchandise, a good deal of which is here exchanged for the cotton produced in the interior. It is a miserable place, consisting of a few booths thatched with reeds, and several wigwams perched on poles, the whole being surrounded by a strong palisade. The surrounding scenery, as throughout these provinces, is lovely—wide reaches of luxuriant jungle, backed by high mountains covered with forests, which are in turn surmounted by the lofty peaks of the Elburz.

Unfortunately, all attempts to turn to account the

great natural advantages and the fertile soil of these regions are rendered nugatory by the unhealthiness of the climate. Abbas the Great, the traces of whose care for the well-being of his subjects have been so often mentioned in these pages, left no stone unturned to improve their condition. In order to repeople them, he transported hither 30,000 Armenians and Georgians, observing (somewhat cynically, perhaps) that, as the country abounded in wild boars and wild vines, it was just the place for Christians. He caused solid stone causeways to be carried through the swampy jungle, and roads to be opened from the seacoast to the interior. He built himself a palace, the gardens of which were celebrated for their beauty throughout his kingdom, and frequently came over the mountains to superintend in person his improvements. What their immediate result may have been, I am unable to state; but at present their remains are hardly visible, and since then the population has been steadily decreasing: no wonder either, for the air is pregnant with fever and the damp heat which prevails for five months of the year is intolerable. It was with supreme satisfaction that, after three days' experience of Ashorada, I received an intimation from the Swedish captain to the effect that he would be ready to start westwards on the 15th.

We touched again at Enzelli on the next day, and on the succeeding one arrived at Astara, the frontier town between Russia and Persia. Three hours further on we halted at Lenkoran, and on the 18th reached

Baku, the best port in the Caspian, and, as before stated, the intended terminus of the railway from Poti and Tiflis. The town, which is situated on an arid slope and has a population of 30,000 souls, contains nothing of interest; but about ten miles to the north of it stands one of the most ancient temples in the world, where the sacred fire has been burning uninterruptedly for centuries, perhaps since the time of Zoroaster, and still remains unquenched. As we stopped two days, I had time to drive out and see it, and in so doing renewed acquaintance with a wheeled vehicle, a means of locomotion to which I had been a stranger since my entrance into Persia.

The temple, which, with an oratory and two or three chambers for the use of devotees, is enclosed by high walls, is in the form of a small square porch, open on three sides and roofed with a dome, immediately under the centre of which stands the altar. The eternal fire is fed by a current of natural naphtha, issuing from an orifice drilled through the altar and to a depth of eighteen feet below. It was tended, at the time of my visit, by a Dervish from Delhi, who lighted several other currents of the same sort within the enclosure, and gave me an idea of the rites of his religion, whatever it may be, by singing a monotonous dirge, and ringing an accompaniment on a hand-bell before each of the flames. He had lived there in solitude for nearly two years, and shortly expected a successor, likewise from India. This holy shrine, this Mecca of the Guebres, is the purest fountain of their sacred element, and, in the days of Persia's greatness was visited by thousands of genuine worshippers, and even as late as the twelfth century pilgrimages were made to it. But it is now left to the care of a single believer in some obscure Hindoo superstition. No one has, I believe, as yet ascertained how the source of the fire was first discovered, or when the temple became an object of such reverence to the Guebres.

The whole country, for several miles round Baku, has a decidedly volcanic appearance, and would seem to be underlaid by reservoirs of petroleum and naphtha. Close to the temple there is a large manufactory for the purification of the former; and as to the latter, it spurts like gas from a gaspipe, and burns in like fashion wherever a hole is driven two or three fathoms into the soil. On my way home I noticed several of these flaming indications of subterranean gasometers. Nor is it only on land that phenomena of this nature are visible; they exist likewise in the sea, and a calm, windless night gave me an opportunity of witnessing them to great advantage. Soon after sunset the governor of the town, who, with the hospitality universal among the Russian authorities in these parts, had entertained me at dinner, put his barge at my disposal, and I was rowed out of the harbour to a small bay about a mile to the south, where the smooth surface of the sea was rippled by several eddies like diminutive whirlpools. A lighted wisp of straw, of which we had a supply in the boat, was cast into each eddy, and at once ignited the petroleum or naphtha, which, after rising through fourteen feet of salt water, burnt as brilliantly as a cauldron of tar. From one eddy we rowed to another and fired the sea in a dozen places. The effect of this union of two such opposite elements—a union which, were there no wind, would never be dissolved—was strikingly beautiful and strange; especially as, on the night in question, there was not a breath of air to disturb its duration.

On the 21st we again got under weigh and steamed northwards along the low western coast of the Caspian, past several islands,—one of which I was told was an active volcano four years previously,—to Derbend, the capital of the Caucasian province of Daghestan, prettily situated on the slope of a frowning hill and surrounded with vineyards and gardens. Petroffsk was our next halting-place, and on the 23rd, *i. e.* forty-eight hours after leaving Baku, we reached Neun Fuss, where, as indicated by the name, there are only nine feet of water, and we were obliged to quit our steamer for a flat-bottomed barge. Before turning our backs on the Caspian I may mention two peculiarities about it which are not perhaps generally known: its level is sixty-two feet below that of the Black Sea, and though it rises some three feet in summer, in consequence, no doubt, of the greater mass of fresh water discharged into it at that season, it does not, as far as I could ascertain, lose any of its saltness by this temporary dilution.

From Neun Fuss we were tugged, in five hours, to the most navigable of the numerous mouths of the

Volga : it is at least three miles broad, but only three feet deep. Sea-going vessels are thus prevented from entering the river, and all merchandise must be transhipped either inside or outside the bar. Some twenty miles above, on its eastern bank, is Astrakhan, a city containing 50,000 inhabitants, half of whom are Tartars ; it has very wide unpaved streets, muddy or dusty according to the season, many wretched wooden houses, and a gloomy Kremlin, built in the 16th century, and reminding one strongly of the deeds of John the Terrible. Disagreeable traces of the staple industry of the place are seen and felt at every turn in the shape of barrels of Caviare and cured fish, and an oily smell which pervades the whole atmosphere. The sturgeon fisheries in the neighbouring branches of the Volga are very extensive, and so lucrative, that the mayor of the town, one of the largest proprietors, has amassed a fortune of not less than 2,000,000*l.* from their proceeds.

On the 25th July we started up the river, on a comfortable steamboat, which wanted nothing to render its accommodation perfect but sheets to the beds. It was very much crowded with deck-passengers, Russians, Tartars, Persians, going to Nishni Novgorod, and some Caucasian prisoners in chains on their way to the mines of Siberia. The latter seemed to be very well treated by their guards, and to have as much tea to drink as any one on board ; which is saying a good deal, for morning, noon, and night this beverage was being brewed and drunk in tall glasses, with a slice of lemon to flavour it. Of the broad swift-flowing Volga I have little to say: its banks are flat and its scenery is monotonous. We stopped at Sarepta, a flourishing German colony, established a century ago; at Saritzin, whence a railway connects the Volga and the Don; at Samara, where there are some hills about 400 feet high, which our captain informed me were unequalled in height by anything between the Oural and the Carpathians. We also stopped at the cities of Zimbirsk and Kazan, and at many other places which are all duly described in the pages of Murray, and after steaming seven days and seven nights, arrived, on the 1st of August, at Nishni Novgorod.

In the railway-station of that town, I threw away my pen, for Bradshaw there told me that if I halted at Moscow to note my impressions of a hurried view of the burnished cupolas and domes of its Kremlin, or to write a word at St. Petersburg about the gems of the Hermitage and the porphyry and marbles of St. Isaacs, I should miss the train which was to convey me, *viâ* Berlin and Cologne, to Calais; the Dover express which was to carry me into Charing Cross on the 8th of August, and more important than all, the limited mail which was to land me amongst heather and grouse on the 12th.

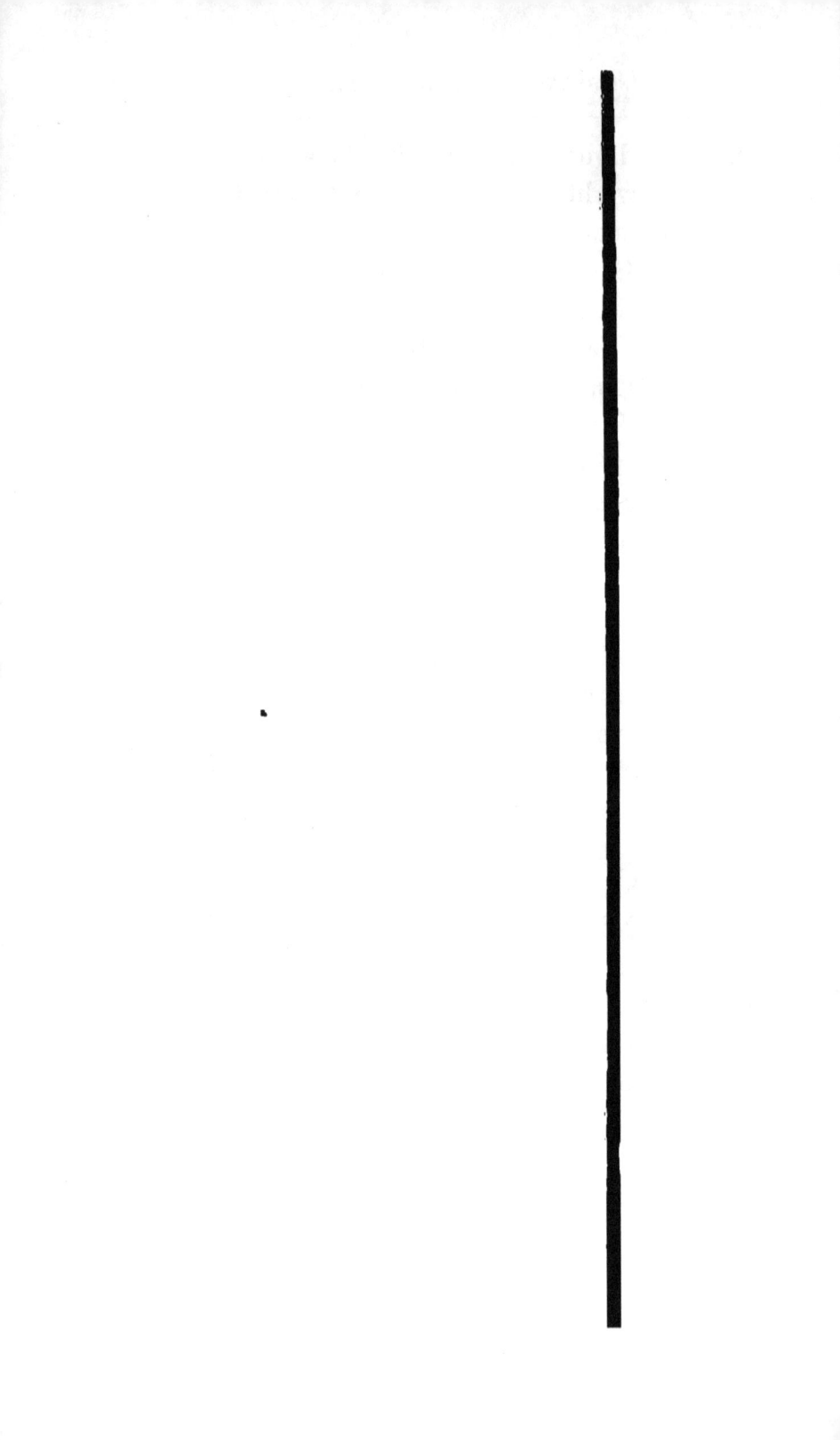

APPENDIX.

ROUTES.

I.

POTI TO TIFLIS.

Total distance, 360 versts (240 miles).
Principal Stations:—
Maran.
Kutüis.
Quiril.
Belagor.
Suram.
Gori.

Railway is opened to Quiril and will soon be completed to Tiflis.

II.

TIFLIS TO JULFA (Persian Frontier).

	Versts
Nawo Akstaf	107
Euruslam	50
Dilijan	19
Yelenawka	33
Erivan	60
(Erivan to Etchmiadzin, 19).	
Nakhitshevan	120
Julfa	40
	*429

III.

JULFA TO TEHRAN.†

	Miles
Marande	42
Tabreez	43
Hadjivava	28
Turkmanchai	50
Mianeh	27
Zenjan	55
Sultania	25
Kasvin	90
Seffer Kodjer	32
Tehran	67
	459

IV.

TEHRAN TO ISPAHAN.

Kinarigerd	20
Koom	45
Sin-Sin	28
Kashan	32
Kohrood	20
Sow	18
Mourcha-Kar	28
Gez	24
Ispahan	16
	231

* Equal to 286 miles.
† Distances are calculated in Persia by farsaks (parasangs), about four English miles: those here given are in accordance with the amount charged for post-horses per farsak.

V.
ISPAHAN TO SHIRAZ.

	Miles
Marg	12
Mayar	24
Koomeshah	24
Aminabad	28
Yezdicaust	16
Shulghistan	20
Abadeh	20
Sormak	16
Khonehkhorreh	28
Dehbeed	20
Moorgâb	28
Sivend	33
Persepolis	16
Zergoon	17
Shiraz	17
	319

VI.
SHIRAZ TO BUSHIRE.

Khonehsemon	32
Dasht-i-Arjeen	12
Kazeroon	31
Direez	10
Bushire	79
	164

VII.
SHIRAZ TO YEZDICAUST (hill-road).

Zergoon	17
Mayeen	30
Rezabad	30
Assopas	16
Kooski-zerd	24
Dehgerdov	24
Yezdicaust	32
	173

VIII.
TEHRAN TO KERMANSHAH.

	Miles
Kolmeh	24
Khaneabad	32
Kushkek	24
Noveran	36
Zerreh	32
Melagird	18
Hamadan	24
Sahadabad	27
Kangawar	24
Sahna	24
Bisitoon	16
Kermanshah	25
	306

IX.
TEHRAN TO RESHT.

Kasvin	99
Kharzan	32
Mangil	22
Rustamabad	22
Kudum	20
Resht	24
	219

X.

ENZELLI TO LONDON by Steamboat, touching at Astara, Lenkoran, Baku, Derbend, Petroffsk, and inclusive of stoppages.

	Days
Astrakhan	7
Nishni Novgorod (by steamboat)	7
Moscow (by railway)	1
St. Petersburg ,,	1
London ,,	4
	20

London: Printed by SMITH, ELDER and Co., Old Bailey, E.C.